THE ONE AND THE MANY:
ENGLISH-CANADIAN SHORT STORY CYCLES

The search for the 'Great Canadian Novel' has long continued through-out our history. Controversially, to say the least, Gerald Lynch maintains that a version of it may already have been written – as a great Canadian short story cycle. In this unique text, the author provides a fascinating literary-historical survey and genre study of the English-Canadian short story cycle – the literary form that occupies the middle ground between short stories and novels. This wide-ranging volume has much to say about the continuing relationship between place and identity in Canadian literature and culture.

Initially, using Stephen Leacock's *Sunshine Sketches of a Little Town* for illustrative purposes, Lynch discusses two definitive features of short story cycles: the ways in which their form conveys meaning and the para-mount function of their concluding – or 'return' – stories. Lynch then devotes five discrete but related chapters to six Canadian short story cycles, spanning some one hundred years from Duncan Campbell Scott to Thomas King, and tracing some surprising continuities in this distinc-tive genre. A number of the works are discussed extensively for the first time within the tradition of the Canadian short story cycle, which has never before been accorded book-length study. This engaging and intelli-gent volume will be of interest to the general reader as well as specialists in Canadian literature.

GERALD LYNCH is a professor in the Department of English at the University of Ottawa.

The One and the Many

English-Canadian Short Story Cycles

GERALD LYNCH

To David,
in friendship,
Gerald

UNIVERSITY OF TORONTO PRESS
Toronto Buffalo London

© University of Toronto Press Incorporated 2001
Toronto Buffalo London
Printed in Canada

ISBN 0-8020-3511-6 (cloth)
ISBN 0-8020-8397-8 (paper)

Printed on acid-free paper

Canadian Cataloguing in Publication Data

Lynch, Gerald, 1953–
    The one and the many : English-Canadian short story cycles

    Includes bibliographical references and index.
    ISBN 0-8020-3511-6 (bound)   ISBN 0-8020-8397-8 (pbk.)

    1. Short stories, Canadian (English) – History and criticism.*
    2. Canadian fiction (English) – 20th century – History and criticism.*
    3. Cycles (Literature).   I. Title.

    PS8191.S5L96 2001   C813'.0109   C00-932717-7
    PR9192.512.L96 2001

University of Toronto Press acknowledges the financial assistance to its
publishing program of the Canada Council for the Arts and the Ontario Arts
Council.

This book has been published with the help of a grant from the Humanities
and Social Sciences Federation of Canada, using funds provided by the Social
Sciences and Humanities Research Council of Canada.

University of Toronto Press acknowledges the financial support for its
publishing activities of the Government of Canada through the Book
Publishing Industry Development Program (BPIDP).

For Jo

Contents

Acknowledgments

Parts of the introduction appeared first or were reprinted in *Dominant Impressions: Essays on the Canadian Short Story* (1999), *Stephen Leacock: Humour and Humanity* (1988), and *Canadian Literature*. Different versions of chapters 1 and 4 appeared in *Studies in Canadian Literature*, and a version of chapter 5 was also first published in *Canadian Literature*. Grateful acknowledgment is made to these publications, more particularly to their editors and readers for suggestions on improving the work. I am also grateful to the Social Sciences and Humanities Research Council of Canada for a Canada Research Fellowship in the late 1980s, and to the University of Ottawa for two sabbatical leaves over the past decade.

Specific indebtedness is given in the text and notes, but I want here generally to express my gratitude to the many who have contributed to this work over the years: my colleagues in the Department of English at the University of Ottawa; graduate students in our seminars on Canadian short story cycles; and associates in English Departments across the country. I am grateful to the readers for the University of Toronto Press and the Aid to Scholarly Publications Program, to UTP's Jill McConkey, who was encouraging and helpful, to Judy Williams for excellent editing, and to Frances Mundy. As ever, I am indebted most to my family for their good-humoured support, especially to Mary Jo, but to our children as well: Bryan, Meghan, and Maura.

Preface

This preface is more a continuation of the acknowledgments, because I want first to situate this study in the context of those writers and books that led me to the subject of English-Canadian short story cycles, and to credit what guided my work and helped me keep faith in the value of the project, such as it has.

I first became interested in the short story cycle as a distinct literary form while working on my Ph.D. dissertation on Stephen Leacock in the early 1980s, specifically while writing the two chapters on *Sunshine Sketches of a Little Town*. But it wasn't until the thesis was finished that I paid due attention to the changes Leacock had made to the original version of the *Sketches* between its serialized publication in the *Montreal Star* and its appearance as a book later in 1912. Only then did I come to recognize that formally the *Sketches* was something more than a book of stories with a continuing setting in Mariposa while yet being quite different from a conventional novel – that it constituted a distinct form falling somewhere between the miscellany of short stories and the novel. And I began to suspect that there was something about this fictional form that was well suited to the Canada represented by Leacock in *Sunshine Sketches*. In thinking so, I was merely appreciating that *Sunshine Sketches* is what Leacock implicitly claims for it in his preface: an 'arduous contrivance' (xvii). Because my thesis became a book on Leacock devoted largely to an analysis of *Sunshine Sketches* and his other story cycle, *Arcadian Adventures with the Idle Rich* (1914), I do not include in the present study a separate chapter on the *Sketches* as a short story cycle. However, in the introduction I do return to Leacock's revisions to the *Sketches* for what remains perhaps the best illustration of how story cycle form can be employed to advantage – of how form and genre communicate meanings.

The more theoretically generative moment in my study of the short story cycle was reading Forrest L. Ingram's *Representative Short Story Cycles of the Twentieth Century* (1971). Although I hope to have qualified and extended some of his insights about story cycle form, it is important to recognize that Ingram said those things first, and was the first to draw extensive attention to story cycles as a distinct genre. With only an exception or two, I am much more in the position of seconding and nuancing for a Canadian context his critical-theoretical proposals – am much more Ingram's debtor than his better.

In the present study, my practice of literary criticism is predicated on the belief that genre conveys some stable and many evolving cultural values. What may seem less obvious, or more contentious, the influence of genre can work independent of the individual writer's particular knowledge of his or her tradition and its relation to the conventions of his or her chosen genre. Question-begging notwithstanding: it is enough that writers share over time and space in an evolving national culture. For me, this generic principle was first suggested in Northrop Frye's concept of an 'imaginative continuum,' which was given expression at the end of his original conclusion to the *Literary History of Canada* (1965). Since first encountering that concept as an undergraduate, I have become familiar with Mikhail Bakhtin's equally inventive notion of 'genre memory' (Morson and Emerson, 89), to which Bakhtin first gave expression (in English translation) in *Problems of Dostoevsky's Poetics* (1963). I have learned much, too, from Alistair Fowler's *Kinds of Literature* (1982), which for me is still the most sensible and accessible work on genre. Fowler's borrowed and improved concept of genre as 'family resemblance' (41) doesn't simplify; it makes the muddled matter workable as he proceeds to sort out what genre is and how it works in literary culture. Still, I make no pretence to being an advanced genre theorist, and I would not want Fowler (or Wellek and Warren, whose *Theory of Literature* [1962] was my other touchstone) blamed for any glaring ignorance that stubbornly shines through.

And now for a necessarily Canadian word about the hyphenation in my subtitle.

Few English-Canadian critics have written successfully about the French-Canadian short story, let alone the story cycle. W.H. New's introduction to the anthology *Canadian Short Fiction* (1998), Wayne Grady and Matt Cohen's introduction to *The Quebec Anthology, 1830–1990* (1996), and Sherrill Grace's 1980 essay 'Duality and Series: Forms of the Canadian Imagination' are noteworthy, if all-too-brief, exceptions. I am not about to increase their number. I would observe, though, that the first French-Canadian novels were *conte/récit*-based *romans* (novels that were collections or rewritings of folk tales and sketches), such as those of the *père et fils* writers: Philippe-Ignace-François Aubert de Gaspé's *conte*-dependent novel *L'Influence d'un livre* (1837), and the father's, Philippe-Joseph Aubert de Gaspé's, *Les Anciens Canadiens* (1863). Even at the end of the nineteenth century, the accomplished Louis-Honoré Fréchette was still writing what are basically tall tales thinly disguising the very Catholic pattern of transgression and punishment. Although these French-Canadian reworkings of folk tales are far removed from the short story cycle as the present study will define the genre, they yet can be seen to share roots with the English-Canadian story, fibrous beginnings in the widespread shorter prose forms that preceded them (parable, exemplum, fable, tale, sketch, and so on). And though the twentieth century has produced a number of accomplished French-Canadian short story writers – for instance, Jean-Aubert Loranger, Albert Laberge, Anne Hébert, Jacques Ferron, Roch Carrier, Hubert Aquin, André Carpentier, Monique Proulx, and, outside of Quebec, Gabrielle Roy and Antonine Maillet – and though some have published collections of stories that exhibit unity (say, the Gaspé tales of Ferron), none has written what this study considers a short story cycle. From my limited reading of French-Canadian short fiction, it would appear that neither the short story (*nouvelle*) nor the story cycle has had the tradition in French-Canadian literature that it has for English-Canadian writers and readers (whereas the novella has continued to possess a cachet in French-Canadian literature that it has never held in English-Canadian; as has the *conte/récit* as opposed to the *nouvelle*). All of which is prelude to my apologetic declaration that *The One and the Many* focuses exclusively on the English-Canadian short story cycle. But this should not be taken as concession of limitation, or only literally so. The English-Canadian short story cycle is a field so varied and rich, and consequently so challenging and rewarding, as to justify my hope that this study will serve as but an *entrée* even to the hyphenated subject.

Following an introduction that discusses the history of the short story and story cycle, and theorizes about the form of the story cycle, in five chapters *The One and the Many* offers extensive and intensive analysis of six Canadian short story cycles, beginning with D.C. Scott's *In the Village of Viger* (1896) and concluding with Alice Munro's *Who Do You Think You Are?* (1978). Between these two literary-historical markers come two early, and very different, Modern story cycles, J.G. Sime's *Sister Woman* (1919) and F.P. Grove's *Over Prairie Trails* (1922); one from the middle of the century, Emily Carr's *Klee Wyck* (1941), which pairs well with Grove's *Trails* in the third chapter; then one late-Modern (some would say early postmodern) example of the form in George Elliott's *The Kissing Man* (1962). Readers might question the inclusion of Carr's first autobiographical memoir/sketch-book in a study of short story cycles, and perhaps wonder as well about *Over Prairie Trails*. But I am interested primarily in short story cycle form as it bodies forth thematic, historical, and cultural matters, and not very interested in the various generic labels applied to the shorter prose forms that make up these particular works; because, too, as I will show, these two texts are composed of stories exhibiting in their cyclical arrangements the designs of fiction; and because *Trails* and *Klee Wyck* are very good examples of innovative Modern uses of short story cycle form. To go already to Fowler: all six of my primary texts share a distinct 'family resemblance' as Canadian short story cycles.

Other readers might wonder why I haven't devoted a chapter to a story cycle published after *Who Do You Think You Are?* in 1978. Or why I didn't begin earlier with, say, Thomas McCulloch's *Letters of Mephibosheth Stepsure* (serialized 1821–3) or, more likely, Thomas Chandler Haliburton's first series of *The Clockmaker* (1836). I would answer that, although the story cycle continued to flourish through the 1980s and 1990s in the capable hands of such writers as Sheldon Currie, Edna Alford, Mavis Gallant, Sandra Birdsell, Robert Currie, Isabel Huggan, George Szanto, M.G. Vassanji, Thomas King, Rohinton Mistry, George Elliott, Derek McCormack, and many another, Munro's only fully formed short story cycle impresses me as offering the most fitting place to end my study (if followed by a rolling stop in the conclusion that returns to Leacock via Munro and then to King's *Medicine River*). Apart from its inarguable virtuosity as a contemporary short story cycle of character *and* place, Munro's *Who* displays and interrogates a number of techniques and subjects – essentialism, authority, gender, metafiction – in a manner that is suggestively postmodern, if not as experimentally so as in the fictions of such contemporary workers in cyclical forms as McCormack and Diane Schoemperlen. Besides which, in my view it is wise procedure to let the passage of time help literary critics settle, if only for themselves, which writers and works are deserving of more attention or recuperation, especially so if the decision determines inclusion in a generic and necessarily selective literary-historical study such as the present one.

As for extending the historical dimension and beginning with McCulloch or Haliburton, I have a number of reasons for not having done so, but will mention only three here, and only in respect to the more likely candidate. *The Clockmaker* belongs to the eighteenth-century European genre of sketch books; it does not exhibit the kind of cyclical form that I consider definitive of short story cycles (though it possesses some of the cycle's more obvious features); and its central character, Sam Slick, does not change from the opening sketch to the last (the Squire 'improves' somewhat under Sam's tutelage, true, but in the process he becomes less prominent, a silenced second banana). Add to this that there is dispute over which sketches actually comprise the first series of *The Clockmaker*, whether the twenty-one published originally in Joseph Howe's newspaper, the *Novascotian, or Colonial Herald* from 23 September 1835 to 10 February 1836, or the thirty-three in book form close to a year later (see Nesbitt, 6–8, and Parker, xxviii), and the questionable claim of Haliburton's landmark fiction to story cycle status is further problematized. I don't dispute *The Clockmaker*'s important, if distant, place in the genre's beginnings in Canada, only insist that my starting point, Scott's *In the Village of Viger* in 1896, is the first fully formed Canadian short story cycle – the *go*, as it were, following McCulloch's *on your mark* and Haliburton's *get set*.

And by way of final apology: I am aware that many readers will balk or blanch or stew or steam (or all four) at my proposal that the short story cycle constitutes a distinctly Canadian genre (not, note, an exclusively Canadian genre). Such a seeming retrograde argument smacks of the grand thematic criticisms that, if most often misrepresented and undervalued, for decades nonetheless licensed critics and readers with the facility to reach for totalizing images and metaphors that would suspend the animated whole of Canadian literature in one of its supposedly dominant expressions (as documentary, as garrison, as victim, as 'nordicity,' as syndrome). Here, I will assert only that the discipline of Canadian literature is by definition a nationalist intellectual-cultural practice. I agree with Tracy Ware when, in a review of the over-eager critical collection *New Contexts of Canadian Criticism* (1997), he writes (having first acknowledged the virtue of cultural inclusiveness), 'but I cannot see how any "representations of Canada" can transcend nationalism' (238). The work towards understanding and possessing an evolving Canadian literary culture is not an attempt to fix an essentialist and exclusivist identity, neither by theme or image nor by genre. Rather, for me this critical practice participates in shaping answers to such questions as: What as Canadians have we been? What as Canadians do we want to be? The balance achieved in the most successful short story cycles between the individual stories and the whole fiction – hermeneutically circumscribing as that must remain – along with the open-endedness displayed by the concluding stories of most cycles – returning home with a difference – *and* the infrequent appropriate closure, these features continue to make this genre a significant contributor indeed to the perpetual musing on Canadian identity. To borrow from A.M. Klein's 'Portrait of the Poet as Landscape,' 'these are not mean ambitions,' and it should always already be much 'merely to entertain them.' Or to deflate: the study that follows is obviously not the work of a critic who fears the occasional 'slap of the flat of the [nationalist] platitude.'

As W.H. New has observed, 'the first point to make is that it is not subject alone but also the importance of the literary form to the subject that demands recognition, and that such recognition is the first step to re-evaluating the genre of short fiction in Canada' ('Back,' 257). And though the situation has changed for the better since W.J. Keith described it in 1985 (see Bentley, *Mimic Fires*, and Trehearne), his observation still provides the broadest justification for such a study as *The One and the Many*: 'Canadian literature,' Keith wrote, 'has seldom been considered in terms of any consistent historical continuity. Nor are there many generic studies to demonstrate the debt, in poetry or fiction or whatever, of one literary generation to another. The existence of a Canadian tradition has sometimes been asserted, sometimes questioned, but rarely traced with any care' (*Canadian*, 4). The six story cycles that are analysed at length in this study were chosen in the first place because they struck me as excellent examples of the permutations of the form in Canadian literature. As my work on story cycles proceeded and I read more and more in the genre, it also struck me that these six books were the story cycles that imagined and explored most rewardingly the subjects of place and identity in Canadian literature, and the connections between them. This, in any case, is my humble hope for *The One and the Many*: that it provide one critic's exploration and analysis of what it has meant to be Canadian over roughly one hundred years as that condition, being Canadian, expresses itself and unfolds its meanings in some of the best fiction produced in Canada in *and by* the genre of short story cycles.

THE ONE AND THE MANY:
ENGLISH-CANADIAN SHORT STORY CYCLES

Introduction:
The Canadian Short Story
and Story Cycle

The short story is the youngest of the canonic genres, beginning only about the middle of the nineteenth century. Regardless, its literary historians and theorists will often open their discussions by casting back to the Story of Job, even unto pre-literate oral histories, in the hope that the narratives of various cultures can be made to appear as proto short stories which were subsequently mnemonically assisted by the 'incidentals' of versification. Just so, academics will dress their new subjects in the respectable robes of a literary history. Contrarily, Canadian critics and scholars, having long recognized the high achievements of Canadian short story writers in this at once oldest and newest of the genres, have tended the other way. They most often present the Canadian short story as a recent phenomenon, as a product of the rise of Canadian cultural nationalism during the 1960s (the third such upsurge, following those of the nation-building 1860s and the postwar 1920s). Or such well-intentioned critics pay undue attention to one kind of Canadian short story: the exquisitely crafted Modern story, that highest achievement in prose fiction of concision, indirection, and unhappy endings. Or, increasing the impoverishment of the historical sense, they focus yet more narrowly on the contemporary, the postmodern short story, like narcissistic children who see their older siblings as endearing attempts towards this present perfection.

The Canadian short story has a history with sketchy beginnings at least as far back as the early nineteenth century. And its most interesting development over the past hundred years has been in the story cycle, a form in which Canadian writers have achieved considerable eminence – a form that has become a recognizable subgenre of the short story, and arguably a discrete genre in its own right.[1] I am not suggesting here at the outset that the story cycle has been ignored by American and British writers (or by Irish, French, Australian, South American, and Russian writers, or for that matter by the writers of any other national literature) – it hasn't, clearly – only that Canadian writers have demonstrated both a strong preference for and high accomplishment in this form from the late nineteenth century onwards. I am not claiming that the short story cycle is somehow inherently a Canadian genre, only that it is distinctly and distinctively a Canadian genre.[2] If I am right in this, then the history of the Canadian story cycle warrants and should reward extensive and intensive study. Notions of a Canadian cultural lag notwithstanding, our writers have been composing some of the best works in this (sub)genre since its beginnings. And more than this, the enduring achievements of Canadian writers in the form can be shown to say much about our relations to place and identity, and about the interdependence of the two in Canadian literary culture.

In this introduction I outline a brief history of the Canadian short story, then consider some of the fundamental questions about the story cycle and its practice in Canada, reflecting on its emergence and development and giving, mostly by way of illustration and reference, an idea of its diversity, continuing popularity, and distinguishing features.

The Short Story and the Canadian Short Story

Attempts at defining and distinguishing among genres, let alone prose fictional forms, are often productive only of categorizing ends, as Mikhail Bakhtin says as cavalierly of those who theorize the novel (*Dialogic*, 8). The many expert contributors to *Short Story Theory at a Crossroads* (Lohafer and Clarey), perhaps the single most useful text on its subject (but see also May), can justifiably be said to arrive collectively at a tautological definition of the short story as a story that is short.[3] I don't intend that observation as a wholly facetious compliment. In these times of rampant genre confusion, such elementary observations are often those of lasting usefulness. And genre theory can be a labyrinthine thicket indeed, covering ground that, on one side, categorizes compulsively with a neoclassical dedication to the rules and, on the other, wants to do away with the notion of identifiable genres altogether. When the generic status of even the novel can be made to appear both questionable and predominant,[4] it is time to adopt Alistair Fowler's conception of genre (derived from Wittgenstein by way of Dugald Stewart) as kinds of literary works that share a 'family resemblance': 'Literary genre seems just the sort of concept with blurred edges that is suited to such an approach. Representatives of a genre may then be regarded as making up a family whose septs and individual members are related in various ways, without necessarily having any single feature shared in common by all' (41). Familiarity and common sense tell us when we are reading short stories and, to turn Mavis Gallant's slightly different observation (xiii), as Canadian readers we know when we're reading Canadian stories: the author is Canadian or the setting is Canadian. Mordecai Richler is a Canadian writer, Montreal is a Canadian setting; ergo, *The Street* is a book of Canadian short stories (a story cycle in fact).

But the first tasks of the present study must be to establish that there is such a thing as a generic family of Canadian short story cycles, that its members constitute a historic continuum of shared features, techniques, and subject matter, and that its concerns are identifiably Canadian. Doubtless already there are some readers who resist the quasi-mystical implications of the initial assertion, borrowed from Fowler, that literary influence can work along generic lines much as genetic influences pass along the spiralling helixes of a family's DNA. Such readers of Canadian literature, and of short story cycles especially, might cite John Metcalf's *What Is a Canadian Literature?* where he argues at undue length (45–87, some one-third of the book) for the unimportance of D.C. Scott's short story cycle *In The Village of Viger*, the very work that provides the primary text of chapter 1 of the present study. Metcalf's evidence is all thumpingly material: *Viger* had a modest initial print run in the US and was not published in Canada until 1945, where it enjoyed similarly scant sales. So how justify claims for its importance? Metcalf's weightiest piece of evidence is that he phoned some of his writer-friends, such as Alice Munro, who assured him that they had never heard of Scott's seminal story cycle.

Against this theoretically naïve argument I would bring the Bakhtinian concept of 'genre memory' (the phrase is actually Morson and Emerson's, 89).[5] Genre memory holds that writers cannot help but be influenced by the various historical-cultural contexts traced in and by the literary form, the genre, in which they choose to work. As Bakhtin writes: 'We are not interested in the influence of separate individual authors, individual works, individual themes, ideas, images – what interests us is precisely the influence of *the generic tradition itself* which was transmitted through the particular authors' (*Problems*, 159; see further, 106, 121). Although in the present study I *am* very much interested in those elements Bakhtin dismisses (for me, literary criticism still means most when it offers close and contextualized readings of important imaginative writing and does not simply refer to the primary material by way of illustrating increasingly abstract theses), Bakhtin's assertion as regards influence and genre is nevertheless to the point. For example, in famously choosing to re-form *Who Do You Think You Are?* as a story cycle, Alice Munro could not help but do so under the influence of the literary-cultural events that contributed to the form of Scott's *Viger* (1896), Leacock's *Sunshine Sketches of a Little Town* (1912), George Elliott's *The Kissing Man* (1962), Hugh Hood's *Around the Mountain* (1968), and so on – whether she had read those earlier story cycles or not. And Bakhtin's concept of genre memory is not especially radical. T.S. Eliot meant much the same, if observed in a retrograde fashion, when he stated in 'Tradition and the Individual Talent' that 'what happens when a new work of art is created is something that happens simultaneously to all the works of art which preceded it' (15). Jorge Luis Borges meant similarly in making such an apparently absurd statement as that Kafka influences Hawthorne, that 'Kafka modifies and refines the reading of [Hawthorne's short story] "Wakefield." The debt is mutual' (57). And Northrop Frye, too, was hinting at the same mysterious processes by which the cultural memory of imaginative literature operates when he speculated in the conclusion to *Literary History of Canada* on what he termed the 'imaginative continuum.' Frye's remarks are particularly germane not only in answer to critics and readers who share John Metcalf's opinion but also in support of my critical stance in the present study: 'A reader may feel the same unreality in efforts to attach Canadian writers to a tradition made up of earlier writers whom they may not have read or greatly admired. I have felt this myself whenever I have written about Canadian literature. Yet I keep coming back to the feeling that there does seem to be such a thing as an imaginative continuum, and that writers are conditioned in their attitudes by their predecessors, or by the cultural climate of their predecessors, whether there is conscious influence or not' (250).

Granted, here the beliefs of Bakhtin, Eliot, Borges, and Frye do not make for logical arguments any more demonstrable than Metcalf's, and maybe even less so according to the letter of Metcalf's rules of influence. Their views do, however, carry a good deal more considered weight on matters that cannot be settled with sales figures and phone calls. More important, the credos of those theorists attest to the power of literature and genre to transmit influence, information, and cultural values; and, as important, they do so from variously divergent ideological perspectives. Metcalf's view – and it remains too prevalent in Canadian culture, or it wouldn't be worth contesting here – is self-servingly short-sighted. With regard to Canadian literature, it repeats the error, a parody of Mark Twain's denial of the premature notice of his death, of endlessly announcing the birth of Canadian literature as coincident with one's own arrival on the scene.

There is a tradition, a continuum, of Canadian short story cycles reaching back at least to Scott's late nineteenth-century *In the Village of Viger*. And in order to understand its emergence and development, it proves necessary first to look briefly at the genre of the short story itself and its Canadian expression.

Among fictional prose narratives there are short stories, longer stories (novellas), and the longest (novels). It is a given for those theorizing the short story (*Short Story Theory at a Crossroads* provides ample testimony) that much of what remains most lastingly productive was said with Aristotelian precision by Edgar Allan Poe in his mid-nineteenth-century review of Nathaniel Hawthorne's *Twice-Told Tales*. Working out of the same Romantic aesthetic that made the lyric the dominant poetic form for a century afterwards, Poe asserted the primary point that short stories had to be short enough to be read in one sitting, else his chief aesthetic virtue of unity of impression is lost; which is to say, if readers have to interrupt their reading, the dominant effects devolving from *concision* of presentation cannot be achieved. Thus was first uttered the mantra of twentieth-century literature classrooms and creative writing workshops (especially those adhering to New Critical principles): every word of a short story must count towards the tell-tale tally, whether a climactic horror, a Joycean epiphany, or a dramatically ironic insight. To such an end – and Poe implies as much – short stories might better be composed backwards.[6] Thus too the short story, and most obviously in its high-impact Modern manifestation (the version most readers think of, from Chekhov to Joyce to Norman Levine), has often been said to be closer to poetry than to the traditional novel (which only further stirs the genre pool unhelpfully).

Inarguably there is much literary-historical, descriptive, and experiential truth in these sketched first principles of short story construction and study, these strongest family features of the genre: brevity, concision, unity of impression and effect. But they fall far short of telling the whole story of the Canadian short story, which, as Frank Davey has argued (142–3), developed from and in traditions somewhat outside those of the Anglo-American model whose history is seen to move with manifest self-ratifying destiny towards a valorization of only the Modern short story.

It can remain a pleonastic fact that short stories must first of all be short. (The word *is* a relative adjective, though, and the historical variability of attention spans might well make us wonder what experience of duration inspired Poe's 'single sitting.' More seriously, this qualifying of the genre's key term 'short' supports Fowler's observation that, when it comes even to the most basic definitions of genre, 'to begin is almost to end,' because even with as supposedly distinct a genre as classical tragedy, 'the common features are few and indistinct' [39; see also Bakhtin, *Dialogic*, 8]). But doubtless the time it takes to write a short story had as much to do with the form's popularity among nineteenth-century Canadian writers as the time it takes to read one. In this way, the two activities – time to write, time to read – are creatively related, attaching author to audience in the formation of a new genre and the making of literary culture. Or put concretely, in a sparsely populated pioneer country such as nineteenth-century Canada's especially, occupied early on by besieged mothers and fathers beleaguered by trees, who apart from such a resentful maverick as John Richardson could or would devote time to writing novels? Interestingly, this lack of time as a result of domestic responsibilities was still being given in the mid-twentieth century by such Canadian women short story writers as Margaret Laurence and Alice Munro as the main pragmatic cause of their writing short stories instead of novels.[7] Although such considerations of length, especially as regards available time, may not be theoretically exciting, they do remind us that the Canadian short story is a product of specific contexts and culture in a nineteenth-century environment that differed markedly from the American, with *culture* defined in the most inclusive way. As readers and critics – old and new, historian, historicist and poststructuralist – we ignore this ground of literature at the risk of falling into prejudice or receding into historical irrelevance.

When in his landmark study of the Canadian and New Zealand short story, *Dreams of Speech and Violence* (1987), W.H. New premises that the short story is the marginal genre, he builds on Frank O'Connor's view that the short story voices 'submerged population groups' (20). In historically marginal cultures such as Canada's and New Zealand's, writers have found the marginal form accommodating of their situations and ambitions. Canadian and New Zealand writers use the short story, perhaps all unconsciously, as a kind of cultural-political protest, subversively, and with a sophisticated irony that remains mostly lost upon the central, dominant, financially rewarding, self-regarding cultures in which they need to succeed, America's and Australia's (see also Knister, Introduction, xi). New's theorizing has about it the ring of truth. Tested in pseudo-scientific fashion, its validity can be shown elsewhere. Ireland's writers, working on the margins of *the* dominant English literature culture, have thrived not only in the form of the short story (and, interestingly, in the story cycle) but also in what many of them still consider the colonizer's language. The Americans themselves dominated the form – with Poe, Hawthorne, and Melville – when throughout their so-called Renaissance they were defining and asserting their culture's unique value as against the British; in other words, when as a culture they would have been feeling most anxiously marginal. And consider: the British have lacked in great short story writers, with D.H. Lawrence being the most notable exception (cf. O'Connor, 19–20).

Foregoing further definitions, then (see New, *Dreams*, 6–17), and without distinguishing among such mini-forms as the parable, the exemplum, the sketch, the anecdote, the tale, and the short story, we might simply observe the enduring centrality of short fiction in Canada's literary history.[8] Our first internationally acclaimed author was a writer of short fictions: Thomas Chandler Haliburton, a colonial man whose *The Clockmaker* (1836) – the Sam Slick stories – testifies to a keen, not to say an anxious, awareness of his position on the margins of two great cultures. Moreover, the first serialization of his *Clockmaker* comprises a sequence of stories linked by character, place, and style, as this form came increasingly to dominate the genre of the short story in Canada as distinct from England and America. The comic-satiric sketch and story in which Haliburton excelled continued to flourish through the middle of the nineteenth century, and by far the most important later nineteenth-century magazines for its publication were the highly influential *The Week* (1883–96) and *Grip* (1873–94), and the more ambitiously popular *Canadian Magazine* (1893–1939). Although primarily an organ of social-political culture, *The Week* published short fiction (and the literary journalism of Sara Jeannette Duncan in her regular 'Saunterings' column). *Grip* published a great number of parodies, sketches and satires of the kind that would later win Stephen Leacock international acclaim (in fact, Leacock published his first comic piece in *Grip* while still a student at the University of Toronto). The work of some other of the prolific writers of comic stories, such as Susan Frances Harrison, E.W. Thompson, Grant Allen, and James McCarroll (pseudonym Terry Finnegan), continues to be recovered and valued for its contribution to the development of the Canadian short story (for example, see Peterman on the recuperation of McCarroll's voluminous writing).

The romantic short story also flourished throughout the nineteenth century in a popular magazine culture that included such publications as Montreal's long-lived *Literary Garland* (1838–51), Susanna and Dunbar Moodie's *Victoria Magazine* (1847–8) out of Belleville, Halifax's the *Mayflower* (1851–2), Toronto's *Anglo-American Magazine and Canadian Journal* (1852–5), [Rose-Belford's] *Canadian Monthly and National Review* (1872–82), the *New Dominion Monthly* (1867–79) and the *Canadian Illustrated News* (1869–83), to name the most successful. Short stories were contributed to these publications regularly by Eliza Lanesford Cushing, Harriet Vaughan Cheney, sisters Susanna Moodie and Catharine Parr Traill, May Agnes Fleming, Rosanna Mullins Leprohon, Ethelwyn Wetherald, Susan Frances Harrison, Agnes Maule Machar, Louisa Murray, and Joanna Wood, to name but the most prolific and those who are becoming better known. The short stories in these magazines, pioneering a somewhat alternate Canadian literary culture, were written predominantly by women who throve on the margins of patriarchal society. Their stories are not 'merely' sketches, or effusive romances, or amateurish (and therefore dismissable) in any sense. As Gwendolyn Guth has shown, they are fully realized short stories as accomplished and important in their historical-cultural contexts as any that came before or afterwards. And their continuous publication makes somewhat less startling the yet surprising appearance of J.G. Sime's short story cycle *Sister Woman* in 1919.

In 1896, at the beginnings of the Modern short story, Duncan Campbell Scott published his seminal story cycle *In the Village of Viger*, comprising a virtuoso's gallery of nineteenth-century story forms, from folk tale to Gothic to local colour – and again with most being romantic rather than realistic in mode. At about the same time, Charles G.D. Roberts invented the realistic animal story (with subsequent help from Ernest Thompson Seton); and Sara Jeannette Duncan continued publishing stories, many of which (such as the title story from her masterful *The Pool in the Desert*, 1903) are equal to those of Henry James in the particularized turnings of their psychological realism and to those of William Dean Howells in their attention to the specificity of place.

Canada's next most famous writer after Haliburton was of course Stephen Leacock, and Leacock was not only a humorist too, like Haliburton, but also in his fiction a writer exclusively of sketches and short stories. After him, through the Modern period, the Canadian story continued to fare well in the hands of such practitioners as Sime, Duncan Campbell Scott, and Raymond Knister (in 1928 Knister dedicated the first anthology of Canadian stories, which he edited, to Scott). Frederick Philip Grove's *Over Prairie Trails* (1922) remains a signal achievement of the period and genre (*Trails*, another story cycle, is mixed genre actually, what would now be called creative non-fiction). Morley Callaghan performed his own version of a Hemingway pruning of prose even as he moved the Modern Canadian story into an urban setting with brief fictions of very un-American, visionary, sacramental, and Catholic dénouements (cf. Davey, 145). And through the 1930s such well-known Canadian writers as Dorothy Livesay, A.M. Klein, and Ted Allan published in such periodicals as the *Canadian Forum* stories that demonstrate the marked influences of the Depression and the social realism (and attendant ideology of socialism/communism) that many writers throughout the world turned to as the most apparently efficacious means of alleviating their fellow citizens' troubles (see Doyle, 'Just'). It would seem that global hard times came closer than any cosmopolitan Anglo-American aesthetics to making the literary world one in its fictions.

The mid-century saw a great number of writers who would go on to achieve international reputations as novelists, such as Robertson Davies and Margaret Laurence, first come to attention as writers of humorous sketches and psychologically realistic stories. Also at this time Sinclair Ross began publishing his naturalistic dust-bowl endurance stories, stories that remain unmatched for the skill with which they unflinchingly depict men and women struggling together in elemental conditions. (If not for its lack of continuing characters and a return story, a collection such as Ross's *The Lamp at Noon* would satisfy my definition of a story cycle, as discussed below; certainly *Lamp*, with its similar settings and relentless readdressing of naturalistic-existential themes, comes closer than any other miscellany to qualifying as a story cycle.) These writers (and other notables such as Jack Parr) were able to achieve a measure of national recognition because of the currency of such popular weekly supplements to newspapers as the *Star Weekly*, such magazines as *Maclean's* and *Saturday Night*, and such literary periodicals as *Queen's Quarterly* and *Tamarack Review* (the last of which was edited by Robert Weaver, a key figure in the development of the contemporary Canadian short story, both for *Tamarack* and for his weekly CBC *Anthology* series on radio). These venues provided publication for writers too numerous to name during what was both the heyday and swan song for short story writing and reading in Canada (see Weiss). Ironically, not only the popular short story but the well-crafted Modern version as well was probably assisted in attaining this high point of reputation in the early to mid-twentieth century by the falling off of literary attention spans (short stories *are* short), before the full occupation of an electronic mass media bent on rendering literary pursuits obsolete and drawing off the advertising revenue that was the lifeblood of the magazines.

The establishment of the Canada Council towards the end of the 1950s did much to increase an interest in Canadian literature inside and outside the burgeoning university community. A hopeful number of nationalistic publishers, literary periodicals, and Canadian literature courses were suddenly established thanks to the largesse of taxpayers, via the Council, and to material causes such as the availability of affordable paperback editions of Canadian books like McClelland and Stewart's New Canadian Library under the general editorship of Malcolm Ross. This interest and government (taxpayer) patronage complimented the third upsurge both of Canadian cultural nationalism and of short story writing. But the increased activity in the 1960s and 1970s, particularly as regards the short story, was not sustained through the 1980s and 1990s, and seemed at the end of the century to be falling off rather precipitously.[9]

Regardless, the critical achievements of Canada's short story writers in the contemporary period are well known and require no rehearsal in this brief sketch interested more in the earlier history of the genre.[10] The efflorescence of talent and styles since about 1960 would make even an ambitious listing of writers still too highly selective to serve any but an unnecessarily contentious and idiosyncratic agenda. Suffice it to say that in the 1960s and 1970s, and to a lesser degree in the 1980s and 1990s, the Canadian short story has continued to enjoy a moderate popularity of practice, if not of sales. It should be observed too, though, that the enduring interest in the short story is largely an academic matter literally, as the practice of short story reading in the wider public seems set on sharing the fate of poetry. That said, few critics or readers would contest, surely, a severely limited list giving the most important short story writers of this period which is headed by Hugh Hood, Norman Levine, Mavis Gallant, Alice Munro, Alistair MacLeod, and Margaret Atwood. After that, I think it safe to say, readers of the present study must feel free to indulge their own turn-of-the-millennium fetish of list-making.

What does need to be said is that many Canadian novelists who first found success in the short form are better there than in the novel (here, names are uncalled for). One of the causes of this wayward development from good short story writer to middling novelist is market considerations given inflated importance by publishers' delusions about what readers want. Another cause is that writers must use their time economically, considering the risk-reward ratio of writing a novel as compared with time spent on financially unrewarding short stories, which is a cause that inversely parallels the reasons for the attraction of the short story to nineteenth-century Canadian writers. But whatever the reasons – and they would include mistaken perceptions of aesthetic merit and the mega-lomaniacal tendencies of modern life – the novel has also become the form in which fiction writers feel they must prove themselves. And publishers do encourage them to think so: both Laurence and Munro had to resist pressure from their American publishers to turn story cycles into novels (Hoy, 67–8). Although it is critically cockeyed to see the short story as the apprentice work of future novelists, readers might well wonder about the novels that will be (and are being) written by writers who have not learned to hone their prose and trim their tales in the discipline of the short story. One palpable observation: novels have certainly been getting bigger and baggier at the turn of the twentieth century, reverting to the dimensions of their nineteenth-century ascendancy, when minute repre-sentationalism was understandable given the unavailability of shared pho-tographic and cinematic versions of events. But if literary attention spans have been dwindling, and they have, we might well wonder: Are these all-new jumbo narratives being read at all? Or are such tomes not per-haps being bought and displayed as quaint cultural kitsch, like man-size hookah pipes in the smoke-free home?

Stubbornly, many of Canada's most accomplished novelists do con-tinue to write short stories that are among the best being published any-where (and the names Atwood, Shields, and Vanderhaeghe come readily to mind). In Alice Munro Canada has produced a writer exclusively of short stories who is widely acknowledged to be among the best ever in English. The form would indeed seem to hold an enduring attraction for Canadian writers, even if very few collections of short stories are pub-lished any more by Canada's globalized corporate publishers, and by fewer and fewer of our literary publishers. Everyone wants a novel, and publishers' declarations that story collections do not sell, and therefore cannot be successfully published (that is, marketed), become self-fulfilling prophecy. If New's theory of marginality helps explain the traditional and (at least to some extent) lasting appeal of the short story for Canadian writers, what then might its weakening, assisted by (im)pure marketing interests, portend? That Canada's is no longer a marginal culture? That the concept of a marginal culture no longer appertains in our webbed world? Or that, as a distinct culture, we are being drawn closer to the expanding American centre, that place where incisive irony bewilders and where literary fiction, like much else, is successful or not in terms exclu-sively pecuniary and megalomaniacal – that place where the title of Alice

Munro's masterful cycle of stories, *Who Do You Think You Are?*, was changed to *The Beggar Maid*, because the American publisher found the original idiom too mystifyingly Canadian (Struthers, 'Material,' 29)? Tellingly, Munro's original title points emphatically, aggressively, to the question of identity, the revised one somewhere else.

The Short Story Cycle and the Canadian Story Cycle

In the first essay of *The Dialogic Imagination*, Bakhtin writes of the power of 'the novel' to exact a generically normative influence on all other genres – to 'novelize' the other genres is his translator's word (5–6). And at first blush this idea could be seen to explain the tendency of the various prose mini-forms to gather into different kinds of collections – such as instructive epistles, folk-tale collections, sketch books, short story cycles – that are then viewed as exhibiting a sort of novel envy. If we accept Bakhtin's grandiose concept of the novel as a literary anti-system, as a self-criticizing anti-generic force, as *the* generic site of 'polyglossia' (12) – as, really, more humankind's creatively liberalizing impulse than its literary product (as in, say, the English novel from the middle of the eighteenth century), then his argument for 'the novel's' universal weightiness is compelling, if bombastic still. (I would even suggest that the brilliantly repetitive Bakhtin, in overextending his critical type, the novel, risks the definition error of vacuousness that Fowler warns against [33].) Interestingly, in view of his contention regarding the 'ability of the novel to criticize itself ... a remarkable feature of this ever-developing genre' (6), it could as well be argued that the short story cycle is the next stage in the evolution of the novel, as some of those implicitly novel-critiquing features of the cycle are discussed below. Still, many features of short story cycles do make the form accord neatly with Bakhtin's description of developments in other genres as a consequence of the novel's presumed generic gravity: 'They become more free and flexible, their language renews itself by incorporating extraliterary heteroglossia and the "novelistic" layers of literary language, they become dialogized, permeated with laughter, irony, humor, elements of self-parody and finally – this is the most important thing – the novel inserts into these other genres an indeterminacy, a certain semantic openendedness, a living contact with unfinished, still-evolving contemporary reality (the openended present)' (7).

Bakhtin talks of the novel both as a generically renovating, revolutionary force in human history and as the product we think of when we think of 'the novel' – say, *Tom Jones, Wacousta, Crime and Punishment, Ulysses*

– and I choose to conceive of it in the latter, more mundane sense. That way, I can argue that the shorter prose forms have also been exacting a powerful generic influence of their own for the past few hundred years, or longer, and that the novel could as justifiably be viewed as but the most popular fictional form into which the shorter prose forms have extended themselves/infiltrated, with the other form being the later independent-interdependent form of the story cycle itself. Which is to argue that the short story cycle is not so clearly influenced by the rise and ascendancy of the English novel. It is a form, a genre, distinct from it, owing more to common sources with the short story than with the novel. And recall: taking Samuel Richardson's epistolary *Pamela* as a beginning, in one version of the rise of the English novel it emerges from a short prose form, the middle-class-serving collection of conduct letters (Watt). So, it could indeed as justifiably be argued that, especially since the turn of the twentieth century with the arrival of modernism, the novel has been undergoing 'storification.'

But I am being only critically halfhearted with the observation that the story cycle displays these characteristic features of both Bakhtinian novelization and the all-inclusive novel itself as he conceived it. Somewhat more earnestly, I would set forth the possibility that the genre of the short story cycle, in implicitly critiquing some of the defining features of the conventional novel itself, can be viewed as displacing/replacing the traditional novel, and not merely as renovating it. However, intriguing as I hope such notions may sound (and more below), my immediate purpose here is more practical. And so to the Canadian short story cycle.

Readers and critics interested in the English-Canadian short story cycle can hesitantly claim predecessors for it (in what Barbara Godard calls its 'venerable history' [28]) in the works of early writers of epistolary novels, collections of letters, and books of loosely linked sketches: in Frances Brooke's *A History of Emily Montague* (1769), in Thomas McCulloch's *Letters of Mephibosheth Stepsure* (serialized 1821–3), perhaps most justifiably in the first series of Thomas Chandler Haliburton's *The Clockmaker* (1836), and in the collections of nature and character sketches of Catharine Parr Traill, Susanna Moodie, and many other sketch-artists of the nineteenth century. Such writings may indeed be seen, if we squint a bit, to anticipate the story cycle, but only to the same extent that transcripts of the political speeches of Joseph Howe to Mechanics Institutes in eastern Canada in the mid-nineteenth century and, a little later, those of Sir John A. Macdonald on the necessity of Confederation can be said to constitute the beginnings of the essay in Canada. Which is to say: only at a stretch.[11] It might also be observed that, from about the mid-nineteenth century onwards, such short fictional and quasi-fictional works would have been influenced by Charles Dickens's *Sketches by Boz* (1836) and *Pickwick Papers* (1837), and that Dickens's very popular first books were likely a seminal influence not only on the English-Canadian short story cycle – especially with regard to Susanna Moodie and Stephen Leacock – but on the story cycle in English literature generally. I suspect, too, that a similar claim can be made for Ivan Turgenev's *A Sportsman's Sketches* (1852), the book which Sherwood Anderson, author of the first Modern American story cycle, *Winesburg, Ohio* (1919), considered 'one of the great books of the world' (in Ingram, 148n12), and which Frank O'Connor enthusiastically described as perhaps 'the greatest book of short stories ever written.' O'Connor goes pertinently further: 'Nobody, at the time it was written, knew quite how great it was, or what influence it was to have in the creation of a new art form' (46).

But, that said, earlier writings are too often called upon to perform distorting turns of anticipation and fulfilment, and, intertextuality notwithstanding, we should be wary of committing what Northrop Frye has described as a kind of anachronistic fallacy. To call something 'pre-romantic,' according to Frye, 'has the peculiar demerit of committing us to anachronism before we start, and imposing a false teleology on everything we study' (*Fables*, 130). It is safer to observe that, to the extent that these writings *can* be said to anticipate the story cycle in Canada – apart from what they are as fictional letters and sketch books – the form first comes into its own in Duncan Campbell Scott's story cycle of a community in western Quebec, *In the Village of Viger* (1896), and, a little later, in Stephen Leacock's humorous treatment of small-town Ontario at about the same time, *Sunshine Sketches of a Little Town* (1912). *Viger* and the *Sketches* were the first to weave for literary artistic purpose, with self-consciously fictional intent, the various strands of the nineteenth-century nature sketch, character sketch, anecdote, tall tale, local colour writing, fable, and romantic tale that preceded the formation of the Modern story and story cycle. Scott's *Viger* is in fact a *tour de force* of those nineteenth-century story forms (Dragland, Introduction, 12), while Leacock's sketches parody many of the same types.[12]

Throughout the twentieth century, the story cycle continued to be well suited to the concerns of Canadian writers intent upon portraying a particular region or community, its history, its characters, its communal concerns, regions and communities as diverse as the world of working women in the Montreal of J.G. Sime's *Sister Woman* (1919), the multicultural Montreal of Hugh Hood's *Around the Mountain* (1967), and the working-class Jewish community of Richler's *The Street* (1968); the dust-bowl prairies of Sinclair Ross's suggestively cyclical *The Lamp at Noon and Other Stories* (1968, though published in magazines over the preceding decades); southern Ontario small-town life some fifty years after Mariposa in George Elliott's *The Kissing Man* (1962); the eccentric west coast islanders of Jack Hodgins's *Spit Delaney's Island* (1976) and the spiritedly impoverished Cape Bretoners of Sheldon Currie's *The Glace Bay Miner's Museum* (1979) in the 1970s; the mostly women's lives of Sandra Birdsell's semi-rural residents of the fictional community of Agassiz, Manitoba, in *Night Travellers* (1982) and *Ladies of the House* (1984), and the Albertan Pine Mountain Lodge (an old folks' home) of Edna Alford's *A Sleep Full of Dreams* (1981) in the 1980s; Thomas King's Leacockean portrayal of Native community life in *Medicine River* (1989) and Derek McCormack's depiction of homosexual life in *Wish Book: A Catalogue of Stories* (1999) in the 1990s. Other story cycles, such as Margaret Laurence's *A Bird in the House* (1970), Clark Blaise's *A North American Education* (1973), Alice Munro's *Who Do You Think You Are?* (1978), Robert Currie's *Night Games* (1983), Isabel Huggan's *The Elizabeth Stories* (1984), and McCormack's *Dark Rides: A Novel in Stories* (1996), focus on the growth of a single character in a particular community, illustrating in the story cycle the interest in individual psychology since the rise of modernism.[13] And any survey of the high points of cyclical story form in Canada must accommodate such unacknowledged innovators in the genre as the Frederick Philip Grove of *Over Prairie Trails* (1922), the Emily Carr of *Klee Wyck* (1941), and the Hugh MacLennan of *Seven Rivers of Canada* (1961), the last of which employs the serial-cyclical form to take in the whole of Canada through its main rivers. But as the present study devotes a chapter to George Elliott's formally more conventional (if stylistically experimental) story cycle *The Kissing Man* of 1962, I decided, after a chapter on *Trails* and *Klee Wyck*, that I couldn't justify a detour into MacLennan's intriguing ficto-geographic experiment with story cycle form.

In addition to providing opportunities for a conventional exploration of place and character, the story cycle also offers formal possibilities that allow its practitioners the opportunity to challenge, whether intentionally or not, the totalizing impression of the traditional novel of social and psychological realism. (And I emphasize here the adjective *traditional*, aware that there are many contemporary novels, such as Thomas King's *Medicine River*, that are patently short story cycles advertised as novels by wary publishers.)[14] Canadian writers who have been inspired to compose something more unified than the miscellaneous collection of stories and who did not wish to forego the documentary aspect of the realistic novel (a fictional strategy that will likely continue to have relevance in a relatively young country), but who were wary of the traditional novel's grander ambitions – suspicious of its totalizations, of its coherent plot, neatly linear sense of time and drive towards closure – have found in the story cycle a form that allows for a new kind of unity in disunity, reflecting a fragmented temporal sense, and incorporating a more authentic representation of modern sensibilities.[15] For example, even such late nineteenth- and early twentieth-century cycles as Scott's *Viger* and Leacock's *Sunshine Sketches* portray the struggles of small communities for coherence and survival under contrary pressures from metropolitanism and modernity, in this form that figures the tension between cohesion and a kind of entropy, solidarity and fragmentation, essentialism and contingency – between things holding together and things falling apart. Later, such writers as Grove, Carr, Laurence, and Munro explore the formation of fictional personality in this form that simultaneously subverts the impression of completion, of closure and totality, suggesting that psychic coherence, essentialism of self, may be as much an illusion in fact as in fiction. Considered in this way, in the deeper disparities between its form and its subject, the story cycle can be seen to display a critical tension between its 'outer form' and 'inner form,' as those determinants of distinctive genre were first termed by Wellek and Warren (231).

Forrest L. Ingram, still the foremost theorist of the short story cycle,[16] provided the first description of its primary distinguishing feature, what amounts to the story cycle's version of the hermeneutic circle: it is 'a book of short stories so linked to each other by their author that the reader's successive experience on various levels of the pattern of the whole significantly modifies his experience of each of its component parts' (19). Ingram describes thus the essential feature of the outer form of the short story cycle: its unique balancing of the integrity of each individual story and the whole collection, what he calls 'the tension between the one and the many' (19). And it proves interesting already to consider Robert Kroetsch's observation of Canadian literature and culture generally in light of this distinguishing feature of the story cycle – its unique balancing of the one and the many. 'In Canadian writing,' observes Kroetsch, 'and perhaps in Canadian life, there is an exceptional pressure placed on the individual and the self by the community or society. The self is not in any way Romantic or privileged. The small town remains the ruling paradigm, with its laws and familiarity and conformity. Self and community almost fight to a draw' (*Lovely*, 51; see also Meindl, 18, 22). The postmodernist Kroetsch's uncharacteristically conservative observation is based, I suspect, on perceptions familiar to numerous other Canadian writers who have generalized similarly: in the attempt to find that elusive balance between the one and the many – for reasons of physical and political environment, for historical reasons – Canadians, unlike Americans, have been more willing to sacrifice the gratifications of individualism for the securities of community. Why? The attempt at a literary-critical answer to that one-word question is part of the purpose of the present study of the short story cycle as a distinctively Canadian genre, and so cannot be stated succinctly and simply. But an initial answer might begin with considerations of physical and ideological environment – a geography that isolates, a philosophical tradition of humanism and conservatism – and of broadly historical determinants (the psychic sense of beleaguerment, and of refusing to choose between opposing positions). Such influences in a developing national culture and character led eventually to various, yet consistent, positions: to the virtual enthronement of compromise as the political modus operandi, to the positing of the middle way as the best mode of ideological travel, to irony as a distinguishing tone of voice (see Hutcheon), and even to finding in the image of the peacekeeper – the one who literally stands between opposing forces – an international *raison d'être*.[17] Such generalizations about national character, however centrist and stereotyping they might sound, are nonetheless necessary to a discussion of Canadian literature and the present study of the English-Canadian short story cycle. Sherrill Grace helps justify such broad cultural observations: 'Before one can decide whether or not the predominance or use of a pattern comprises a "typically Canadian" imaginative act, one must be able to describe the patterns, not the themes, of that imagination' (451). But *are* such generalizations about national character expressed in that literary pattern called the short story cycle? Consider for now this key comparison: it is not serendipity that the seminal work of American literature was considered by Ernest Hemingway (21) to be *The Adventures of Huckleberry Finn*, a first-person episodic novel whose title is the name of its highly individualized hero, a satiric picaresque from the point of view of an outsider ingenuously castigating the institutions of his community. Although I long wished that Robertson Davies had made the claim when he had the opportunity, I would propose that a comparable candidate for our first great work of fiction is Leacock's *Sunshine Sketches of a Little Town*, a book whose title focuses attention on the community and whose viewpoint is very much that of the ironic insider, the Leacock persona-narrator, and a book whose form, the short story cycle, manages to balance the needs of the one and the many in a manner that might also be seen to suggest further a geopolitical appropriateness of this popular form in Canada.

Forrest Ingram has also described a tripartite system of categorizing story cycles according to the ways in which they were conceived and compiled. He types story cycles as 1) 'composed,' that is, cycles which 'the author had conceived as a whole from the time he wrote its first story,' a cycle such as *Sunshine Sketches*; as 2) 'arranged,' that is, ones which 'an author or editor-author has brought together to illuminate or comment upon one another by juxtaposition or association,' a cycle such as *In the Village of Viger*; and as 3) 'completed,' that is, 'sets of linked stories which are neither strictly composed nor merely arranged,' but ones which were completed when their author recognized the links within a group of stories, a cycle such as *Who Do You Think You Are?* (15–18). But here Ingram's ground-breaking study takes us only so far in understanding and appreciating this form that occupies the generic gap between the miscellany of short stories and the novel, between the discontinuous form on the one hand and the totalizing on the other.[18]

A more useful and faithful method of categorizing story cycles is the simpler one of viewing them in terms of what lends the cycle its primary coherence, what holds it together in its cyclical form. There are story cycles that are unified primarily by place, such influential classics of the genre as James Joyce's *Dubliners* (1914) and Anderson's *Winesburg, Ohio*; or such Canadian examples as Scott's *Viger*, George Elliott's *The Kissing Man*, Hood's *Around the Mountain*, Currie's *The Glace Bay Miner's Museum*, Hodgins's *Spit Delaney's Island* (set on Vancouver Island), Sandra Birdsell's Agassiz cycles. In this proposed system the other major category accommodates cycles that are unified by character, such as Grove's *Over Prairie Trails*, Carr's *Klee Wyck*, Laurence's *A Bird in the House*, Munro's *Who Do You Think You Are?* and Huggan's *The Elizabeth Stories* (1984). Two minor categories can be added to these major ones of place and character. There are miscellanies of stories that are unified by a consistent thematic concern – any of Charles G.D. Roberts's volumes of animal stories and especially Ross's *The Lamp at Noon and Other Stories* come to mind. And there are story collections that impress readers as more than usually unified by a consistent style or tone, collections that often also cohere around a central theme or recurrent themes – such as Norman Levine's collections, any of Munro's miscellaneous collections, or Guy Vanderhaeghe's *Man Descending* (1982). I am wary, though, of including collections from these two minor categories in my definition of short story cycles; in fact, I do not include them, simply because on such a basis claims for inclusion can be made for almost any miscellany of stories. As Fowler cautions regarding looseness of generic definition, 'overextending a critical type, as perhaps William Empson did in *Some Versions of Pastoral*, makes it in the end vacuous' (33).[19]

If according to my proposed system the presence of a constituent theme or a consistent style alone cannot be the defining characteristic of a story cycle, it would be mistaken not to take account of the role those aspects play in strengthening the coherence of cycles unified primarily by place and/or character, the two major categories on which I will remain focused throughout this study. And, it should be added, what is true of any broadly categorizing system is true also of the system being proposed here; namely, that these two major categories overlap. With the Grove persona, the familiar trails of *Over Prairie Trails* lend coherence to Grove's story cycle. Hanratty, Rose's hometown, serves also to unify Munro's *Who Do You Think You Are?* Laurence's *A Bird in the House* is unified by a combination of the character of Vanessa MacLeod and Manawaka. In Edna Alford's *A Sleep Full of Dreams*, it is both the character of Arla Pederson and the setting of an old folks' home that lends unity to the cycle. And Thomas King's *Medicine River* coheres around both Will and the home-place of the cycle's title. I would also note here what will emerge convincingly by the end of this study: that where story cycles unified by place are never dependent on a single recurring character, Canadian story cycles unified primarily by a recurrent character *are* reliant also on place. In the Canadian short story cycle, place plays an essential role in the formation of character, while gracing both the character and the cycle itself with additional significant coherence.

But even if this alternate system of classifying story cycles according to what contributes most to their coherence – what, apart from their structure, makes them story cycles – takes us further than does a system that must often speculate on the principles that governed the cycle's composition (Ingram's distinction), it still betrays the spirit of the story cycle, and does so fundamentally. In this regard, categorization of genres is a good way to begin discussing a diverse form, not an end in itself, as Fowler is prone to repeat (24). For there is something troubling in this useful recourse to place and character (let alone a constituent theme or consistent tone). Such a method of subgeneric categorizing can lead to the view of story cycles as failed novels; that is, to judgments based on inappropriate generic rules, the very thing I would like most to avoid. Again as Fowler says, 'When rules of the wrong genre are applied, they naturally seem arbitrary and oppressive' (28). It is the traditional novel, from Richardson to Richler, that presents a continuous narrative of character, place, theme, and style, however minutely particularized or scrambled the chronology of that narrative has become from Laurence Sterne's *The Life and Opinions of Tristram Shandy* (1759–67) to Richler's *Joshua Then and Now* (1980). And, of course, the novel coheres most obviously in being a narrated plot extended over a comparatively lengthy period of time. Short stories, because they so often describe only climactic actions, continue to be distinguished for their concision. Even in a linked series they will always lack the traditional novel's chief advantage as a unified action (whether external or internal), temporally continuous, and couched in a totalizing narrative form. There is something essential to stories that is decidedly anti-novel (*pace* Bakhtin), something (as Poe realized at the genre's inception) that is indeed closer to lyric poetry – the illuminating flash of climactic action temporally suspended rather than the steadily growing light of causal development (see Poe, 480–92 and 443–6). But reviewers and critics too often persist in approaching story cycles with an inappropriate aesthetic; that is, with the wrong eyes, with a sensibility preconditioned by hundreds of years of novel domination. A staggered series of flashes will never a steady beam make. The sequence that is a story cycle signals a different code altogether: the world and life as seen by stroboscope, held still momentarily, strangely fragmented into new arrangements, moving unfamiliarly in the minds of readers accustomed to the spatial and temporal panorama of novels. That steady beam, itself an illusion of novelistic codes, is broken up, perhaps intentionally disrupted in the way that many a Modern novel set about marring its most attractive generic feature.

The success of a story cycle should not be judged, therefore, with regard to its approximation of the achievement of a novel.[20] Its success should not depend on the extent to which it is unified by place, character, theme, or style, nor, for that matter, should it be judged finally by any aesthetic grounded on the desirability for a continuous and complete unfolding and closure. Although the story cycle appears especially accommodating to Canadian writers who wish to examine in their fiction particular places and characters, the form is also paradoxically unique for the ways in which it often reflects the exploration of the *failure* of place and character to unify a vision that remains tantalizingly whole yet fundamentally suspicious of completeness. Place, Viger for instance, does not only hold together Duncan Campbell Scott's *In the Village of Viger*; here, place does and does not unify, for place in this story cycle also fails to lend coherence because *Viger* is about the ways in which the things of Viger the place are threatening to fall apart in the onslaught of metropolitan modernity. Perhaps this suspiciously neat paradox can also be stated in terms of the outer and inner dynamic of the form (which I borrow again from Wellek and Warren, 231), with Viger the setting of the stories, the fictional place, representing the outer dynamic that obviously gives coherence to the stories of this cycle, and with Viger the figure of Scott's vision of a Canadian communal ideal at the turn of the twentieth century, the ideological place, representing the inner principle that is being destabilized by the modern world and, consequently, destabilizes the lives of its residents. To take one more example, this time from the other major category of story cycles: in similar manner the character Rose does not ultimately unify Munro's *Who Do You Think You Are?* That story cycle is also about notions of essential selfhood and character – how they are formed and represented, how individual identity is provisionally achieved – as whole entities in both fiction and life: with Rose, the representation of the destabilized self, as a kind of inner principle threatening ideas of coherent personality, and with Rose the recurrent character who knits the fictions together as the outer dynamic that confirms our expectations of character development. Often each story of a cycle raises such problems of continuity and coherence only to defer their desired solutions to the next story in the cycle, whose conflict both repeats and advances that of its predecessor, until readers reach the final story of the cycle, which, as one result of its cumulative function, now returns them to the preceding stories in the context of the cycle as a whole. Story cycles viewed with regard to their outer and inner forms, whether cycles of character or place, seldom close on a grounding essence or reassuring presence. Some do come asymptotically close, though.

It is understandable, then, that this form came into its own at the end of the nineteenth century and is in the main a twentieth-century form. The popularity of short story cycles coincides with the arrival of the modern world, when the revolutionary impact of Darwin, Marx, Freud, and Einstein was being cumulatively felt and all traditional systems were coming under a destabilizing scrutiny (by these totalizing systems themselves, ironically), including the tradition of the realistic-naturalistic novel. Viewed in this context, the short story cycle can indeed be considered as a kind of anti-novel, fragmenting the continuous narrative's treatment of place, time, character, and plot, and often offering simultaneous multiple perspectives in a manner paralleling that of cubist painting.[21] There were those in Canada at this time, such as Scott, Leacock, Sime, and Grove, who used the fragmented/fragmenting form paradoxically for intentionally totalizing purposes. In 1912 Leacock employed place, Mariposa, to display ironically his ideal of a Tory and humanist community. Yet repeatedly in individual stories, the community, portrayed as robbed from within and without of genuine religious spirit and political leadership by the combined influences of materialism, metropolitanism, and mistaken characters, seems nonetheless always to be resisting Leacock's unifying vision. Those critics who regret that Leacock did not write, perhaps could not write, a novel (and there are many of them) have failed to see just how appropriate his chosen form – the story cycle – is to his lament for an essentially eighteenth- and nineteenth-century social philosophy of tolerance and responsibility in the frenetic modern age.[22] When before him Duncan Campbell Scott conceived of Viger, the small town on the periphery of a Quebec city at the turn of the century, and when his vision showed him, too, that all the values of the traditional humanist and conservative were here under attack from the forces of urbanization and modernity, were in fact threatened with disintegration, what better form could he have chosen to display that situation than the short story cycle? When the modernists Grove and Carr turn the light inward to explore the psychology of the formation of their own personas as artists, they do so in this form that highlights, not consistency and coherence, but formation *as* process in a natural setting, even as re-formation. Given such visions of disintegrative reality, the nineteenth-century novel of social and psychological realism, with its grandly totalizing conventions, would rightly have been considered as formally inappropriate to the insights seeking and forebodings moving towards expression. And what was true of formal appropriateness at the beginning of the century became only more apparent as the decades tore by like fissured beads on a fraying string. At mid-century, in *Orpheus in Quebec* (1942), J.G. Sime makes a striking observation of the kind of formal-generic-cultural appropriateness I'm suggesting here: 'one feels in the cities, I think, the potentialities of quite another kind of art – disjointed, disconnected art that finds its expression in thumb-nail sketches, short stories, one-act scrappy plays, and the like' (34). Since Sime is the author of the most underrated story cycle discussed in the present study, *Sister Woman* (1919), a remarkable fiction of sororal community set in First World War Montreal, I indulge myself in thinking that her closing 'and the like' refers to the subject of the present study – the form she had excelled in some two decades before making this statement – the short story cycle.

To return to more practical considerations of form: story cycles work through a process that Ingram calls 'recurrent development,' 'the dynamic patterns of recurrence and development' (20), and that Robert M. Luscher describes similarly in this way: 'As in the musical sequence, the story sequence repeats and progressively develops themes and motifs over the course of the work; its unity derives from a perception of both the successive ordering and recurrent patterns, which together provide the continuity of the reading experience' (149; cf. Godard, 29–30). In such a pattern, the first and last stories are most often the ones of key significance, with the final story of the cycle being the most powerful, because there the patterns of recurrence and development initiated in the opening story come naturally to fullest expression. Opening stories in cycles of place usually describe the setting of the ensuing stories in a way that presents place as one of the cycle's major dramatis personae. For example, *Viger*'s 'The Little Milliner' and *Sunshine Sketches*' 'The Hostelry of Mr. Smith' do so in ways that also provide a frame for the stories that follow; the first story of George Elliott's *The Kissing Man*, 'An Act of Piety,' locates the community quite literally with regard to compass points and lists neighbours whose family members will become major players in the stories that follow. These opening stories also introduce into the contained, the framed, community a disruptive element: the metropolitan Little Milliner herself, the abandoned woman of *Sister Woman*'s 'Alone,' Josh Smith, Prop. of the *Sketches*, the diseased Irish of *The Kissing Man*, the dehumanizing poverty of Sheldon Currie's 'The Glace Bay Miner's Museum,' the old-age death-in-life humiliation of Edna Alford's 'The Hoyer.' Cycles whose primary unity is provided by a central character begin in bildungsroman fashion, as might be expected, with a story of the protagonist's childhood, establishing a pattern that is repeated with variation in the ensuing turnings of the cycle. In 'Ucluelet,' Carr actually misrepresents her age at the time of actual events in order to foreground her persona in the tradition of orphan-girl fictions; *A Bird in the House* opens with 'The Sound of the Singing,' a story of Vanessa's earliest sense of richness and deprivation in the patriarchal home; 'Royal Beatings,' the opening story of Munro's *Who Do You Think You Are?*, presents the first remembered confusion of love and pain in Rose's life, and begins to deal with the problem of representation – by mirroring, paralleling, doubling, echoing – regarding these determining formulators of her personality.

But as the chapters that follow will show, it is in their variations of organization and their concluding stories that cycles present the most serious challenges to readers and critics (and provide most readerly pleasure, of course). Concluding stories of pure story cycles bring to fulfilment the recurrent patterns, frequently reintroducing many of the preceding stories' major characters and central images, and restating in a refrain-like manner the main thematic concerns. In doing so, concluding stories are in effect the feature that most clearly distinguishes the family of the Canadian story cycle from its near cousins, the series or sequence of stories, and the tonally unified miscellanies. Because I have already published a critical book on Stephen Leacock's writings which deals extensively with *Sunshine Sketches* and *Arcadian Adventures with the Idle Rich* (1914), in the present study I am not writing at length about either of these high points in the development of the Canadian short story cycle. Fortunately, Scott's *Viger* is available as a similar story cycle of small-town place at about the same time; and at least one critic prefers it to the *Sketches* as the 'forerunner of the modern Canadian short story cycle' (Meindl, 18). Because of the paramount importance of the concluding stories of cycles, however, I will round off this introduction by drawing on *Sunshine Sketches* first to show the ways a great writer employs story cycle structure to convey the meanings of his subject – suggesting the ways that genre *is* meaning – and second to illustrate briefly some of the ways in which the concluding stories of story cycles work; in this instance, the ways in which the unsurpassed 'L'Envoi: The Train to Mariposa' closes the short story cycle that is *Sunshine Sketches of a Little Town*.

Leacock made three major structural revisions to *Sunshine Sketches* between its serial publication in the *Montreal Star* from 17 February 1912 to 22 June 1912 and its publication in book form later that year. He added the preface and reorganized the stories, dividing and combining, as follows: the first two instalments for the *Star*, 'Mariposa and Its People' and 'The Glorious Victory of Mr. Smith,' were combined to form the book's opening story, 'The Hostelry of Mr. Smith'; and the sixth instalment for the *Star*, 'Mariposa's Whirlwind Campaign,' was divided to become the fifth and sixth stories of the published book, 'The Whirlwind Campaign in Mariposa' and 'The Beacon on the Hill.' The addition of the Preface is significant because it and the concluding story of the cycle, 'L'Envoi: The Train to Mariposa,' provide an extra-Mariposan frame for the stories proper. That is, Leacock's preface and 'L'Envoi' present readers with different, though complementary, perspectives on *Sunshine Sketches* and

Mariposa, perspectives that differ not only from one another but also from the point of view of the variable narrator of the interior stories (1 through 11). All three perspectives – those of the authorial prefacer, the ironically involved narrator of the interior stories, and the reflective narrator of 'L'Envoi' (another Leacock persona) – are necessary to a rounded view of the town and the book. They give us Leacock's, the prefacer's, advice on how to approach his fiction, the narrator's insider-outsider vision of Mariposa, and the Envoi narrator's retrospective view on how we should think about what 'Mariposa' means as 'home' and the meanings of *Sunshine Sketches* as imaginative literature (the Envoi narrator actually refers self-reflexively to 'such a book as the present one' [141]).

By reorganizing the opening and middle parts of the book, Leacock gave prominence to the character of Josh Smith, who dominates the opening and closing stories on business and politics, and so bestrides the town like a suspect colossus. Also, Leacock's reorganization created in the book's middle – stories 4 through 9 – two three-story sections, of which the first is concerned with Mariposan religion and the second with Mariposan romance. This symmetrical centre of the *Sketches*, like dual triptychs, actually opposes three stories on the failure of Mariposa's institutionalized religion to meet simply, in broad as opposed to high fashion, the needs of its Anglican parishioners with three on the virtues of Mariposa in matters of romance, love, marriage, and family. And this structurally contrived, balanced opposition at the centre of *Sunshine Sketches of a Little Town* should begin to show the ways in which Leacock's masterpiece is a more complexly wrought work than is usually recognized – that it is in fact proof of Leacock's implicit claim in his preface that it is an 'arduous contrivance' (xvii). More pertinently, the revised organization of this short story cycle can be seen aptly to body forth the values of Leacock's humanism, toryism, and eminently practical vision of human community in Canada.

The interior stories of the *Sketches* are grouped, then, into five thematic sections: 1) stories 1 and 2, concerning Josh Smith and Jefferson Thorpe respectively, deal with real and illusory business in Mariposa, with the first including an important reference to and anticipation of the political matters of the two closing stories; 2) using the ship trope, story 3, 'The Marine Excursion of the Knights of Pythias,' portrays in microcosm the social life of Mariposa aboard the *Mariposa Belle*; 3) stories 4 through 6 deal with the religious life of the town; 4) stories 7 through 9 centre on romance and family; and 5) stories 10 and 11 depict the political life of the Mariposans and the shenanigans of their candidates for office. Schematized so, the two-story business and political sections of the *Sketches* (dominated by Smith) can be seen structurally to frame yet again, or to contain further, the social, religious, and romantic concerns of the town. This is what might be expected in the fiction of a career-long professor of political economy at McGill University, and the exigencies of such a writer's priorities offer a reason why the third story, the social microcosm, is not the first in the cycle, as might be expected. In other words, the structure – indeed the restructuring – of the short story cycle that is *Sunshine Sketches* perfectly conveys the priorities of life in Mariposa and, in its pragmatic attitude, Leacock's mind: the practical realities of business and politics first and last, while at the heart of the book – his only fiction written specifically for a Canadian readership, recall – are found what may be called the spiritual realities of religion and love. Such analysis of the organization of the stories of *Sunshine Sketches*, foreshortened though it is, may yet serve to confirm Alistair Fowler's repeated statements that genre does not provide just a vehicle for the conveyance of meaning but that genre *is* meaning. 'Of all the codes of our literary *langue*,' he writes (reforming Saussure's term), 'I have no hesitation in proposing genre as the most important, not least because it incorporates and organizes many others. Just how many other codes are generically articulated remains uncertain. Probably far more than we are aware of. At any rate there is no doubt that genre primarily has to do with communication. It is an instrument not of classification or prescription, but of meaning' (22).

Nowhere does the genre of the Canadian short story cycle more concisely *mean* than in its concluding stories. I call these concluding stories of cycles 'return stories.'[23] As in such return poems as William Wordsworth's 'Tintern Abbey,' Charles G.D. Roberts's 'The Tantramar Revisited,' and Al Purdy's 'The Country North of Belleville,' return stories are defined by their reflections on the passage of time, change, and identity. In 'L'Envoi: The Train to Mariposa,' an anonymous auditor – a 'you' displaced in the City – boards an imaginary train bound for Mariposa and his past, discovers his face mirrored in a darkened window and realizes that he will be unrecognizable to those among whom he once lived happily (though, like Roberts's persona, something also made him leave). But if 'L'Envoi' depicts an abortive return for the materialistic auditor, it remains instructive for that other 'you' aboard the train, the reader, with regard to the importance of recovering the values that Leacock associates with Mariposa. (It is worth opening a lengthy parenthesis here, rather than dropping a note, to observe that there is quite a difference between the way return stories function in Canadian and American cycles, with the latter being more accurately termed something like 'lighting-out stories.' The concluding story of Sherwood Anderson's *Winesburg, Ohio*, the Modern American story cycle nearest to Leacock's *Sketches*, is titled 'Departure,' and when George Willard shakes the dust of *his* hometown from *his* heels, he looks from *his* train window and sees that 'the town of Winesburg had disappeared and his life there had become but a background on which to paint the dreams of his manhood' [247]. Contrarily, Leacock's narrator and auditor finally find themselves together, a community of two, 'sitting in the leather chairs of the Mausoleum Club, talking of the little Town in the Sunshine that once we knew' [145].)

'L'Envoi' already exists within a Canadian tradition that begins with 'Paul Farlotte,' the concluding story of Scott's *Viger*, where the eponymous hero struggles to reconstitute family at the end of a cycle whose stories have repeatedly shown the family to be fragmenting in the onslaught of modernity and metropolitanism. Characteristic of the technique of return stories of cycles, 'L'Envoi' casts readers back into the preceding stories by recasting those stories within a dramatic re-emphasizing of the vision of the whole cycle: here, by boarding the magically transforming train to Mariposa. 'L'Envoi' begins to do so by opening with many references to a quotation-marks-enclosed 'home' (141), because *Sunshine Sketches* has essentially been a reminder of what 'home' means, and because 'L'Envoi' is as a return story a concluding lesson in how memories of 'Mariposa' as 'home' should be employed. It does so also by referring to many of the key figures and events of the preceding stories. For example, the Envoi narrator chastises his auditor for his one-time nouveau-riche dream of making a pile of money in the City and returning to Mariposa to build an ostentatious house, 'the best that money could buy' (141). Such talk of fine houses recalls the various building projects of the preceding stories: Josh Smith's exploitative additions to his hotel in the first; the materialist edifice of Dean Drone's new church in stories 4 through 6 and all the trouble it causes; and by way of contrast, the 'enchanted' new and modest home of Peter Pupkin, Zena Pepperleigh, and their newborn (117). The auditor's betraying desire for material wealth also aligns him with Smith and the mistaken Jefferson Thorpe, and even with the ostentatious Reverend Drone. The auditor is chided for having 'half forgotten Mariposa, and long since [losing] the way to it' (142). As the observation of his dream for a grand house most obviously recalls the enchanted home of the Pepperleighs from stories 7 through 9, which constitute the most favourable treatment of Mariposa, here the restrained criticism of forgetting and disowning reminds readers of the three stories on Mariposan religion, where the past, and indeed Mariposa itself, are metaphorically 'blotted out of existence,' constituting the cycle's most unfavourable treatment of Mariposa (79).

The Envoi narrator then indicates for his forgetful auditor some of the passengers aboard the train, all Mariposans: 'one of the greatest judges that ever adorned the bench of Missinaba County' and 'that clerical gentleman ... who is explaining to the man with him the marvellous mechanism of the new air brake (one of the most conspicuous illustrations of the divine structure of the physical universe)' (143). The references are to Judge Pepperleigh and the Reverend Dean Drone, although neither is named, or needs to be in the return story. In a sense, Pepperleigh and Drone are here accorded a degree of figuration, of abstraction, similar to that which 'Mariposa' itself is accorded in 'L'Envoi,' and in accordance with the prefacer's claim that his characters are types and Mariposa is not one Canadian place but 'seventy or eighty of them' (vii–viii). More important, the references to Pepperleigh and Drone in this return story pointedly recall yet again the most favourable treatment of Mariposan life in the romance stories and the most dispiriting aspect of life in the little town in the stories on religion. In the return story of *Sunshine Sketches*, Leacock would have his readers read clear-sightedly, remembering the reality as well as the romantic illusion of the preceding stories, and be prepared, unlike the homesick auditor fantasizing an idealized Mariposa, to recognize the value of their individual and collective pasts. Such is the value of 'such a book as the present one,' *Sunshine Sketches of a Little Town*. As the train moves towards Mariposa and the return story towards completion of the cycle, the two characters of Pepperleigh and Drone can emerge hazily, heavily coded, to represent the best and the worst of Mariposan life – the site of romance, love, and family; the place of materialism, modern megalomania, forgetfulness, and incipient modern metropolitanism – thereby serving, like the abstraction that is 'Mariposa,' a metonymic function that is highly effective within the structure of a short story cycle.

As the imaginative train crosses the bridge over the Ossawippi and moves ever closer to Mariposa, the Envoi narrator exclaims, 'We must be close now!' In a manner that resembles a technique of the dramatic monologue, the auditor interrupts the narrator with an unrecorded, though apparently apprehensive, remark. In the key passage of 'L'Envoi' the narrator considers the cause of his travelling companion's anxiety:

What? It feels nervous and strange to be coming here again after all these years? It must indeed. No, don't bother to look at the reflection of your face in the window-pane shadowed by the night outside. Nobody could tell you now after all these years of money-getting in the city. Perhaps if you had come back now and again, just at odd times, it wouldn't have been so.   (145)

The mirror image here focuses the central concern of 'L'Envoi' and, indeed, of *Sunshine Sketches* itself: self-identity in relation to Mariposa – modern Canadian identity in relation to its more communally responsible past. The Envoi narrator admonishes his auditor for the relentlessness of his self-serving 'money-getting in the city,' a damning indictment of obsessive pecuniary pursuits that have told on his very physical features, making him unrecognizable to those who have kept in touch with their Mariposan origins, and perhaps unrecognizable to himself. The Envoi narrator is not suggesting that his auditor 'go home again' permanently, only that he should 'perhaps' have 'come back now and again, just at odd times.' That of course is the primary lesson of *Sunshine Sketches*, and it is given in 'L'Envoi,' the return story of the cycle. And this interdependent relation between place of origin and identity is definitive not only of *Sunshine Sketches of a Little Town* but of the preponderance of Canadian short story cycles.

There are numerous other instances of echo, pointed reminder of earlier events, and reiteration of the cycle's central thematic concern in 'L'Envoi,' but I am not as concerned here with exploring further the complexities of *Sunshine Sketches of a Little Town* as with indicating the ways in which its return story functions cumulatively and characteristically of short story cycles. Like *Viger*'s 'Paul Farlotte' before it and the many that will come after, 'L'Envoi' as a return story of a short story cycle depicts provisional possibilities respecting the recuperation of community for its displaced former and current inhabitants and the tentative presence of a sense of self and identity that is intimately connected to place as home. But those possibilities must remain provisional both within these concluding return stories and in the preceding stories of the cycle, preceding stories which the cumulative function of the return story then asks the reader to reconsider. As much as such return stories tempt with hints of comfortable closure, they often also destabilize, resisting closure.[24] This is true also of Grove's 'Skies and Scares,' of Sime's 'Divorced,' of Carr's 'Canoe,' of the prototypically titled return story of George Elliott's *The Kissing Man*, 'The way back,' of Munro's 'Who Do You Think You Are?,' and of the final stories of numerous other short story cycles. It is not that the meanings of all story cycles remain indeterminate; only that open-ended return stories are another of the prominent family features of the genre in Canadian literature. When this convention is worked by writers of Scott's, Leacock's, Sime's, Grove's, Carr's, Elliott's, and Munro's skills, the result is cycles that return to their origins, or their elusive centres, without ever quite closing the circle. Or perhaps the better image is of a discontinuous cyclical narrative that has spiralled its characters and readers about its centre, outwards and upwards, up and down, able to return at any moment to its starting point, and doing so most meaningfully in its return story, if never quite connecting with the closing point of its own mythic origin.

1

'In the Meantime':
Duncan Campbell Scott's
In the Village of Viger

Duncan Campbell Scott's *In the Village of Viger*, published in 1896,[1] is
the first instance in Canadian fiction of the subject of the present study,
the short story cycle, and the first story cycle of place. Raymond Knister
concluded his cautiously stock-taking introduction to *Canadian Short
Stories* (1928), the first such anthology, praising the signal achievement of
Viger: 'a perfect flowering of art is embodied in one volume, *In the Village of Viger*, by Duncan Campbell Scott. It is a work which has had an
unobtrusive influence; but it stands out after thirty years as the most sat-
isfyingly individual contribution to the Canadian short story' (xix).[2]
Knister dedicated the anthology to Scott. And recently, W.H. New has
confirmed *Viger*'s place at the head of the rich tradition of the Canadian
short story cycle (*Dreams*, 42, 48).[3] My purpose in this first chapter is
twofold: to build on what New has said about the cyclical organization of
Viger; and then to focus attention on the primary concern of this seminal
short story cycle as expressed in its cyclical form: the challenge that the
coming of metropolitan modernity poses to traditional conceptions of
family and, by extension, to Scott's complex figuring of community;
which is to say, the challenge the twentieth century offered to an earlier,
though by no means easy, faith in identity grounded in family, community, and place.[4] I am not arguing that the fictional Quebec village of Viger
figures as a haven of some family ideal in opposition to the nefarious big
city,[5] or that there are no other themes, images, and foci through which
Viger can rewardingly be read as a coherent story cycle. There are: structural balance (Gerson, 'Piper's'; New, *Dreams*, 184–5), recurrent imagery
(Dragland, Introduction; Ware, Afterword, 123), gender (Gadpaille, 14),
the temporal motif and Old World versus New World (Dyer), to name
but some that have been found productive. What I am arguing is that

Scott tellingly displays the disruption of traditional family and the destabilization of semi-rural community in *Viger* concurrent with the pressur-
ing advances of modern metropolitanism, thereby suggesting one cause –
and it may yet be a first cause – for those stress-fracturings.

Although very much the conservative in all areas of his life – private
and public, as government official and as poet[6] – Scott was not so reactionary as to dream of somehow stopping, never mind of turning back,
the clock. Rather, *Viger* shows how apprehensive of materialistic definitions of progress he was at the turn of the last century. This story cycle
also suggests Scott's hope that the fictional representation of what was
being lost and precariously preserved might slow that modern clock,
allowing for a more reasonable progress in the transitional period, a
progress which would carry with it into the future those conservative-
humanist values, necessarily renovated, that guide citizens in coming
always to know themselves in relation to place.[7] Viewed as such, the figure of 'Viger' functions as providing a space parallel at the preceding turn-
of-the-century to one of those 'interstitial space[s]' of the recent *fin de
siècle* whose emergence and potential Homi K. Bhabha writes of in *The
Location of Culture* (3): 'These "in-between" spaces provide the terrain
for elaborating strategies of selfhood – singular or communal – that initiate new signs of identity, and innovative sites of collaboration, and con-
testation, in the act of defining the ideal of society itself' (Bhabha, 1–2).

In the Village of Viger deserves and rewards extensive and intensive
critical attention, then, because it stands at the head of the rich tradition of
the Canadian story cycle and because it presents an instance of a very
good writer's use of the form to express his anxieties and hopes at that
period in history when the nineteenth century was becoming the twentieth and rural Canadians were becoming urbanized. Viewed in this light,
the Duncan Campbell Scott of *Viger* keeps company with those late nineteenth-century 'antimodernists' whom T.J. Jackson Lears has described
'as some of the most educated and cosmopolitan products of an urbanizing, secularizing society ... the "point men" of cultural change. They
experienced and articulated moral and psychic dilemmas which later
became common in the wider society' (xv). At times in *Viger* Scott, like
his friend Archibald Lampman (especially the Lampman of such poems as
the dystopian 'The City of the End of Things' [179–82]), seems to despair
of any good coming from industrialization, modernity, and urbanization;
at other times he, like fellow post-Confederation writer Bliss Carman
(who thoroughly enjoyed urban life while cautioning against the detri-
mental effects of over-civilization [see Bentley, 'Carman,' and 'The

Thing,' 28–30]), is more willing to refashion his idea of family and community in view of the inevitability of modernization. As will be seen especially in the discussion of *Viger*'s return story, 'Paul Farlotte,' Scott was able to entertain the hope, or at least to envision the possibility, of a humane modern world emerging, one where such concepts as family, community, place, and identity could be redefined without losing their traditional functions of conserving and transmitting such values as bequeath to individuals and communities their now necessarily adaptable identities.

Much of Scott's poetry and prose suggests that his attitude towards developments around the turn of the century – the whole ethos of progress and materialism, what was dubbed 'the age of plutocracy' – was complex and ambivalent. Here again Jackson Lears proves helpful, as his description of the anti-modern attitude so accurately describes the Scott implied by *Viger*: 'The antimodern impulse was both more socially and more intellectually important than historians have supposed. Antimodernism was not simply escapism; it was ambivalent, often coexisting with enthusiasm for material progress. ... Far from being the nostalgic flutterings of a "dying elite," as historians have claimed, antimodernism was a complex blend of accommodation and protest which tells us a great deal about the beginnings of present-day values and attitudes' (xiii). *In the Village of Viger* should be read in this light: within the contexts of its seminal role in the literary history of the Canadian short story cycle, as an expression in fiction of turn-of-the century anti-modernism, and as hopefully creating an earlier version of that potentially productive 'interstitial space' Bhabha describes. Considerations of the book that ignore these contexts either view *Viger*'s significance as, at best, an interesting if confused example of the local colour vogue in Canada or, at worst, a fabrication of some conspiratorial academic community (Metcalf, *What Is*, 45–87). All such readings short-change the book's currency. In terms of Jackson Lears's more complex reading of similar American texts, such simplifications would render mute *Viger*'s real ability to speak to present-day Canadian readers about their history, the formation and continuing re-formation of their values.

It will prove helpful to have the ten stories of *In the Village of Viger* listed. They appear in this order:

1. The Little Milliner
2. The Desjardins

New has outlined a way in which *Viger* can be seen to comprise two story cycles within a cycle, with each story of the first cycle – stories 1 through 5 – having its counterpart in the second – 6 through 10 – so that 'The Little Milliner' is echoed in 'The Bobolink,' 'The Desjardins' in 'The Tragedy of the Seigniory,' and so on in a sequence of repetition with variation that accords well with the essential dynamic of short story cycles (*Dreams*, 184–5). This pattern may well be present in *Viger*, though if so, it would make taxing demands on the most attentive reader's memory, and risks becoming almost as unrecognizable as the chiasmic rhyming scheme that Dylan Thomas imposed on his 101-line 'Prologue,' where the first line rhymes with the last, the second with the second-last, and so inward to the middle couplet (3–5). And New's compelling analysis does not apply so convincingly when we consider (to take but one example) that Paul Arbique of the fourth story, 'Sedan,' has his most obvious counterpart in the eponymous Paul Farlotte of the tenth and last sketch, the return story: both Pauls are fixated on France and both experience visions that lend their names biblical resonances, especially in terms of the Old Testament dispensation of vengeance (for Arbique) and the New Testament law of love (for Farlotte); and both Pauls are contrasted pointedly in their family relations.

An at least equally convincing argument can be made for a more immediate, if complexly incremental, organizing principle of alternation in *Viger*. The first story, 'The Little Milliner,' concerns an outsider, Mademoiselle Viau, who rejects the offer of Vigerian romance; the third story, 'The Wooing of Monsieur Cuerrier,' concerns the marriage of a Vigerian, M. Cuerrier, to an outsider. The second story, 'The Desjardins,' is about family madness associated with France (Charles's Napoleonic delusions of grandeur), while the fourth, 'Sedan,' concerns madness resulting from an alcoholic obsession with the fate of France in the Franco-Prussian War (1870–1, which dates the setting of *Viger*, in this one story anyway, earlier than might be assumed). The fifth story, 'No. 68 Rue Alfred de Musset,' inversely parallels the refusal of romance in the first story, 'The Little Milliner,' and offers a dark variation on the comic romance of the third, 'The Wooing of Monsieur Cuerrier.' And so on. This organizing principle of alternation also more accurately expresses the progressive and cumulative 'dynamic patterns of recurrence and development' that Ingram (20) and the present study see as definitive of story cycles. Or perhaps 'symphonic' would be a better (if yet another) term to describe the organization of *Viger*. It has the virtue at least of harmonizing with Scott's oft-quoted remark that 'all art, as Walter Pater points out, is constantly striving towards the condition of music.'[8] (And Scott, the accomplished amateur pianist and performer in Ottawa, composed a number of poems on musical models or subjects.)[9] Structurally *Viger* is a story cycle full of parallels, inversions, doublings, and mirrorings, of recurrent motif and leitmotif, and, most appropriately, of echoes and resonances. In its bold opening description of setting that becomes context and theme in the first paragraph of 'The Little Milliner,' and in its related stories of different lengths and tones, stories that provide contrapuntal variations on its theme, *In the Village of Viger* offers indeed a literary equivalent of musical form. As in a suite, say, its dominant theme – the deleterious effects of twentieth-century urban expansionism and modernity itself – develops through resonance and echo to find crescendo-like climax in the concluding story, 'Paul Farlotte,' a return story that movingly brings together the variations on a theme dealt with in the preceding nine of the cycle.[10]

The literary generic form of *In the Village of Viger* – the story cycle – is especially appropriate to its subject. The realistic nineteenth-century novel, the only plausible fictional alternative, would not have been as well suited as the story cycle to portraying the subsumption of the small community of Viger by the expanding metropolis and, along with that uncomfortable accommodation, the threatened fragmentation and disintegration of many of those conservative, humanistic values that Scott held, those traditional nineteenth-century, anti-modern values whose relevance was being challenged by the modern age: organicism, romance, duty and responsibility, work, tolerance, family and community. The discontinuous narrative of the story cycle, with its implied formalistic challenge to the illusive unity of the master narrative of the novel of social and psychological realism, provided Scott with a form ideally suited to the fictional depiction of the dissolution and tentative reconstitution of what may be called Vigerian familial and communal life. The hope of reconstitution is equally important here, because as Bhabha observes of the current popularity of postmodern forms of fragmentation, 'if the interest in postmodernism is limited to a celebration of the fragmentation of the "grand narratives" of postenlightenment rationalism then, for all its intellectual excitement, it remains a profoundly parochial enterprise' (4). The subject of *Viger* may be the pressures exerted from without and within by modernization and urbanization on a small Catholic village in *fin de siècle* Quebec, but its vision is neither naïvely hopeful nor parochial.

Ian Reid has written insightfully of the relation between discontinuous form and fragmenting subject in Sherwood Anderson's *Winesburg, Ohio* (1919), the American short story cycle that most resembles *Viger*. Reid's observations are applicable not only to the relation of form and subject in Scott's story cycle but also to what was said in the introduction of the present study about the formal features of the short story cycle generally (namely, that the story cycle is mainly a modern form that arose both as an alternative to the conventional nineteenth-century novel, *the* most relevant grand narrative, and in response to the challenges of modernism, and about the ways that genre *is* meaning). 'Sherwood Anderson's *Winesburg, Ohio*,' observes Reid,

> stands as an obvious paradigm of the modern short-story cycle. Its form is clearly between an episodic novel and a mere collection of discrete items. The setting is fairly constant in place and time, and many characters appear in more than one story, with George Willard being present in all but a few. But the tight continuous structure of a novel is deliberately avoided: Anderson said he wanted 'a new looseness' of form to suit the particular quality of his material. His people are lonely, restless, cranky. Social cohesion is absent in their mid-western town. Even momentary communication seldom occurs between any two of them. Winesburg is undergoing a human erosion caused by the winds of change blowing from the cities, by the destabilizing of moral codes, and by the intrinsic thinness of small-town life. The 'new looseness' of *Winesburg, Ohio* can convey with precision and pathos the duality that results: a superficial appearance (and indeed the ideal possibility) of communal wholeness, and an underlying actual separateness. (47–8)

Something much the same would appear to be Scott's purpose in *Viger*: to catch the diversity within unity and the richness of life in the small community even as that community appears to be passing out of existence. But pointedly unlike Anderson in *Winesburg*, Scott also wants to commemorate the worthwhile and to preserve it remade in the new literary form of the short story cycle, which, as I have shown, has its own structural tightness. As Scott observed in 'Poetry and Progress' of the relation between modernism and poetic forms: 'The desire of creative minds everywhere is to express the age in terms of the age, and by intuition to flash light into the future. Revolt is essential to progress, not necessarily the revolt of violence, but always the revolt that questions the established past and puts it to the proof, that finds the old forms outworn and invents new forms for new matters' (*Circle*, 142).

Changing times, liminal/interstitial spaces, the meantime – *transition* in its various manifestations is both subject and key to the temporal setting in much of Duncan Campbell Scott's writing (see Dragland, Introduction, 12), whether in such well-known poems as 'The Height of Land' and 'Chiostro Verde' (*Selected*, 52–5, 99–101), which consider the future and wonder whether humanity and its arts are poised on the brink of genuine progress or retrogression and disintegration, or in the so-called Indian poems about half-breeds who embody the violence that ensues as European-Christian civilization is, in Scott's view, in the process of assimilating Indian culture (Lynch, 'Endless'; cf. Dragland, *Floating*, 155–206). In *Viger* this theme of transitional times is expressed in the personal and public displacements that result from, or at the least are accelerated by, the confrontation between the swelling twentieth-century metropolis and the beleaguered nineteenth-century village. As has been stated, *Viger*'s predominant manifestation of the effects of this present confrontation between past and future is the destabilization of the traditional conception of family. Fractured families can be viewed as the most telling sounding board for the various themes played out in *Viger*'s stories: crime, madness, dislocation, urban sprawl, New World versus Old World, failed romance, exploitation of labour, betrayal, and others. Repeatedly *Viger* portrays disrupted families or depicts the absence of what can be called the natural family – father, mother, children – as the chief threat to the survival of those humanistic, conservative values that Scott presents in *Viger* as threatened by modernity.

I want first to look closely at *Viger*'s remarkable opening paragraph with its bold announcement of the book's subject of transitional times – its forthright projection of the entire fictional project that is *Viger*:

It was too true that the city was growing rapidly. As yet its arms were not long enough to embrace the little village of Viger, but before long they would be, and it was not a time that the inhabitants looked forward to with any pleasure. It was not to be wondered at, for few places were more pleasant to live in. The houses, half hidden amid the trees, clustered around the slim steeple of St. Joseph's, which flashed like a naked poniard in the sun. They were old, and the village was sleepy, almost dozing, since the mill, behind the rise of land, on the Blanche had shut down. The miller had died; and who would trouble to grind what little grist came to the mill, when flour was so cheap? But while the beech-groves lasted, and the Blanche continued to run, it seemed impossible that any change could come. The change was coming, however, rapidly enough. Even now, on still nights, above the noise of the frogs in the pools, you could hear the rumble of the street-cars and the faint tinkle of their bells, and when the air was moist the whole southern sky was luminous with the reflection of thousands of gas-lamps. But when the time came for Viger to be mentioned in the city papers as one of the outlying wards, what a change there would be! There would be no unfenced fields, full of little inequalities and covered with short grass; there would be no deep pools, where the quarries had been, and where the boys pelted the frogs; there would be no more beech-groves, where the children could gather nuts; and the dread pool, which had filled the shaft where old Daigneau, years ago, mined for gold, would cease to exist. But in the meantime, the boys of Viger roamed over the unclosed fields and pelted the frogs, and the boldest ventured to roll huge stones into Daigneau's pit, and only waited to see the green slime come working up to the surface before scampering away, their flesh creeping with the idea that it was old Daigneau himself who was stirring up the water in a rage.   (3–4)

The ten stories that follow are illustrations of and variations on the theme of transitional times announced in this opening paragraph: what Viger was, what it is 'in the meantime,' and what it will become. Employing rhetorical strategies that feature irony, litotes, and some misdirection, Scott shows in the opening paragraph that Viger, rather than being 'the pleasant Viger by the Blanche' that he offers in the book's prefatory verses (unpaginated) or the secure mock-Arcadia he will describe in the opening of 'Sedan' (30), is a village in the path of a city about to 'embrace' it – 'not a time that the inhabitants looked forward to with any pleasure.' Readers must immediately wonder just how the city will 'embrace' Viger. Lovingly? Possessively? Protectively? Suffocatingly? As an empire takes a prospective colony? (The possibility of a postcolonial Viger is intriguing, if one I must leave for others to pursue.) Interestingly, this opening paragraph subtly reveals that Viger is, in the narrator's narrating time, already lost to the city, that the historical time of the ensuing fiction is 'the meantime,' a phrase which is repeated in the concluding sentence of 'The Little Milliner' (14). The time of the ensuing stories is, then, the interval between what Viger was and what it has already become for the narrator: an intermediate time – the time of transition which for Scott entails, as it always does in the Indian poems, violence – colloquially a mean time indeed.

The details of the opening paragraph also reveal that Viger's flour mill – one of a rural community's foundational institutions – will remain shut down because flour is produced more cheaply in the industrialized city. Thus Scott introduces the theme of dislocation resulting from technological progress – modern production methods – a theme that figures centrally, as will be shown, in the organic-versus-mechanical opposition of the return story, 'Paul Farlotte.' (In the opening of 'Josephine Labrosse,' going to work in the city is presented in terms that could easily be mistaken for taking up prostitution [66–7]). The ominous advance of such metropolitan/modern changes are signalled further by the foreboding 'rumble of the street cars,' and in the portrayal of the city as a colonizing Pandemonium on the horizon, advancing northwards and lighting up the 'southern sky ... with the reflection of thousands of gas-lamps' (see *Paradise Lost*, 1.726–30). The north-south axis often provided a moral-ethical analogue in Scott's work, with the north suggesting a reservoir of potential spiritual renewal – in a manner that anticipates such Canadian modernist poets as A.J.M. Smith and F.R. Scott, such contemporary poets as Al Purdy, such fiction writers as Leacock, who in 'L'Envoi' suddenly locates his Mariposa distantly north of the city (the fictionalized Toronto), such painters as Lawren Harris and Emily Carr, and such historians as the W.L. Morton of 'The North in Canadian Historiography' – and with the south being best characterized by Scott himself in these lines from 'The Height of Land': 'The crowded southern land / With all the welter of the lives of men' (*Selected*, 53).[11]

Scott's apprehensiveness about the effects of the northward-pushing modern world on Viger is figured next in the opening paragraph by a catalogue of emphatic, repetitive negations that already place the figure of Viger under effective erasure. After the embrace of the city, there will be 'no unfenced fields,' 'no deep pools,' 'no more beech groves,' and 'the dread pool ... would cease to exist.' The first two negations diminish Viger spatially along horizontal and vertical axes, with psychological-cultural repercussions of constrained and shallower lives; the next two figure temporally as a loss of memory, which shuts off access to realms of edenic innocence and darker experience, and with the whole constituting a loss of what might be expressed in the useful cliché 'fullness of life.' The ugliest image in this paragraph, the 'green slime' that comes 'working up to the surface' of Old Daigneau's pit – an abandoned gold-mine shaft – might be seen further as proleptic of the evil effects of the pursuit of material wealth, another theme that recurs in *Viger*, and figures centrally in such dark stories as 'No. 68 Rue Alfred de Musset,' 'The Tragedy of the Seigniory,' and 'The Pedler.' In losing Old Daigneau's pit Viger is deprived not only of a communal site for memory and a scene for folk-tale invention – significant positive linkages – but also of a kind of stigmatic reminder of its human fallibility and incipient tendency to behave contrary to its own best interests.

Even in so seemingly insignificant a detail as the loss of its frog population (and note that frogs are mentioned no fewer than three times in this opening paragraph), Viger can be seen symbolically to lose a means of access to the heart of nature, both outer nature and inner human nature. For as much as frogs were 'breathers of wisdom' for Archibald Lampman (7; see Bentley, 'Watchful'), they are in one of *Viger*'s two happy stories, 'Josephine Labrosse,' subconscious messengers of good tidings from Viger. There, the somewhat ironically named city clerk, Victor, cannot remember that his new-found love, Josephine, lives in Viger. At the nadir of despair, he has a dream:

> He dreamed that he was sailing down a stream which grew narrower and narrower. At last his boat stopped amid a tangle of weeds and water-lilies. All around him on the broad leaves was seated a chorus of frogs, singing out something at the top of their voices. He listened. Then, little by little, whatever the word was, it grew more distinct until one huge fellow opened his mouth and roared out 'VIGER!' (69)

The frogs, doomed to extinction locally, function positively in the suggestively collective unconscious of the city clerk, directing him away from his dehumanizing office life towards Viger and his future wife and family. (Given Scott's lifelong devotion to Archibald Lampman and his work, I suspect here, too, a kind of intertextual wink at Lampman's sonnet sequence 'The Frogs' [7]. And I trust it is worth extending this parenthesis to observe one further point of relevance: the similarity between this dream of Victor's return to Viger and the dream-vision in the closing sketch of Leacock's story cycle *Sunshine Sketches of a Little Town*, 'L'Envoi: The Train to Mariposa,' wherein the imaginary train arrives in the Mariposa station to another small-caps announcement, 'MARIPOSA! MARIPOSA!' just as the would-be returnees are drawn back into the leather chairs of their urban Mausoleum Club [145]; in *Sunshine Sketches* the attempted return to the threatened small town fails literally buts succeeds figuratively; in *Viger* it is successful, though only for the lover, Victor, and only temporarily, since, as the opening paragraph of *Viger* indicates, it is to an ultimately much changed Viger that Victor dreams his way.)

Thus the opening paragraph of *Viger*'s first story informs readers that Viger's radical transformation is certain and proceeds to suggest what the loss of 'Viger' portends literally and figuratively on a number of levels.[12] As will the remainder of 'The Little Milliner' itself, the rest of the stories portray the transitional throes of Viger 'in the meantime,' with disintegrative modernity first fracturing the integrity of traditional conceptions of family, the nineteenth-century or 'Victorian' idea of the family. Doubtless it is for such reasons that the houses of Viger are portrayed in the opening paragraph as clustering for protection around the defiant 'slim steeple of St. Joseph's, which flashed like a naked poniard in the sun.' St Joseph, as well as being the patron saint of workers, was the protector of the Holy Family, and he remains the patron saint of families, of fathers, who are noticeably either absent or dangerously present in *Viger* (as they are missing in Scott's Indian poems), and of Canada itself.[13] It may be, therefore, that the name 'Viger' is intended to connote the French words *vigilance* and *vigie* (look-out man), which would accord with St. Joseph's role as patron and protector. (And of course *viager* means 'for life.' Readers who think these suggestions strained might ponder the aptness of the name 'Josephine' – a female Joseph – in that one of *Viger*'s two happy stories, 'Josephine Labrosse,' where the father's absence leaves its three generations of women in desperate circumstances.)

In accordance with the dominant theme announced in the opening paragraph of *Viger*, the first story, 'The Little Milliner,' proceeds immediately to offer an instance of metropolitan intrusiveness in the person of the pathetic Little Milliner, Mademoiselle Viau. Her house is built on what had always been open ground, so that there is a suggestion of, if not violation, at least crowding of Vigerian space. '[M]en from the city came and put up the oddest wooden house that one could imagine. It was perfectly square' (4); put up rather than built, this house is hardly a home, and its box-like architecture is ugly and sharply exclusive. Suggesting confrontation, this house is erected directly across the street from that of Viger's resident seamstress, Madame Laroque, and as milliner Viau competes successfully with Laroque, who, as the local gossip, is a kind of *spiritus loci*. The Little Milliner lures away Laroque's younger clientele especially, thereby revealing the changing tastes within Viger for metropolitan fashions, for city things, with attendant implications for the future of Viger. (Scott may be writing here a version of the Carlylean philosophy of clothes, whereby the rural dress more favourably expresses the Vigerian spirit; in 'Paul Farlotte,' the return story, the communally responsible Paul wears 'a curious skirt-coat that seemed to be made of some indestructible material, for he had worn it for years, and might be buried in it' [81].) Against community, the Little Milliner lives privately, driving the busybody Laroque to distraction. She rejects a Vigerian suitor (7), precluding symbolically the possibility of a harmonious union between the small community and herself, the first emissary from the city, by literally shutting her door on a potential romance which, in the Vigerian scheme of things, would have led to marriage and family.

Most relevant, though, is one of the Little Milliner's mysterious family relationships. She has an unnamed male relative who is a thief. It would seem that some in the city are compelled, significantly for unspecified reasons, to steal, and are shot for doing so. (This theme of property crime will also recur with variation in two later stories, as embezzlement and purse-snatching, when in 'The Tragedy of the Seigniory' [60] Louis Bois wastes his absent master's money on lottery tickets, and when Henri Lamoureux causes a communal disaster by stealing from the eponymous Pedler [76].) Although the Little Milliner is admirable for her devotion to family, and though she is certainly much more demure victim than corrupting victor, it is nonetheless her family connection *in the city* that makes her life miserable and her stay in Viger transient. Because of that family connection in the city, the Little Milliner is symbolically a corrupter of Viger. As the Widow Laroque finally fumes, criticizing the transience and anonymity in connection to community that indicate two important features of the coming metropolitan modernity: '"It will not do!" said the widow. "Somebody builds a house, no one knows who; people come and go, no one knows how ..."' (13; and see 11).

The concluding paragraph of 'The Little Milliner' (13–14) begins with an abrupt temporal shift of 'three years,' with a movement, that is, into or closer to the present time of the narrator. There is in its description of the seamstress's abandoned house a strong impression of decay and death, of 'white curtains pulled down' and a dead geranium that 'looks like a dried stick' (this last is an important image that recurs in the return story, as will be shown). Although the Little Milliner's abandoned cottage presents an image of the sort of dangerously pathetic death-in-life epitomized in Miss Havisham of Dickens's *Great Expectations*, the final sentence of this concluding paragraph contains images both sinister and hopeful: 'In the meantime, in every corner of the house the spiders are weaving webs, and an enterprising caterpillar has blocked up the key-hole with his cocoon.' The natural weaving spiders now successfully occupy the place of the unravelled Little Milliner, while a hopeful caterpillar is undergoing an occluding metamorphosis (perhaps Scott would have us see only so far inward and outward, whether into another's private life or the future of the surrounding Viger community). There is, to be sure, a sense here of the natural/organic order reclaiming the violated space of Viger. But there are also in these images suggestions of entrapment and portentous change. Granted, the temporal shift and the repetition of 'in the meantime' from the opening paragraph contribute to a sense of hopeful reclamation and comforting closure, of the story's having come full circle (as the stories of local colour fiction often do, returning the calamitous inhabitants of small towns safe and sound to where they began: think of the numerous adventures of Anne Shirley, or of the excursion of the Mariposa Belle). But it is more disturbingly likely that the changes symbolized in the Little Milliner and her folly-house abandoned to spiders and cocooned caterpillars signify that Viger will not be permitted to shut out the problematic influences of accelerating modernity. 'It seemed impossible that any change would come,' as the opening paragraph of the story puts it: 'The change was coming, however, rapidly enough.' Metamorphosis is distinguished biologically for rapidity of morphological change, as Kafka's Gregor Samsa awakens to discover. And it is much to be doubted, from the evidence of 'The Little Milliner,' that Viger will emerge into the modern age transformed into *Mariposa* (the Spanish word for butterfly). But regardless of these questions that persist, and should remain, in determining a final reading of these highly suggestive closing images, the opening story clearly depicts the introduction of trouble into 'Viger,' both village and book – trouble in the form of crowding, transience, alienation, and crime – modern trouble introduced in association with a disturbed city family. The ensuing stories of the cycle pick up and play upon these initial themes of 'The Little Milliner' – including its few hopeful notes – until the return story, 'Paul Farlotte,' brings them to rest.

It is perhaps enough to observe the way in which the second story, 'The Desjardins,' concerns inherited family madness. Adèle and Philippe Desjardin, already recalling and amplifying the (perhaps) mistaken familial devotion of the Little Milliner of the first story, decide to care for their mad brother Charles. In what may be the first use of the device, Scott creates in Charles Desjardin a madman who believes he is none other than Napoleon Bonaparte. Charles is a pathetic figure who parodically suffers the seasonal vicissitudes of his hero's career as summers of triumphant campaigning are followed by dark Russian winters: 'The sleet dashes against [Charles], and the wind rushes and screams around him, as he ascends the little knoll. But whatever the weather, Philippe waits in the road for him and helps him dismount. There is something heroic in his short figure' (20). Thus Scott contrasts the false heroism of the deluded madman to the true heroism of the caring brother, Philippe, whose devotion to an ideal of familial duty almost compensates for his and his sister's sacrifices, and who possesses, ironically, the Napoleonic 'short figure.' Certainly the conjunction of the two views of heroism, opposed within the one family in this very short story, suggests at least that Scott's understanding of family is not congruent with the idealized picture of the sentimental fiction of the turn of the preceding century.

Finally, it should be noted that once again the unnatural demands of a fractured family – two brothers and a sister, with no mention of a mother, but with a mad paternal line into the past – again preclude budding love, in this instance the romances of Philippe and Adèle Desjardin with members of the Vigerian community. The Desjardins, an old family, live on the perimeter of Viger; family madness prevents their entrance into the fuller life of the community and, consequently, the continuance of their family name. As Philippe declares melodramatically to his stunned sister when they realize that their inheritance of madness has come home again: "'We must cut ourselves off; we must be the last of our race"' (18). That French family name, *Desjardin*, would be translated into English as 'of/from the garden.' The humanist and conservative Scott may be implying that there is a fault in the family of man, an ineradicable flaw that has its roots in *the* Garden and is also associated with the wrong kind of hero-worship, an (as it were) original social sin of excessive pride and self-centredness which, from a Christian humanist's point of view, can be endured only with the kind of familial caring practised by the loving Philippe Desjardin.[14] Such a suggestion of the damning effects of pride and individualism is supported by the description of Desjardin *père*, who was 'inhospitable, and became more taciturn and morose after his wife died. His pride was excessive and kept him from associating with his neighbors, although he was in no way above them' (16). So it is probably not fortuitous that Charles identifies with Napoleon, the early nineteenth century's romantic icon of liberty and sublime ego.

In the fourth story, 'Sedan,' Viger is shown to have the small town's dark underside of intolerance expressed as racism. At one point in the story a drunken mob goes forth in darkness to deliver a 'sound beating' (34) to an innocent German immigrant (an event that finds echo in Alice

Munro's 'Royal Beatings,' where the small-town victim dies as a consequence of his beating [*Who*, 9]). The display of this unattractive Vigerian characteristic takes place again within a fractured family. Paul Arbique, a type of the *miles gloriosus* (a negative type in answer to Monsieur Cuerrier's positive in the third story), and his resentful wife have no children: 'They had only had one child, who had died when she was a baby, and this want of children was a great trial to Paul. They had attempted to fill her place by adopting a little girl, but the experiment had not been a success, and she grew to be something between a servant and a poor relation working for her board' (32). Irrationally, if it is not out of jealousy, Madame Arbique 'had taken a dislike to the child, and she simply neglected her.' In doing so, Madame Arbique continues the characterization of dominant, shrewish, even witch-like women which was begun somewhat favourably with Madame Laroque and continued in the third story, 'The Wooing of Monsieur Cuerrier,' with Diana who, in league with Laroque, schemes to foil the romance of Monsieur Cuerrier and the fair Césarine. In 'Sedan' it is a man, Paul Arbique himself, who acts as block when he stands between Latulipe (the adopted daughter) and Hans Blumenthal, 'the German watchmaker' (33). Such blocking characters also repeat with variation the theme that was introduced in 'The Little Milliner' when Mademoiselle Viau shut her door on Vigerian romance. Moreover, Paul is a drunkard whose affliction is, like the Desjardins', hereditary, a family matter: 'Madame Arbique knew he would drink himself to death, as his father had done' (36). Because Latulipe leads a limbo-like existence within the Arbique family and Viger itself, she sympathizes with and eventually marries Hans, the other outsider in Viger who is her adoptive father's sworn enemy and symbolic killer.[15] In doing so, she and Hans may well represent a commendable instance of New-World family (and perhaps even Hans's profession as watchmaker implies that time is on his and Latulipe's side). Of course, the absence of Arbique children already suggested figuratively that Paul, fixated dipsomaniacally on the past, had no future, and in this respect his fate may adumbrate one possible future for romance-foiled, family-fractured Viger itself. In the end, though, Paul's thoughts 'were hardly of the war, of the terror of the downfall which had a little while before so haunted him' (37); that obsession, it is suggested, had merely allowed him to express his own brand of inherited madness: alcoholism. This is important to stress with regard to the present reading's emphasis on fractured families, because it is hereditary alcoholism and not his inability to leave behind the Old World and commit to life in the New that is the first cause of Paul's downfall. More broadly, it may be that the inherent madness seeking expression here is the cohesive group's primordial need for a scapegoat, as Paul Arbique's self-ratifying Viger wants to exclude newcomers such as Hans and the adopted Latulipe from the communal family.

'No. 68 Rue Alfred de Musset' focuses on yet another fractured family, a sister and her dying brother. The sister, Eloise, schemes to get out of Viger at any price; she comes very close to prostituting herself in achieving her end. She wants out of Viger for no other reason than that she 'must do something' (40). To do so, she commodifies herself as an object to be appraised physically: '"Look at me, Maurice – tell me now – " She stood with her head thrown back, and poised lightly, and with a little frown on her face. "Superb!" said her brother.' The furniture she later displays to entrap unwary suitors is described in terms that might well suit Eloise's equally offered body: '"You have rarely seen things so exquisite; the secretaire has a secret cabinet, the chest is carved with a scene of nymphs in a wood ..."' No wonder 'the young man [the dupe] began to regard her with some interest; he remarked to himself that she was a lovely girl' (43). In the execution of this plan to nab a rich husband, Eloise depletes what little physical strength remains to her devoted brother. Negatively mirroring Philippe Desjardin's commitment to fraternal responsibilities, Eloise exploits her brother's sense of familial duty, declaring in a manner that brooks no contradiction, '"I must go; it is my duty; you do yours"' (46); after which her brother wonders, '"I wish I knew what my duty was."' Is his familial duty to instruct his younger sister in moral-ethical matters or to help her carry out her reprehensible intrigue? The weak and weakened brother chooses to assist his sister and is resigned to his death. She nabs her Pierre; theatrically 'she g[ives] herself to him' (48), in a phrase that, like her negative mirroring of Philippe and Adèle Desjardin, ominously echoes the union of Latulipe and Hans in the preceding story, where Latulipe is said ironically by the narrator to be 'giving herself to the enemy' (37).

Also, Eloise's 'career' (as the story's closing sentence sardonically labels her future life: 'This was the beginning of her career' [49]) inversely parallels the Little Milliner's movements: Viau desires to reside quietly in Viger, Eloise will do anything to get out; the one rebuffs romance from within Viger, the other schemes to marry well and out; the one's downfall results from her tangled family ties, the other ruthlessly exploits her sick brother to launch her gold-digging career (in the end, though, it is revealed that Eloise lusts not for gold but to become 'powerful' [48]). Scott would have us make such comparisons in the alternating arrangement of the cycle's first and fifth stories: notice, for instance, that he associates both women with the floral symbol of folly, the geranium (5 and 40). He would have us appreciate that Eloise's overriding ambition to go to the city is but the present expression of an inhuman ruthlessness teased into the open, especially as that inhumanity affects none other than the last of her immediate family. In having Eloise's devoted brother pretend a kind of madness (again recalling 'The Desjardins') in order to serve his sister's inflamed ambition, Scott may even be hinting that Eloise is actually the one maddened by her obsessive desire for a career in the city, suggesting that she has been infected by the modern disease whose chief symptom is the insatiable desire for an 'action' that Viger does not, cannot, and should not afford. Her first words in the story, revealing an undefined mental excitability and employing a metaphor of illness, give the only motivational clue to her subsequent behaviour: '"Maurice, Maurice, I'm sick of life. I will be an adventuress"' (39).[16] Perhaps what we have in this story is Scott's intimation of those diseased desires born fitfully of modern life and an industrial consumer capitalism, of those fevered needs that were truly beginning to exercise their gigantic appetites in the swelling cities of the turn of the last century – of those consumptive longings for a vaguely understood satisfaction, of needs created by a system that dislocates to disintegrate, then creates a craving for mythic wholeness, or 'fulfilment,' and knows the real rewards of eternal deferment.

Fractured families and ensuing confusion continue to figure with varying importance in all the other stories of *Viger*, sometimes simply as the absence of any form of traditional family, and usually only as the implied cause of confusion. The sixth story, 'The Bobolink,' tells of an old man and a blind girl who form a tenuous bond, creating a mock-familial relationship (unrelated children call him 'Uncle'), and share only an impermanent affinity apart from whatever families they may have (she, Blanche, named apparently for Viger's river, is simply the 'daughter of his neighbor Moreau' [51], so there may be a complex pun in the girl's first and last names). In what begins as a tale of local colour about a lovable village cobbler and his avuncular relations with children, especially the bathetically blind Blanche, Scott employs the image of a caged wild bird to suggest something of the existential condition. As much as Blanche is permanently imprisoned in her blindness, the old cobbler is trapped in 'his silent cabin' (54), and their ersatz family emerges finally as something of a self-deception. This may seem a harsh reading of a 'sentimental fable,' as New describes it (*Dreams*, 182), but in having the children figuratively laugh at the old man behind his back (51), Scott does suggest that there may be much of self-deception in the old man's pleasant life 'by the Blanche' (as the prefatory poem to *Viger* ends). And the story leaves it at that, as a sadly mild revelation of human limitation and the capacity for self-delusion.

However, 'The Bobolink' is highly suggestive allegorically, though an allegory of just what is far from determinable. New is most convincing (as is his analysis of the form and reading of *Viger* generally compelling [*Dreams*, 177–86]) in his bi-cyclical pairing of 'The Bobolink' with 'The Little Milliner.' He writes of them as follows in his point-form schematization of *Viger*'s stories: 'two stories of innocents in flight, the first hounded into departing, the second released into freedom and regret' (184). That may be all that can be said.[17] But perhaps the trapped bird that the old cobbler captures and Blanche frees is emblematic of the spirit of Viger itself, since the blind girl does bear the name of the stream that runs through the village. Perhaps the blind Blanche also anticipates, in the manner of story cycles, the blind Pedler of the ninth story, the legendary figure who will suggest more forcibly that the village can be greedily blind to its own best interests in the crowding modern world that stalks it. To entertain such readerly thoughts with regard to what is precious in 'Viger' is to be left like the old cobbler and Blanche themselves, wiser but sadder, 'not untinged by regret' (54) at 'the evidence of change and loss' (Bentley, 'The Thing,' 42).

'The Tragedy of the Seigniory,' the most *conte*-like of these Viger stories set in Quebec, tells a very Catholic and grotesque tale of transgression (stealing, symbolic murder of a virtual son) and punishment (death, perhaps damnation). In doing so it echoes 'The Desjardins' in melodramatically tracing the last of a noble Vigerian family whose one remaining servant is corrupted by greed associated with a city lottery. Like the pretentious and dangerous Church of England church in Mariposa (53), the manse here is described in the opening paragraph as 'set upon a rise, having nothing to do with the street, or seemingly with any part of the town' (55). So, as in 'The Desjardins,' the context of the tragedy is alienation from the life of the village and, I would argue, the absence of conventional family relations. Louis Bois is isolated, alone, and addicted to gambling, and those conditions can be read as cause and effect, and as expressions of the age.

'The Pedler,' a kind of seasonal folk tale, is, like the preceding two, not directly relevant to the theme of fractured family (though, it can be said again, no natural family appears in this story either). It shows instead how incipient materialism – Henri Lamoureux's passing of a counterfeit coin to steal a red purse from the Pedler (76) – puts paid to a communal Vigerian ritual. This loss recalls the first paragraph of *Viger*, which lists among the coming changes the loss of Old Daigneau's abandoned gold-mine shaft, with its suggested mnemonic significance as a caution against the pursuit of wealth. Notably, the Pedler as a communally ritualistic type can be seen to echo forward to 'the grinder man' of George Elliott's 'The way back,' the return story of the cycle *The Kissing Man* (1962), the book which provides the primary text of chapter 5 of the present study. The obvious difference between the two figures is that where the grinder man facilitates the reintegration of someone into the small-town community, the Pedler points up a characteristic – material acquisitiveness, property crime – that will contribute to the spiritual subsumption of Viger by the city (and that way also recalls the preference of the Vigerian girls for the Little Milliner over Madame Laroque).

As he does in many of his Indian poems, Scott shrouds the retreating figure of the blind, robbed, and humiliated Pedler in a chastening meteorological event: 'one of the sudden storms had gathered the dust at the end of the village and came down with it, driving every one indoors. It shrouded the retreating figure, and a crack of unexpected thunder came like a pistol shot, and then the pelting rain' (77). Blind like Blanche, the Pedler assumes symbolic proportions that make the figure folkloric, perhaps mythic, something like Finn MacCool in Irish mythology, sleeping beneath the country and waiting to awaken; or like Klein's drowned poet in 'Portrait of the Poet as Landscape,' waiting to surface (104); or like Al Purdy's disappearing iconic cowboy, 'clopping in silence under the toy mountains / dropping sometimes and / lost in the dry grass / golden oranges of dung' (*Being*, 72). The Pedler had visited Viger seasonally – 'He used to come in the early spring-time' (74), the story begins – providing occasion for a communally ritualistic meeting place and exchange, not inviting the mad acquisitiveness that Lamoureux now expresses. And then the Pedler too is lost, though he may, like those other mythic figures, be potentially available for retrieval: 'Some venturesome souls who looked out when the storm was nearly over, declared they saw, large on the hills, the figure of the pedler, walking enraged in the fringes of the storm' (77). He recalls the lost Daigneau of the opening paragraph of *Viger*, 'stirring up the water in a rage' (4). Such figures do not go gently, it must appear.

Even in such an ostensibly happy story as 'Josephine Labrosse' – the romantic comedy as prose tale – the family unit is fractured, the father being dead and the family, three generations of women, facing penury. As in such romantic comedies as *A Midsummer Night's Dream* and *Twelfth Night*, there is much confusion in this story, as to motive, identity, place, and gender role. Figuring, too, the ways in which romance, love, and marriage emerge more from a figurative thicket than from rational choice, 'Josephine Labrosse' has recourse to dream and the unconscious in solving one of the lover's, Victor's, critical problems in finding his Josephine (the frog dream discussed above), who has already found him through the machinations of her mother. Dreaming also plays an important role in *Viger*'s only other happy story, the romance of Monsieur Cuerrier and Césarine; there (24), the dream may be warning Cuerrier that Madame Laroque has set her cap for him and that such a match would be marriage to an untamable shrew. There, too, Cuerrier's, the aging bachelor's, declaration that he will marry is met by his friend's question, "'So, are you not mad?"' To which Cuerrier replies, "'No, I'm not mad"' (23). This brief interchange regarding mental instability not only points up the irrationality of romance and love but, following immediately on 'The Desjardins,' repeats discomfortingly – makes a joke of – the theme of insanity. In fact, the two comic stories of *Viger*, which end happily and in traditional fashion with the promise of restorative marriage, are heavily ironic, if promising nonetheless.

Josephine Labrosse's future husband, the somewhat nebbish Victor, is partly tricked into the attachment by the mother's allowing Josephine's rough and romantic cousin to appear as a competing suitor. Not only does this story open with the narration of Madame Labrosse's going to the city in a way that is surely intended to be mistaken for prostitution, but there is even a suggestion that the mother regards her daughter at one low point as goods in the display window that has failed to support them (68) – and in this perception, on which the mother may well be acting, scares up the black hare of manipulative Eloise Ruelle virtually prostituting herself. The conclusion of the story is also slightly disturbing in its association, through the repetition of a song, of Josephine with her wild relative, the rabble-rousing François Xavier Beaugrand de Champagne (73). However, the outcome in 'Josephine Labrosse' is unequivocally hopeful and Viger-enhancing. In fact, the full budding of love between Victor and Josephine, however arranged, is to Viger what the meeting of Peter Pupkin and Zena Pepperleigh, which is also arranged, is to Leacock's Mariposa (91–2): a rapturously joyful and celebratory moment in which Josephine's caged bird sings its heart out, and which concludes in a family scene of promising domesticity: 'Is it her own heart she hears, or is it Victor's? No need of words now. How the bird sings! High and clear he shakes out his song in a passionate burst, as if all his life were for love. And they seem to talk together in sweet unsaid words until he ceases. Now they are seated on the sofa, and Madame Labrosse comes in' (72). So, as much as the female deception in 'Josephine Labrosse' recalls Eloise Ruelle's nastier exploits, it also remembers the earlier comic machinations of Monsieur Cuerrier in spiriting off the fair Césarine, the compensatory union of Latulipe and Hans at the end of the bleak 'Sedan,' and, happily, the sadly freed bird of 'The Bobolink.' In accordance with the story cycle's dynamic of recurrent development, the fourth instance of the motif of marriage – following 'Cuerrier,' 'Sedan,' and 'No. 68' – can be seen to repeat and to play a variation on the themes of deception in romance and compensatory strategies, fusing the earlier three instances in cumulative fashion for a most hopeful outcome.

Still, the earlier, ostensibly comic 'The Wooing of Monsieur Cuerrier' can nonetheless be read as an unnatural, therefore an unpromising, May–September romance, as the story's opening description of setting suggests: 'It had been one of those days that go astray in the year, and carry the genius of their own month into the alien ground of another' (21). Readers must entertain doubts whether Cuerrier and Césarine's marriage will be a fruitful one. Unpromisingly, Cuerrier estimates his suitability as husband to Césarine wholly in materialistic terms, 'calculating how much he was worth, valuing his three farms in an instant. He felt proud after that, and Césarine Angers did not seem quite so far off' (25). Not only is Césarine Anger's surname suggestive of disruption, but it is immediately following his calculations that Cuerrier has his dream, which can also be read now as warning him that he is making a mistake in figuring the younger women into his connubial ciphering and that Madame Laroque, shrewishness notwithstanding, may in fact be his natural mate. Significantly, surely, Césarine is an outsider who deprives Madame Laroque of Cuerrier, and so sets up yet another sympathetic vibration with 'The Little Milliner,' with the note that showed the new seamstress taking trade from the Vigerian stalwart. But mine is doubtless becoming too severe a reading of the first comic story in *Viger*. 'The Wooing' does end hopefully, with the mismatched pair escaped to their honeymoon and with Césarine decorating her hat with flowers plucked by a bucking Cuerrier (29). To return to the story's opening metaphor, perhaps a pod from the aging tree that is Cuerrier will find productive accommodation in the 'alien ground' (21) that was the fair Césarine.

Viger's return story, 'Paul Farlotte,' plays a final variation on the cycle's dominant theme of fractured and mending family, but does so now in concert with a number of the other motifs of the cycle's preceding stories: madness, duty, industrialization and progress, Old World and New, self-sacrifice, among others. Like the final stories in the best cycles (a selection of which will be discussed in ensuing chapters), 'Paul Farlotte' functions as peroration to *Viger*, returning to the story cycle's dominant theme and refiguring it in a powerful, because cumulative, manner, reiterating key images and even repeating phrases from earlier stories. But perhaps the first thing that should be noted about 'Paul Farlotte,' as the information will help justify my claim for its paramount function in the cycle, is that Scott seems to have written it specifically as the final story for *In the Village of Viger* (Groening, 501–2). (Alice Munro would do likewise, during the flurry of final revisions that would finalize her only short story cycle, with the return and title story of *Who Do You Think You Are?* [Hoy, 59–62].) Moreover, Scott clearly signalled his belief in *Viger*'s integrity as a story cycle by 'refusing in his lifetime to allow any of [its] stories to be separately reprinted or anthologized' and by insisting to Ryerson Press, who wanted to reduce the number of stories, that they could publish it in 1945 only in its original form of 1896 (New, *Dreams*, 178).

The introductory paragraph of 'Paul Farlotte' describes 'two houses which would have attracted attention by their contrast, if for no other reason. One was a low cottage, surrounded by a garden, and covered with roses ... The other was a large gaunt-looking house, narrow and high' (79). In the process of binary opposition, the two houses are linked closely by their radical differences (because an opposite depends for definition on its other). In fact, the two are linked literally by the shadow – an ironically ominous adumbration – of a roadway tree, which 'seemed, with its constant movement, to figure the connection that existed between the two houses' (80). The low cottage suggests humility, and its associations are with organic order and the traditional floral symbol of love; the other building, described as a weather-flayed survivor of battles (its 'martial air'), hints at spiritual emaciation and, as the ambitious pride of its male occupants soon proves, a modern mechanical Babel. In these two houses, located significantly 'to the west' and thus more 'New World' (79), live two very different kinds of family, though both are fractured families. Paul Farlotte, of the low cottage, is a gardener, a teacher, and a bachelor; the orphaned St Denis children, occupying the gaunt-looking house, are cared for by their eldest sister and brother, Marie and Guy, acting as surrogate parents.

The St Denis men, like members of many another family in Viger, are cursed with a form of madness, obsession-compulsion: the deceased St

Denis *père* was, and his living son Guy becomes, wholly absorbed in perfecting a matchbook-making machine, a machine which is represented solely by a mechanical 'wheel' (84) whose perfect realization quickly becomes an end in itself. This fixating image of a mechanized cycle that destroys family is, in this return story of the story cycle, countered by the movement of the natural diurnal cycle, the shadow which joins the fates of the two houses and brings saviour Paul Farlotte to the St Denis children. Ironically, the realization of the perfected mechanical wheel would destroy a Vigerian cottage industry whereby the locals – among whom are numbered the St Denis females – earn small cash making match-books. Thus the situation in this return story echoes the theme of modern-industrial displacement that was implied by the reference to the closed flour mill in the opening paragraph of the first story, 'The Little Milliner,' and expressed throughout *Viger* in the displacements undergone by the likes of Eloise Ruelle and her brother Maurice, the Labrosse family, the Pedler, and others. Scott may also be lamenting in this critical event of the return story the fracturing – ultimately a form of maddening – of the human sensibility itself that results from the enforced drudgery of modern industrial methods of production. If this is the case, he was participating in a critique of the separation of work and culture that had been made since at least the early nineteenth century, and most famously by the Thomas Carlyle of *Past and Present* (1843), the John Ruskin of *The Stones of Venice* (1851–3), the Matthew Arnold of *Culture and Anarchy* (1867), generally by the teachings of Marxism and particularly, from about 1880 onwards, by the work of such Fabian Socialists as William Morris.[18]

Paul Farlotte's family still resides in France, and his enduring dream is to return for a visit with his old mother before she dies, which makes France his beloved motherland in two respects, both of which are essential to his identity (as is his dependence for consoling 'comfort' on the 'wisdom of Montaigne,' the humane, sceptical, and above all *practical* Montaigne (89)). As he remarks to Marie, he 'has tried to make this little place [his home in Viger] like it [his birthplace]' (83), and perhaps too faithfully so. But each time Paul had been about to realize his dream, his financial resources were spent instead on the St Denis family, who continue to be threatened with destitution because of the absorbed obliviousness of their natural male provider dreaming his nightmare of mechanical perfection. Paradoxically the value of the perfected machine is said by Guy to reside wholly in his 'mak[ing] a fortune out of it' (86). Paul Farlotte loses his dream of return to his natural family because he assumes responsibility for his neighbour's family: ultimately he loves his neigh-

bours as he – more than he – loves himself. The St Denis men strive obsessively to realize an apparently unattainable dream of perfection –
something mechanical and inhuman, as perfection must remain[19] – to the
exclusion of all concern for their natural family. And it bears repeating in
other words: the St Denis men shirk that which Paul shoulders – familial
duty – and Scott underscores the contrast by having Paul sacrifice his ties
to natural family and native place to assume the family responsibilities of
the St Denis men in his adopted country.

Farlotte's decision to become surrogate father to the St Denis children,
which entails relinquishing his dream of return, is summarized in *Viger*'s
return story in terms of a resolute dark night of the soul:

> All night long Monsieur Farlotte walked in his garden, patient and
> undisturbed, fixing his duty so that nothing could root it out. He found the
> comfort that comes to those who give up some exceeding deep desire of the
> heart, and when next morning the market-gardener from St Valérie, driving
> by as the matin bell was clanging from St Joseph's, and seeing the old teacher
> as if he were taking an early look at his growing roses, asked him, 'Well,
> Monsieur Farlotte, when do you go to France?' he was able to answer
> cheerfully, 'Next year – next year.'   (88)

Farlotte knows he will never return to France. After a whole night alone –
'undisturbed' referring to his solitary vigil and not to any simple noctur-
nal inner peace won without a quest – after a night of focusing on his
duty, 'he was able to answer cheerfully,' with the 'able' suggesting that he
has endured a dark night indeed. (Interestingly, and again ironically, St
Denis, or Denys, is the patron saint of France; perhaps even more interesting, hagiographic legend traces Denis, the first bishop of Paris, back to
St Paul.) The above passage's allusions and references to Gethsemane,
'duty,' finding 'comfort,' sacrifice, St Joseph, and 'growing roses' suggest
in the complex manner of masterful fiction that Paul Farlotte finds in the
New World, by re-creating it, the essence of what he has 'cheerfully'
given up: homeland, family, a new identity in a new place. He '[fixes] his
duty so that nothing could root it out,' in effect putting down new roots
in the New World. These allusions, images, and references also suggest
that the unarticulated reasons for his decision devolve from both hard-
won humanistic beliefs and a Christian vision of community that, as I've
said, literally find expression in his selfless love for his neighbour. In its
emphasis on familial 'duty' (which has also just been ascribed to Farlotte
by Marie [87]), Paul's decision brings to cyclical fulfilment the theme that

was introduced in 'The Little Milliner' with Viau's tragic devotion to her male relative, and most impressively in Philippe and Adèle Desjardin's caring for their mad brother Charles. Directly echoing Philippe Desjardin, who 'seemed to find some comfort' (18) in giving up his desire for marriage and family, Paul Farlotte 'found the comfort that comes to those who give up some exceeding deep desire of the heart.' And his resolve in 'fixing his duty' might even be said to offer a cure for Eloise Ruelle's fevered exploitation of the word in her perverse command to her brother Maurice: 'it is my duty; you do yours' (46).

There are, it can now be said, two sorts of family madness in 'Paul Farlotte': the hyperrational and egomaniacal pursuit of perfection by mechanical means, a fixation which leads to obsessive-compulsive psychosis (thus echoing the Desjardins' nominal reminder that perfectibility is not possible for fallible man, and the implicit caution as to human limitation of 'The Bobolink'); and Paul Farlotte's vision-haunted madness that leads to his relinquishing a lifelong dream for the sake of others – the 'madness' of irrational, though reasonable, Christian love, which was seen figured variously in the other romantic attachments of *Viger*. Paul Farlotte's love reconstructs family where family had been disintegrating; his love is the glue that bonds a fracturing family one to another and (the application of glue being what it is) to himself. Thus he is the gardener who cultivates the best roses in the country (80; as Ware notes [Afterword, 123], gardening 'unites labour and art'), symbolically providing an alternative to those other isolated and withering gardens in Viger (those of 'The Desjardins' and 'The Tragedy'). Thus too Paul becomes an *imitatio* of St Joseph, protecting another 'Marie' and her 'children,' reconstituting another 'holy' family, which is doubtless why St Joseph is mentioned not only in the passage above but at the end of the story, when 'the bell [is] ringing from St Joseph's' (89), recalling the image of St Joseph's spire flashing 'like a naked poniard' in the first paragraph of *Viger*.[20] Most subtly telling in this respect is the recurrence in the return story of the 'dry stick' image from the first story, 'The Little Milliner.' There, it is Viau's abandoned and withered geranium which 'looks like a dry stick' (14); here, it is in reference to 'a superstition in the village that all [Farlotte] had to do was to put anything, even a dry stick, into the ground, and it would grow' (80). Along with its framing function, the allusion is of course to the legend wherein God signals a reluctant St Joseph that he is to head the Holy Family by having him stick his staff in the ground and causing a lily to grow atop it.

The St Denis family is holy at the end of 'Paul Farlotte' not because it is divinely sanctified but because it constitutes that rarity in modernizing Viger – a functioning family. Nonetheless, Scott does administer an authorial blessing by having his narrator echo God the Father's approval of Christ's baptism when, at the conclusion of 'Paul Farlotte,' the apparition of Paul's mother looks upon her son's decision to give up his dream of visiting her and smiles, 'as if she were well pleased' (89; see Matt. 3:17). Note too that Paul Farlotte is a modern-day Saul/Paul who is figuratively waylaid by a vision on the road to a mistaken destination. In his aspect as maddened visionary, Farlotte could be said to occupy the 'beyond' that Homi Bhabha describes as a kind of psychic analogue to his culturally potentially rich 'interstitial space.' 'Being in the "beyond,"' Bhabha writes, 'is to inhabit an intervening space, as any dictionary will tell you. But to dwell "in the beyond" is also ... to be part of a revisionary time, a return to the present to redescribe our cultural contemporaneity; to reinscribe our human, historic commonality' (7). 'Being in the beyond' may unfortunately echo (perhaps only for me) Leacock's parodically thaumaturgical *Behind the Beyond*. Regardless, Scott leaves Farlotte in a culturally-spiritually creative space, genuinely so, wherein his mother is to him – to invoke the authority and faith of George Steiner – a 'real presence' (81).

Read in this way, 'Paul Farlotte' can be seen to offer one possible answer to the questions that Scott implicitly asks throughout his *fin de siècle* short story cycle: What is 'family' to mean in the alienating, dislocating, industrializing, urbanizing, maddening modern world that is coming? What do we want family to be? What do we as Canadians want to be in the coming century that Prime Minister Laurier would soon promise us was Canada's?[21] The return story suggests that if 'family' is to maintain functional meaning in the New World and modern times, exclusive definitions of the word must be broadened to include (or properly 'to embrace' [3]) neighbours such as the St Denis, communities such as transitional Viger, the city even, and, ultimately, the family of humankind – enlarged in an ever-increasing (to borrow the title of Scott's last book) 'circle of affection.' Certainly Paul Farlotte's decisive act of charity and love, enacted at home, and the foregoing reading of that act, would be congenial to the moral-aesthetic of the Scott who wrote as follows in his 'At the Mermaid Inn' column of 19 March 1892:

The promptings to kindness result in a greater humanity, to abstinence in a more sublime self-control. And who shall measure the effect, or set a bound to the force of the objective value of service? The washing the disciples' feet, the acts of tenderness and mercy start at once a thousand roots of peace and promise in the heart. By these present virtues we communicate with the millennium; we are part of that circle of goodness and beauty which shall widen out into eternity. By this service we are linked to the past and its throes are triumphant in us. So between the two abysses we stand conservators of the past, pioneers of the future. But we are most of all pioneers, the function of our service is one for progress, for advance; by these acts of humanity and usefulness we increase the store of the beauty and goodness of the race. No individual excellence was ever lost; today we are protected by the valour of one of our ancestors, who stood in the breach of the wall and would not let the enemy pass. And will we not by our present self-control make the task of life easier for someone who is to come after us. Beauty is not a term of form alone, it is the secret and ever-present essence of the spirit of absolute truth, of supreme goodness, so that each service, each stroke of kindness, each expression of geniality is one more beauty.   (37)

By way of concluding I observe just how apt was Scott's choice of fractured family as sounding board for the various expressions of dissonant modernity played out in *Viger*. Because the institution of family is the intermediary between the individual and society, and the relay between past and future – those 'two abysses' – with strong roots into the past and green shoots into the future, it would have been for the conservative-humanist Scott the primary social organism for countering the denial of communal and individual identity which time (modernity) and space (the encroaching city) threaten. To fracture the institution of family is, therefore, to disrupt that which facilitates the transmission of values and cultural continuity itself. To trace the expressions and to suggest the causes of that fracturing, and then to refashion 'family' as Scott does in *In the Village of Viger*, is an admirable achievement of imagination informed by memory and hope, to all of which the short story cycle is ideally formed.

2

Fabian Feminism: J.G. Sime's
Sister Woman

J.G. Sime's *Sister Woman* (1919) has been called one of the most 'stylistically accomplished works' of early-twentieth-century Canadian literature
(New, 'Back,' 257), and 'a technically and thematically sophisticated landmark in women's writing in Canada' (Campbell, 'Gently,' 40). More
recently, Misao Dean included *Sister Woman* in her wide-ranging study of
the cultural interplay between the gendered self and its social construction in Canadian fiction, *Practising Femininity* (1998). W.H. New included 'Art' from *Sister Woman* in his anthology *Canadian Short Fiction*
(1997), and Sandra Campbell and Lorraine McMullen reprinted the story
'Munitions' in their anthology *'New Women'* (1991). Under the auspices
of the Early Canadian Women Writers series edited by McMullen, the
Tecumseh Press republished *Sister Woman* (1992) and Sime's ambitious
1921 novel *Our Little Life* (1994), with excellent scholarly-critical intro-
ductions by Campbell and K. Jane Watt respectively. Yet apart from this
work and a couple of graduate theses, Sime has continued to remain comparatively unknown, 'virtually invisible not only to accounts of Canadian
literary culture but to other explanations of the historical period of her
finest work' (Watt, 'Passing,' unpaginated preface).[1] I would be surprised
if more than a handful of workers in remote areas of the field of Canadian
literature had heard of Sime or her strikingly original story cycle.[2] At the
risk of sounding colonially extravagant for making the claim (though I
don't think the situation of neglect can be exaggerated), I would contend
that J.G. Sime is Canada's most underrated writer of the Modern period –
and is so in comparison with such celebrated writers as Sara Jeannette
Duncan, Stephen Leacock, F.P. Grove, and Morley Callaghan. Sime was
not as prolific as any of these contemporaries, but then she was much less
recognized and encouraged. Still, she produced a substantial body of

diverse works that deserve and reward attention, the most impressive of which is the story cycle *Sister Woman*.

Because extravagant claims can eventually do more damage than good in the project of recuperating earlier Canadian writers, I would like momentarily to divert the natural course of this introduction and simply present the opening paragraph of 'Art,' which, if not selected at random, is not atypical of Sime's writing:

> There is nothing so wearisome in all the wearisome possibilities of this world as to be talked to about Art. I dislike to be talked to about anything beginning with a capital letter – Love, Art, Vice – anything of that sort. The more people talk about such things the less do they do them; and unless you do a thing what can you possibly have to say that is worth listening to about it? I haven't known many criminals – to give them their technical name – but I'll be bound that if I did know them they wouldn't talk to me about Vice. They might spin me a yarn about housebreaking, perhaps, and very diverting it would be, but they wouldn't call it by the name of Vice. They would call it – whatever the slang for burglary may be. As to lovers – none that I have known ever talked of Love – while artists are generally too busy to be talking much at all. Art, indeed, may be described as a thing to be done and not talked about. I daresay the War will help it [Canadian art] on its way – so far, at least, as not talking about it is concerned. But why, as Mr. Granville Barker says, worry with it at all? If it is there you can't miss it, and if it isn't there no talking about it will produce it. Let it take its chance with love – which is much in the same box. (224)

It may be unsafe to say uncritically (if safe in so far as in keeping with this interdiction against talking about Art) that, for present purposes – simply to display Sime's ability – here is a passage that speaks for itself. Yet consider: 'Art' is the twenty-third of twenty-eight stories that have talked insistently, implicitly and explicitly to the reader about Love and Vice, *and* Art, in numerous subtle and self-reflexive turns. Note too the range of reference that boldly links art, crime, and love; note further the Tennysonian hope that War might change decadently exhausted things for the better, including that thing called 'love,' a word whose referent is, by this point in *Sister Woman*, if not virtually identical with the lives of women, clearly in women's safe-keeping. And note finally the nice touch where the last sentence talks seriously of 'love' in the lower case.

But having violated this far the interdiction, I may as well observe further that the near-identity of love and art is central to Sime's vision, being integral to her faith in the potentially meliorative function of writing, to her identification of women's lives and love, and to her implicitly socialist politics. Those subjects will be discussed presently. My point here is that you have only to begin reading *Sister Woman* to recognize that you are in the presence of a writer of remarkable skill and bold intellect: 'it is there [and] you can't miss it.' And a writer, I will argue, who chose the form of the story cycle to distinguish herself from the turn-of-the-century women writers writing novels on the Woman Question that provides the prologue's bemusing occasion for the stories of *Sister Woman* (8). Yet most readers and critics have somehow managed to 'miss it,' to bypass the challenges and pleasures of this writer confidently possessed by turns of a Duncan-like wit, a light-handed Leacockean litotes, an intellect as formidable as Grove's (or Duncan's or Leacock's), and a modern style that expresses itself in prose as sharply direct and indirect as Callaghan's. Why is that – or has that been, one hopes – the case?

The 'canon question,' like the Woman Question that inspires New Woman fiction, is worth pondering further. What recuperation Sime has benefited from has been wholly the result of recovery projects motivated by a feminist critical agenda, which understandably values her writing within the limitations of its own ideological work. But as regards the place of *Sister Woman* in the continuum of the Canadian short story cycle, the feminist aspect of the work is, if not the least interesting, then its most obvious feature. Of course such statements of interest, ideological work, and valuation mainly reveal any critic's bias (subject position) at a certain point in time and cultural space (here, my particular interests in the genre of the Canadian short story cycle at the beginning of the twenty-first century). So be it. I am not laying claim to greater 'truth value' than that revealed by Sime's feminist critics. Canadian literature and genre are the interests that attracted me to *Sister Woman* and Sime. But I would nonetheless contend that most readers not primarily feminist in their critical attitudes, and after the initial surprise at Sime's forthright presentation of women's lives, would find the preponderantly feminist readings of *Sister Woman* a somewhat redundant exercise. I dwell on this contentious point because I fear that, restricted to feminist readings, Sime could actually be done further disservice. And I trust this lengthy qualification is understood in light of the primary gratitude readers and students of Canadian literature should feel towards McMullen, New, Campbell, Watt, Dean, and Tecumseh Press for the work they have done in drawing attention, including mine, to Sime's writing. Nor is this to say that Campbell and Watt make no mention of Sime's reformist politics; they do, but only in passing.

Sister Woman is an eccentric work of fiction, for both its story cycle form and its at once conservative-maternal and radical feminist treatment of its subjects, with those formal and substantive differences doubtless also accounting for its comparative invisibility in the evolving canon of Canadian literature (see Gerson, *Purer*, 153). For the majority of those Canadian readers of the post–First World War era, accustomed in their fiction to variously sympathetic treatments of the rural in humorous tones of local colour (Montgomery, Leacock), to wilderness romance adventures (Seton, Roberts, Gilbert Parker), and to the compromising solutions of New Woman fiction (Duncan, Lily Dougall, Joanna Wood; see Dean, 57–63), *Sister Woman* could only have affronted their sensibilities with its claustrophobic urban world of sharp unappealable judgments. It is one thing to read of the lives of Scott's colourful Vigerians under pressure from the tumescing metropolis and quite another to be confronted by a twenty-eight-story volume of Little Milliners at once adrift and imprisoned in exploitative urban spaces.

That comparison is not as straining for continuity as might first appear. A high proportion of Sime's sister-women are actually seamstresses (the younger Sime herself apprenticed as a dressmaker [Watt, Introduction, xiv]). True, Sime's seamstresses are just about all immigrants from the British Isles and France, but they are as displaced in the New World's opportunistic city (a fictionalized Montreal) as is Scott's urban Little Milliner plunked down in semi-rural Viger. In fact, an initially useful way of imagining the disruptive modern world of *Sister Woman* and its impact on its first readers is to conceive that the sister-women of Viger – Madame Larocque, Adèle Desjardin, Latulipe Arbique, Josephine and Madame Labrosse, Marie St Denis – have finally been embraced by the encroaching modern city that imminently threatens in *Viger*'s splendid opening paragraph, or to imagine that the ambitious Eloise Ruelle has fulfilled her ill-considered wish for a career in the bright, if gaseous, lights of the big city to the south. Conceived so, *Sister Woman* nicely continues that anti-modern strand originally picked up by Scott in Canada's first short story cycle (and subsequently explored by Leacock in *Sunshine Sketches*, 1912). It does so at a time when Canada was most hurriedly becoming an urban country, when the workplace and living conditions brought about by industrialization had long since been viewed in Europe as dehumanizing (by such as William Morris), and it weaves that anti-modern strand into what must indeed have struck readers as the new and strange communal tapestry of *Sister Woman*. Moreover, comprising the 'short and scrappy' sort of modern stories Sime would later say were best suited to the modern ethos (*Orpheus*, 45), the women's tales retailed in *Sister Woman* just about all have sad, if not tragic, endings. For such reasons, *Sister Woman* may well have been, and may remain, the kind of fiction only literary critics and serious students appreciate. There are other possible reasons for its languishing, and I will take up some of them below.

Sister Woman was first published in London, England, by Grant Richards in 1919. That publisher and date have some significance for the present study. It was Richards who finally brought out James Joyce's controversial *Dubliners* in 1914, after its long and discouraging search for a publisher. Subsequently *Dubliners* became the first internationally celebrated modern short story cycle of place, with its concluding 'The Dead' providing a symphonic instance of a return story that must surely move readers of any time and place. And as much as Joyce, the self-styled outsider, intended nothing less than a severe moral history of his Irish-Catholic European city, Sime in *Sister Woman* wrote a moral history of working women in patriarchal capitalism, a gendered slice of life in a New World city. As Campbell has observed, Sime was well suited to such a fictional program of championing the downtrodden and the outsider by the condition of her own marginalized life as a single immigrant woman in Canada (Campbell, Introduction, x).

The year 1919 is significant because that was when Sherwood Anderson's *Winesburg, Ohio* was published, it being the first modern American short story cycle of place (see 38–9 above). It must always appear remarkable that this new generic form, the story cycle, emerges at roughly the same time in Canada, the United States, and Ireland, if employed for the different purposes of subversion which the histories of those dissimilar contexts invoke and provoke. And though no one would dispute that *Sister Woman* is feminist fiction (its pleonastic title constitutes something of a sororal brick to the head),[3] it yet clearly plays off and against the compromising New Woman novel that had preceded it in Canada and the Anglo-American world – and does so formally precisely because it is a story cycle. Thus the present chapter argues that Sime's *Sister Woman* is best understood generically in the new tradition of the short story cycle that was begun in Canada by Scott and continued by Leacock, and was emergent internationally in *Dubliners* and *Winesburg, Ohio* (and before *Winesburg* in Sarah Orne Jewett's *The Country of the Pointed Firs* [1896]). These story cycles and their authors made innovative uses of short stories in cyclical structures to give voice to Frank O'Connor's 'submerged underclasses' in opposition to a social system identified generically with the novel (see O'Connor similarly on *Winesburg* [39–

41]). To repeat, then, it is only by reading *Sister Woman* in the formal-generic context of the Canadian short story cycle that its original contribution even to feminist fiction can be fully appreciated.

Sister Woman comprises twenty-eight stories framed by a very brief prologue and epilogue. The first feature of its organization as a story cycle worth remarking is the actual number of stories, twenty-eight, which corresponds both to the time for the moon, traditionally associated with the female, to make one orbit, or cycle, of the earth (with a bit to spare), and corresponds also with the period of a woman's menstrual cycle. It is too odd and large a number of stories for Sime to have arrived at it randomly, so twenty-eight may indeed have been chosen for its associations with women and the completion of natural cycles. Such associations complement Sime's continual recourse to a maternal feminism grounded in nineteenth-century natural science, the maternal feminism which essentializes women as mothers and mates, though much more as mothers in *Sister Woman*. (As I will show, the radical aspect of Sime's feminism rests in this priorizing of the maternal over the spousal role, as well as in her refusal of the happy, compromising endings of New Women novels.)[4] Further, there is some evidence that the volume as a whole is indeed organized to reflect either the phases of the moon or the flux of hormones (estrogen and progesterone) in the progression of a woman's menstrual cycle (Sime did spend her working life as nurse to Montreal's leading gynecologist; but interestingly, in a cycle of twenty-eight stories that treats of a great many aspects of women's lives, from abortion to prostitution to sexual longing to coquetry, there is no reference to menstruation). The moon does wax and wane from new to full, and *Sister Woman* moves from a despairing first two stories of women brutally victimized, through a developing arc of endurance stories, to a closing return story of a woman who struggles to redefine the words 'marriage' (in the *absence* of a husband) and 'love' in a triumph for which the words 'gynocentric' and 'full' would be accurately descriptive.

But the primary structuring principle of *Sister Woman* as a story cycle is framing: by the prologue and epilogue, by the fairly consistent frame narrator who provides the opportunity for most of these women's stories, and by the framing of the twenty-four interior stories by the first two ('Alone' and 'Adrift') and the last two ('The Bachelor Girl' and 'Divorced'). The last story, 'Divorced,' also constitutes the definitive return story of *Sister Woman* as a story cycle by taking the recurrent theme of women's freedom within patriarchal capitalism and moving matters to a higher level with a vision of idealized love that would appear to be identical with and exclusive to women, or at least to the childless woman of this return story. I use the conditional voice here not only because 'Divorced' is finally but one of twenty-eight stories, however paramount its role as the return story of *Sister Woman*, but also because there is another story, 'A Page from Life,' the only story that adopts a male point of view, where a man proves himself capable of a similar kind of mystically intuitive love.

Having touched on the aesthetic aptness of numerological matters, I might also remark here again that the excessive number of stories in *Sister Woman* also contributes most to its few aesthetic flaws. There are simply too many short stories. Some strain for effect and others are sketchy pieces that do little but justify the charge of repetitiveness that the mostly confused reviewers levelled at the book (Campbell, Introduction, xxvi–vii). *Sister Woman* has other faults: frequent dialect fiction in thick stretches that makes the reading more a chore than a pleasure (she had thought at one time of doing a whole novel in dialogue [Sime, *Thomas Hardy*, 56]), and seem to little point other than to display the writer's considerable skill at rendering brogue phonetically; a recurrent tendency towards sentimentality (Pacey, 'Fiction,' 185), especially as regards babies (perhaps the pitfall of a writer who never married, was childless, and had a decades-long affair with the prominent Montreal gynecologist); a repetitive recourse to the idealization of maternal feminism that, whatever the reader's biases, becomes at times but a metaphysically signifying tag and is, quite simply, too simple a solution to the socio-economic issues which *Sister Woman* engages. By no means are those minor flaws, but in *Sister Woman* they are the sort of faults that a powerful imagination and intellect sometimes allow in an otherwise excellent work of literary art.

Of course, such criticisms of style – of repetitiveness, dialect, sentimentalism, and gestural mysticism as regards motherhood – must be understood in view of the feminist didactic intention that dictated the style of these stories, the (as I will argue) mild socialist-realist aesthetic that eschews ornamentation and features directness and clarity for the sake of wide accessibility and influence. It could even be said that the stories of *Sister Woman* are hardly Modern short stories at all; but for 'Divorced,' the return story (and one or two others to a much lesser degree), they achieve few moments of insight or Joycean epiphanies for their subjects; they are not especially interested in the well-made plot or unity of impression and effect, apart from the dominant impression that these are sympathetic representations of working-class women's generally drab lives. What they are preponderantly are biographical sketches stately (by the frame narrator) for illustrative-educative purpose, in a way that recalls the eighteenth-century story and, before that, medieval exempla and parables. Mary Louise Pratt, quoting H.S. Canby, is especially helpful on this aspect of the form of *Sister Woman*'s stories:

> The exemplary or illustrative trend in the short story traces back not just to the medieval exemplum or the biblical parable, but to the use of the short narrative in eighteenth century periodicals like London's *The Spectator* and *The Rambler*, where it merges with the essay. In the eighteenth century, says H.S. Canby, 'the novel developed freely. But the short story, by custom, remained a pendant to the essay, was restricted to the purposes of illustration. In this age, as never before or since, it was bound up to the service of didacticism. Its range was small. Its success was remarkable' [Canby, 26]. ... Outside literature, the exemplary narrative is always a fragment of a larger discourse, never a complete whole. (Pratt, 103).

Where the pre-modern Duncan Campbell Scott exercised a range of nineteenth-century story forms in *Viger*, Sime reaches back to earlier practices, in a manner that is yet typically Modern in its participation in the myth of discontinuity, its rejection of immediate predecessors in favour of earlier and more austere craftsmen (T.S. Eliot's relation to the metaphysicals, especially Donne, is the obvious example; in Canada, A.J.M. Smith and F.R. Scott enact similar leaps of literary faith).[5]

In *Sister Woman* the biographical stories serve as exempla in a total design that is as powerful as it is compelling. The external 'larger discourse' to which Pratt refers (if not in this way) is, as I've been hinting, the discourse of socialism. Perhaps the best evidence of this is simply that most of the stories of *Sister Woman* persistently establish and keep attention focused on the working conditions of their subjects, and their themes are always bound up with economic circumstances. Two of Sime's later books are especially useful for the light they cast on the form and intent of her story cycle, *Orpheus in Quebec* (1942) and *Brave Spirits* (1952; Frank Nicholson is given as coauthor). *Orpheus* is a musing upon the kind of art that may arise in the aftermath of the Second World War, and *Brave Spirits* is a memoir that might usefully have been subtitled 'Famous Writers I Have Known and Their Influence on Me.' In *Orpheus* Sime speculates that Quebec's and Canada's indigenous art form will be music, a music inspired by the St Lawrence River (suggestively an extension into aesthetic matters of Donald Creighton's 'Laurentian Thesis' of 1937).[6] She also considers what new forms of literature may arise, and one is a form that sounds very much like the short story cycle Sime had fashioned in *Sister Woman* some twenty years before: 'one feels in the cities, I think, the potentialities of quite another kind of art – disjointed, disconnected art that finds its expression in thumb-nail sketches, short stories, one-act scrappy plays, and the like' (34). That is an aesthetic which also suits such of her literary descendants in both Montreal and the short story cycle as the Hugh Hood of *Around the Mountain: Scenes from Montreal Life* (1967) and the Mordecai Richler of *The Street* (1969). Sime observes further that modern Canadian society itself lacks the coherence necessary to the novel as it was understood in the eighteenth and nineteenth centuries (45); and she prognosticates, long after her own dealing with the theme both in *Sister Woman* and *Our Little Life*, that for Canada explorations of the subject of immigration could prove to be its original contribution to world literature; and concludes by suggesting further that the divided loyalties and lives of immigrants and modern women have much in common (42–3).

Brave Spirits is the more interesting work, though, as in it Sime remembers the most influential people in her life as a writer. For those few readers acquainted only with Sime's fiction, her memoir reveals her to be an even more fascinating figure than they may have projected. She was personally acquainted with an impressive array of mid- and late-Victorian writers. And with early Modern writers too: to take but one instance, she participated as subject in some failed experiments in mysticism with the young William Butler Yeats (and Sime's father was one of a very few to encourage the young poet). But of all the literary luminaries she met, the two most influential were William Morris and Mrs Oliphant (the mid-Victorian popular novelist who was also a distant relation), and these two neatly contribute to the shaping of Sime's thinking on social-political matters and on women's lives respectively. The portrait of Mrs Oliphant is engaging in itself, but for present purposes its most significant feature is the somewhat cold and independent woman's last words of general advice to Sime: '"Marry the first man who asks you and get yourself a baby as soon as you can. For that is the only thing that matters in this world"' (55). It may strike present-day ears as comically retrograde, that kind of maternal feminism, until readers notice the cavalier way in which the male of the species is used. Any man will do, motherhood's what matters. Such advice could be interpreted as promoting as radical a feminism, a sorority of self-sufficiency, as any since. Oliphant's are last maternal words which Sime put into practice, if not in her own life, then in *Sister Woman*'s ultimate picture of woman alone and as keeper of the ideal of love.

Important as Mrs Oliphant was to Sime as the model of an independent woman writer and as wise woman, the legacy of William Morris influenced her at least equally through the period of *Sister Woman*. In 'A Whiff of William Morris as a Socialist,' she tells of encountering Morris when she was eleven years old as he was speaking to a group of workers. She was immediately fascinated (*Brave*, 7), and it was a lasting impression repeatedly fortified through the late 1880s and the 1890s by frequent attendance at Morris's Sunday evening lectures for his Hammersmith Socialist Society in the Kelmscott stable of his house outside London. On first encounter, she describes him as 'pointing out how we might all, if we only would, share with each of our fellow creatures the comforts and conveniences that were within our reach' (7). She concedes that initially she could not connect Morris's vision of love with the love (no doubt upper-case) she had read of in novels: 'I couldn't recognize the kinship between that love and the love with which my novels had made me familiar.' But she makes clear that Morris was a prime, perhaps *the* prime, and lifelong influence on her thought; and if she is frustratingly non-specific about just what it was she took from Morris, she reveals in the following statement that it may well have been Morris's well-known championing of the value of work as the foundation of art and social justice: 'He set before us a vision of the sort of life that anyone with a morsel of the artistic build in him would like to lead and to see his fellowmen leading. It seemed a simple proposition (not so very unlike that of the early Christians)' (12).[7]

Fabian Socialism was so called after Quintus Fabius Maximus, the second century BC Roman general who, with his tactic of avoidance, of wearing the opposition down slowly, defeated Hannibal in the second Punic War. In Fabian Socialism this avoidance tactic translates into its first principle of gradualism as opposed to communist (Marxist-Leninist) revolution. Besides having been the political affiliation of her hero Morris, Fabianism possesses a number of features that would have appealed to Sime. It was very much a middle-class and intellectual social movement of the late nineteenth century; and its two prime directives of gradualism and permeation didn't make overly taxing demands on its adherents (Weintraub, 10). As Margaret Cole describes the essentials of the movement, 'the main characteristics of Fabian thinking ... are, first, that it is eclectic' (27), second 'democratic' (28), and third 'gradualist' (29); she adds endearingly that its adherents are optimists and enthusiasts (32). As Rodelle Weintraub observes in his introduction to *Fabian Feminist*, middle-class professional women were among those groups especially attracted to Fabian Socialism (10). The history of Fabian Socialism and of Morris's involvement in it requires no rehearsal here. Suffice it to say that the history of British socialism itself and of Fabianism constitutes a sequence of factionalisms into various societies that seems to prove nothing so well as Freud's concept of the narcissism of small differences. Regardless, as Cole, who had deep and personal ties to the Fabian movement, attests, despite his early setting up of his own socialist shop, 'William Morris remained a Fabian' (3). The main point of contention between Morris and the Fabians was that Morris, something of a lifelong anarchist, never wanted a political party, but rather saw his prime duty in teaching, and teaching through art (Cole, 20). In this, he was in sympathy with the Fabians' most popular proselytizer, George Bernard Shaw, to whom Sime also had a close connection, and whose own Fabianism contained – or didn't contain rather, but expressed explosively – a strong strain of radical feminism.

It was at a Morris lecture that Sime first became aware of Shaw (and Oscar Wilde, H.G. Wells, and others). For a time she boarded with Shaw's sister, Lucy, and an essay in *Brave Spirits* recalls her close association with the Shaws.[8] It is not difficult to make a case for the influence that Morris's talks and his arts-and-crafts movement had on *Sister Woman*, especially as regards Sime's continual valorization in her story cycle of woman's domestic work as art, and particularly the repeated recognition of the art-craft of seamstresses: in *Brave Spirits* she writes of her acquaintance with embroideresses from Morris's workshops, one of whom was Yeats's sister Lily, whom, she says, Yeats considered 'a real artist' (62). It is only a little more difficult to imagine the impact on Sime of Shaw's histrionic addresses to the Fabian Society, yet such a reception must surely have occurred. Shaw's radical feminism is best appreciated in his *The Quintessence of Ibsenism* (1891), which began as a talk to the Fabian Society in 1890 and was repeatedly published. So it is possible to picture, if somewhat fancifully, the impressionable Sime sitting spellbound through Shaw's performances of Shavian wit. Whatever the actual case may have been, biographical and circumstantial evidence indicates that Sime would surely have encountered, quite likely in person and undoubtedly in print, volleys of Shaw, such as the following gems from the *Quintessence*'s 'The Womanly Woman' chapter:

> Now of all the idealist abominations that make society pestiferous, I doubt if there be any so mean as that of forcing self-sacrifice on a woman under pretence that she likes it; and, if she ventures to contradict the pretence, declaring her no true woman.   (124)

> The truth is, that in real life a self-sacrificing woman ... is not only taken advantage of, but disliked as well for her pains.   (125)

The sum of the matter is that unless Woman repudiates her womanliness, her duty to her husband, to her children, to society, to the law, and to everyone but herself, she cannot emancipate herself ... In that repudiation lies her freedom; for it is false to say that Woman is now directly the slave of Man: she is the immediate slave of duty; and as man's path to freedom is strewn with the wreckage of the duties and ideals he has trampled on, so must hers be.   (130–1).

Below, in the context of discussing particular stories from *Sister Woman*, I will have recourse to some possible specific influences of Shaw. For the present, I would conclude this detour into influences on Sime and *Sister Woman* (and I don't doubt but there are other influences in the life of such a well-read woman, though I would contest whether or not they were equally formative or forceful) by recalling that those primary influences are the conservative Mrs Oliphant for a form of maternal-radical feminism, William Morris for the valuing of women's domestic work, and Shaw for a witty form of firebrand Fabian Socialism permeated by an unequivocating radical feminism. The gradualist and permeative character of Fabianism was expressed practically in an educative thrust, which can be seen in the framing epilogue and prologue of *Sister Woman*, where the intention also is clearly to educate the male interlocutor in (*pace* Freud) what modern women want. Thus the mode of the stories within the frame is as illustrative exempla, and Sime's intention is didactic in a way that anticipates later socialist realist aesthetics (see Doyle, 'Just'). Unsurprisingly, all three of her primary influences – Oliphant, Morris, Shaw – viewed literature as their main tool for educating the masses and achieving their ends.

Ultimately, though, in *Brave Spirits* (in 1952, that is) Sime declares her differences from Morris and Shaw in their socialism (though never from Mrs Oliphant as a model of an independent woman writer).[9] In retrospect she rejects Morris's utopian vision, believing that it lacks the vital 'sharpness' necessary to true literary art, and dismissing any art tainted by a programmatic ideology. In her brief monograph on Thomas Hardy, she already criticizes his later novels for committing 'the great sin against art – that of writing to the order of a philosophy of life instead of to the order of life itself' (45). Always with Sime, as is evident much later in *Orpheus in Quebec* and the numerous recollections of writers in *Brave Spirits*, the implied aesthetic is an eclectic mixture; here, of the modernist-realist and the didactically *engagé* that has affinities with the high Victorian moral-aesthetic. As Watt describes it, though, the *Sister Woman–Our Little Life* period was suggestively a socialist-realist stage through which the middle-aged writer Sime passed: 'At this stage of her career, at least, Georgina Sime believed in a direct link between literature and the realm of the political. Her work was not only about formal experimentation, about the possibilities of differing engagements with genre and form, but was about "saying something" [in reference to Sime's criticism of a novel], about moving literature away from a decadent artfulness into an engagement with contemporary society through an exploration of individual situations' (Introduction, x).

Sime's reputation may well have been low, then, because of the implied socialist politics that underlies *Sister Woman* and *Our Little Life* (though in the end 'politics' may be the wrong word; 'attitude' may be more vaguely accurate). It is likely that *Sister Woman*'s challenging view of patriarchal systemic unfairness and capitalist-consumerism/commodification made – and makes – the story cycle at least as 'threatening' today as when it was first published. As the frame narrator (a Sime persona) of the stories declares in frustration to her smug male interlocutor in the epilogue: '"you've got to start the world again"' (292); that is, tear it down and start over if the injustices to working women that her stories body forth are ever to be rectified. That is the most extreme statement of Sime's exasperated narrator, at her most threatening-challenging. Thus *Sister Woman*'s socialist-feminist critique, with its disturbing mixture of a conventional maternal feminism and insistence on women's independence, would have contributed significantly to Sime's continuing undervaluation. And historically, Sime would have suffered under the conservatively Canadian response/lack of response to a woman writing powerfully and frankly about working women's lives. In her two books of fiction, and more so in *Sister Woman*, her subject matter is highly risqué and dealt with more frankly than anything in Grove or Callaghan, whose later introduction into Canadian fiction of such taboo subjects as women's sexual desire and prostitution (in *Settlers of the Marsh*, 1925, and *Such Is My Beloved*, 1934, respectively) gave them much censorious trouble. Still, such material would have been more acceptable in male-authored fiction. Furthermore, though Sime lived in Montreal for some forty-three years and didn't begin writing till moving there, she seems to have been viewed, at worst, with critical suspicion, when included at all in surveys and Canadian literary histories, and at best as providing an immigrant woman writer's view of Canada (Logan and French, 305; see Campbell, Introduction, xv).

It is understandable that Sime's few critics have focused attention on the feminist aspect of *Sister Woman*, on what Campbell calls Sime's 'gyn-cocentric empathy' (43), abundant and obvious as it is. The stories are so stridently about the lives of working *women* that it would be as critically irresponsible not to give due emphasis initially to a feminist reading as it would be to ignore the question of identity posed by Alice Munro's *Who Do You Think You Are?* New accurately, if yet only partially, describes the form and function of *Sister Woman* this way: 'Sime's remarkable work adopted an interrupted narrative form in order to expose the inadequacies of a normative social pattern that consigned women to second-class status and abandoned them to penury, divorce, stillbirths, single parenthood, and domestic service' ('Back,' 257). Watt is closer to the mark with her description of the story cycle as one dealing with 'women's varied and conflicting relationships to power, and the economic and social conse-quences of any divergences from the path of "normal" morality' (Intro-duction, ix). But once this has been observed, we are left to wonder what *Sister Woman* and Sime have to say about the material causes of such conditions.

The 'normative social pattern' operative in the world of *Sister Woman* is clearly and primarily patriarchy. But what should then become appar-ent is that this story cycle, with but a couple of exceptions, focuses atten-tion as relentlessly on the various economic conditions of its female protagonists. It repeatedly presents even its sympathetic female narrator in an employer-employee relationship with her subjects, and frames its twenty-eight stories between an epilogue and prologue that has the narra-tor wanting to enlist her male interlocutor in a campaign to right the wrongs of women's lives. As has been shown, it is only when that invita-tion to a co-operative war on systemic injustice fails that she calls him to a revolutionary effort to 'start the world again' (292). Interestingly, in New's series of victim positions above, 'penury' begins it and 'dom-estic service' ends it, and of the three coming between, 'single parenthood' also elicits associations of unfavourable economic circumstances. With the exceptions of the prologue and epilogue, and a few money complaints of characters in the stories, Sime is never obvious in the way of most socialist-realist fiction. She insists that her stories and their implied critiques speak for themselves. Still, in its 'gentle scan' (the epi-graph from Robert Burns) of economic conditions for working women around the time of the First World War in Montreal, *Sister Woman* implicitly indicts capitalism as much as patriarchy (only hinting in its epilogue at the connection more recent feminist arguments have made obvious between the two).

Unlike prefaces and afterwords, prologues and epilogues are integral to the fiction they frame. In *Sister Woman*, they are composed mostly of dialogue between a woman who is the author of the stories proper and a representative, initially sympathetic, man.[10] It may not matter a whole lot whether this female narrator is identical with Sime herself,[11] but she does seem to be the same mainly consistent narrator who is involved in an employer-employee relation with many of the female subjects of the stories (a questionable conceit). If the title of the book has not adequately prepared the reader for tendentiously gendered fiction, the prologue leaves no doubt as to the didactic purpose of these sororal stories. The first-person narrator of the prologue demonstrates admirable patience and restraint in the onslaught of her boorish male interlocutor's opening statement, '"You women don't know what you want"' (7). Clearly the two could soon be on confrontational ground, as his repeated use of the phrase 'you women' invites and challenges. Repeatedly and tactfully the narrator coaxes and provokes her male companion, such as when she will not allow him to make their conversation a discussion of the dreaded '"Woman's Question"' (8) by insisting that her subject is '"The woman's and the man's"' question. (In a witty womanly way, the narrator says that she will 'skirt the question.') It is a Fabian manoeuvre, her avoidance of confrontation and her determination to focus on educative necessity for the greater good of permeating one somewhat thick skull. Repeatedly from this first interchange, the female narrator betters her male interlocutor in the match of wits, so much so that his only response is to 'sit and puff.'[12] Early on the narrator offers a justification of the stories that will follow – to articulate what women want – though their literal occasion has not yet been mentioned. When the male complains, '"You talk plenty ... you women,"' the narrator responds, '"You have to talk to find out what you think, when you're a woman."' Along with its good-natured complaint against women's exclusion from other ways to solidarity (media, education, public platforms, and so on), such a statement can be seen to priorize female speech, even to distinguish a kind of female physical expressiveness vis-à-vis an implicitly male mental life. But most obviously the narrator's statement implicitly criticizes the self-involved male who, without being told, would '"never find out that anything was wrong with us."' Thus the statement opens the needed space for the twenty-eight illustrative stories that follow.

Another noteworthy feature of the prologue is the amiability of the man and woman, their obvious friendship, because their relationship will be strained by the time of the epilogue. Here, they both laugh, and do so as a consequence of the narrator's witty repartee. As she writes towards the prologue's conclusion, 'At that we laughed again. When people like each other and are happy they laugh easily' (8). That is a hopeful view both of relations between the sexes and of the function of humour (a 'kindly' humanizing view of humour actually, which inevitably recalls Leacock's theory; and, I might add, a didactic use of wit that recalls Shaw's great value as a Fabian proselytizer). But this friendly situation cannot continue, because the answer that *Sister Woman*'s stories articulates in answer to the man's final patronizing, '"State your grievance, madam!"' leaves him in a precarious position indeed with regard to his continuing comfort and his relations with his female friend.

The prologue concludes with the narrator's writerly response to the man's challenge: 'I took the cover of my typewriter and sat down before it ...' (ellipses in original). That creative response is remarkable for a number of reasons: it makes the stories of *Sister Woman* a repetitive performance of Sime's female grievances;[13] its suggestion of female display is subtly provocative, I think (the epilogue concludes in an even more suggestively sensuous fashion, again with the typewriter: 'I ran my fingers over the typewriter keys – and felt them lovingly. ...' [293]); and the typewriter, the modern mechanism, is displayed as an aid, an ally really, to women's advancement. The writing of women's stories is going to convey the grievances and implicit challenge to patriarchy, not talking to men about them. Finally, as has been said, the prologue unapologetically introduces the stories to follow as illustrations, as exempla, making clear the didactic purpose of the whole project of *Sister Woman* – repeatedly to show this unnamed, so representative and powerful, male interlocutor what he will ultimately refuse to see and understand.[14] *Sister Woman* does so in the genre of the short story cycle, which is perfectly formed to recurrent and developing variations on a theme, and to challenging convention.

The first story of the cycle (an obvious key position, as I have argued in the introduction), 'Alone,' must have been shocking for its time on a number of scores, and it was doubtless meant to score shockingly on the prologue male and readers of *Sister Woman*. But I want first to jump to the epilogue and so to finish the framing device that does so much to make *Sister Woman* the protesting whole that it is. The epilogue (292–3) is even shorter than the brief prologue, and it is most obviously the book's structural return story, in that it returns to the time and place of the prologue. (The final story proper, 'Divorced,' constitutes a thematic return story.) The male interlocutor initially responds puffily to the preceding onslaught of twenty-eight stories illustrating for his benefit women's grievances. Yet he comments, '"It sounds simple."' Here, his repeated questions to the narrator – '"So that's all ... that's all that women want? ... That's all you have to say"' – alert the narrator both to the unexpected degree of the man's resistance/thickness and alarm her as to the enormity of the campaign for justice she wishes to inaugurate with her writing. She answers him with an alarmed '"*What!*"' and observes with some little irony, 'I was startled, and I confess I raised my voice a little.' She needs to draw her breath before continuing, then says with true oracular pre-science (it is 1919): '"Why, I'm not even started yet."' The male's continuing unresponsiveness, or inappropriate responsiveness, pitches her into her one paroxysm of revolutionary, contra-Fabian fervour: '"I ..." I positively stammered in my hurry – "I've got reams and reams and reams to say," I said to him. "Oh, so you think it's simple, do you? Well, let me tell you what we women want is simple – but the world isn't simple. Don't you see," I said, "you've got to start the world again if – We can't fight the world the way it is. You – you've got to ... "' But the man refuses from his comfortable position to answer this clarion call to what can only be revolution against the whole order of things – 'the world' – that has trapped Sime's sister-women in the various positions of compromise and power-lessness that the twenty-eight stories have preponderantly depicted. The narrator's final response to this refusal is the literary self-reflexive turn quoted earlier: 'I ran my fingers over the typewriter keys – and felt them lovingly. ... ' The repetition reaffirms a return to the Fabian principles of gradualism, permeation, and education; like Morris and Shaw, Sime will seek to achieve her ends through literature.

A quite disquieting conclusion, nonetheless, one that locates the only chance of a loving partnership in the woman writer's somewhat exhibitionist (or performative) relationship with her typewriter. As Campbell observes ('Gently,' 49), 'the final sentence of *Sister Woman* focuses on woman and typewriter, not woman and man. The symbol of women's entry into the business world also becomes the instrument of female expression. Sime subverts the traditional happy ending as the female narrator caresses – "gives her hand" – not to man but to machine.' And that is the finished frame containing the exempla of *Sister Woman*, one which in closing has dispensed with the bonhomie laughter of the prologue, and presented the woman alone and poised at the keys of her typewriter, planning, it must be, to coax from the machine yet more stories that will articulate women's grievances as powerfully. Going by this reading of only the prologue and epilogue, which total fewer than four pages of prose, is it any wonder that this story cycle never found popularity? Readers and critics of any time can countenance unhappy endings, but only the bravest spirits can face such direct and energized challenges to their complacency and comfort. Such implied provocation is what the interior stories of *Sister Woman* present by way of uneditorialized exempla.

As Campbell has also observed (Introduction, xvii), the first and last stories of the cycle, 'Alone' and 'Divorced,' form a pair, what I would call a kind of thematic frame within the structural frame of the prologue and epilogue. In fact, the first two and last two stories form this second, reinforcing frame (with 'Adrift' and 'The Bachelor Girl' respectively). The first two stories are all the more impressively risky given the frame narrator's intentions of leading the receptive male interlocutor out of the friendly prologue and into the world of women's stories. Campbell may be right in describing the stories of *Sister Woman* as 'gynocentric dialogue,' because the 'real communication in them is usually between woman and woman.' Nonetheless, the pretext remains that these stories are told for the benefit of the male interlocutor (Dean, 120n12, agrees). That is the narratological occasion of *Sister Woman*. And it is an important one, given Sime's implicit Fabian socialist ideology, because her purpose is educative, becoming revolutionary only in the heated response to the bullheadedness of the man in the epilogue. This is not to say that her real sister-woman needed no such illustrative instruction, only that Sime chose the more difficult challenge of preaching to the most unconverted and powerful.

The titles of the first two stories, 'Alone' and 'Adrift,' and of the last two, 'The Bachelor Girl' and 'Divorced,' signal their status as pairs constituting a thematic frame within the frame of the prologue and epilogue: all four portray women in different states of despairing loneliness and problematic independence. Pairing – with one story building on the theme of the preceding one or answering it thematically – is also the primary cyclical feature of the interior stories of *Sister Woman*. 'Alone' and 'Adrift' announce the theme of women's freedom and independence that will be the subject of a high proportion of the stories of the cycle, and the final two treat that subject in extreme situations, with the return story, 'Divorced,' doing so most positively. This thematic movement from the first two stories to the last two also constitutes the main movement of the story cycle, and, given that there are twenty-eight stories, it describes something of 'A Circular Tour' (to borrow the title of the twenty-second story) from the old moon of systemically enforced isolation to a new moon of chosen independence that includes a redefinition of love exclusive to women. But as the final two stories show (as does the epilogue), in

Sime's vision, for a woman to choose independence from an abusive husband (and for Sime in her conventional attitude no woman would divorce herself from even a tolerable mate) is to opt for a condition of suffering and frightening freedom, despite the mostly mystical consolation of 'Divorced.' The main difference between these bracketing pairs of stories, though, is that the women of the first two have their 'freedom' thrust upon them as punishment by a patriarchal system that will not permit their unconventional choices, whereas the women of the final two stories have chosen a freedom that, if travestied in 'The Bachelor Girl,' in 'Divorced' yet contains the promise of a spiritually creative independence.

The first story, 'Alone,' accosts the male listener/reader of the prologue with the short sad tale of a young immigrant-British housekeeper, the mistress of her employer who lies dead in the house below. She was pregnant by him and has had an abortion. As the story sums itself up in one typically succinct paragraph: 'He was dead and her baby had never been born. She was alone' (19). 'Alone' intentionally jolts the reader, as well as the prologue male, but it also serves the typical function of first stories in cycles by introducing the subject that the ensuing stories will take up and vary, and which the return story 'Divorced' will bring to completion: the real 'Woman's Question' of female freedom within consumer-capitalist patriarchy. The opening informs readers that 'Hetty Grayson waked up' (9), perhaps declaring Sime's secondary intention of rousing her sister-women to their condition as well as showing women's situations to the prologue male. As her name indicates, Hetty Grayson lives in a gray world that denies her not only husband and child (son?) but also the ability to see her way out of an intolerable situation. She cannot see even the extent of the room in which she is confined and has confined herself, 'looking out into her little room through a mist of misery.' Campbell observes that the repeated use of setting as women's confining space is a unifying feature of the stories of *Sister Woman* and (no doubt thinking also of Virginia Woolf) recognizes it as a typical strategy of women writers: 'The settings of many of the stories are also linked: women brood in lonely rooms. Like many women writers, Sime uses spatial imagery to suggest the isolation and restriction of her character's lives' (Introduction, xvii). When Hetty does take in her room, everything she observes is of her dead lover-employer's doing: 'he had chosen ... he had given ... he had hung up with his own hands ... It was his room really, not hers.' Hetty's room, owned and fashioned by her lover-employer, is as much her death chamber as is the room in which he is stretched out below. As she lies on the death-bed that has been made of her life, that life passes before her eyes, until she returns irrevocably to this tomb of her own.

As Hetty's life passes before her, readers are introduced to the theme of immigration that will be a feature of many of the ensuing stories (anticipating what Sime would say in *Orpheus in Quebec* [42–3] about the potentially original material for Canadian fiction in immigrants' stories, and about the similarly divided lives of immigrants and modern women). Readers see Hetty propositioned on the street by a strange man (11), as are a number of the characters in these stories, and significantly this sort of verbal assault is presented as an unremarkable occurrence (in 'Mr. Johnston,' the tenth story, salesgirls are cajoled into climbing ladders so that men can look up their dresses, and are regularly rubbed against by male co-workers and a supervisor who has to be repulsed tactfully). In one short paragraph Sime plays significantly on the word 'engage': Hetty's lover first 'engaged her as his housekeeper,' but by the end of the paragraph 'their eyes had met ... he had engaged her' (11, ellipses in original), establishing a complex of associations that continue centrally in *Sister Woman*. Men have economic power over women; they use that power to engage women in economic and romantic relationships; but the love that arises is no less real for being so contractually founded. Throughout the stories, too, Sime will repeatedly show a pointed facility for conveying the forlorn isolation and utter dependency of the Hettys of the world: her lover-employer 'lay dead downstairs. And she couldn't go and lie beside him because there were other people in the house now, and his sister was sleeping just below. She had to keep it a secret ... even now. He was dead. She was alone. She had nothing and nobody ... and there was nothing anywhere, ever any more. And the sun was rising on a new day' (12, ellipses in original). The sun may also rise on this woman's world in which Hetty is hardly living at all, but it illuminates nothing but her bereft condition. Such women as Hetty, disempowered in capitalist patriarchy at any time, risk everything when they behave in a manner that flouts the self-serving rules of that system. The story cycle that is *Sister Woman* presents thus a vicious circle indeed, and it begins that way with 'Alone.'

Hetty, having entered into a secret mock-marriage with her lover-employer, at first enjoys the life of near-wife and mock-mother to a Chinese servant, 'Ling the Chinaman' (15). As Campbell first observed, Sime's feminism is a 'maternal feminism,' and Sime is not being ironic in her depiction of the pleasure that Hetty, and many other of her characters, derives from the role of nurturing mother.[15] Hetty 'was puzzled at her joy in doing' domestic chores for her lover-employer; 'and yet, behind, somewhere, it all felt infinitely old' (13), as old in Sime's view as marriage itself – tolerable, conventional versions of which Sime does not challenge. Hetty is in every sense (to borrow the title of Sime's first book, a non-fictional work in the tradition of conduct literature, and a study which valorizes women's domestic work) *The Mistress of All Work* (1916). Sime's feminism may appear an odd brand of feminism indeed, and I don't pretend to make it more palatable to contemporary readers. Consider, though: nothing in *Sister Woman* is more powerful, or more powerfully rewarding, than motherhood ('Motherhood' is the title of the eighth story of the cycle). Motherhood is the near-equal of the upper-case Love itself that is idealized in the return story 'Divorced.' And recall Mrs Oliphant's advice about marrying the first man who proposes and getting pregnant (*Brave*, 55): men are finally incidental to the idealization of maternity and love in Sime's world of sister-women, as disposable as the epilogue's male interlocutor when he refuses to co-operate. Sime's feminism is what Campbell describes it as, maternal feminism, but more than that: both conventional-maternal and radical. Only a myopic view of the past presumes that the genuine radical thought of an earlier day would not be as radical today or, even more myopically, has to be radical in a recognizable way.

But Hetty Grayson of 'Alone' is caught up in a traditional women's world fashioned by patriarchy, imprisoned in it, and figuratively killed by it. Two moments in front of mirrors signal the extent to which her sense of identity is dependent on the man who has died. In the first she sees herself as 'not herself ... it was how he would see her if he could be looking through her eyes' (14). And in the second: 'The face looked at her. It was stern and white, and its cheeks were wet with tears, and its swollen eyes looked at her as if from a great distance' (19). Obviously, Hetty's experience of schizoid dissociation suggests a reading of the conclusion of 'Alone' that would have Hetty either mad or about to commit suicide: 'And then suddenly the eyes changed. There was no longer any questioning in them. And in the glass Hetty Grayson saw the figure raise its arms and coil up the heavy hair that hung all about it, and make itself neat ... rapidly ... unselfconsciously. She seemed to be just watching it; she had no connection with it. And then she saw it pause a moment with its closed hand at its mouth. And she saw its lips move, and she seemed to see – or was it hear? – the words somewhere: "And then it'll not be a secret any more!"' (20, ellipses in original). As much as the death of her lover, the systemically enforced, socially deplored abortion deprives Hetty of what was for Sime a woman's prime identity as a mother: 'And she had learned what it means to have small hands at your heart ... small hands tugging. She had learned the longing of the woman to give her breasts to her child' (17, ellipsis in original). But as 'Alone' shows a number of times, the unjust situation had since deprived her of any sense of identity, because for Hetty, under the victimizing dispensation of the first two stories of *Sister Woman*, to commit to a love outside the bounds of normal social relations is literally to lose herself in the identity of the man: she 'had lost herself in him again' (20). Also, significantly the longer passage above draws attention to her abundant hair, for there is something almost Pre-Raphaelite in Hetty Grayson, something of the confined and maddened maid of Shallot; and that suggestion would be in keeping with the many hints throughout *Sister Woman* about the dangers of Romance in women's lives.[16] It is most likely that Hetty too is to become a suicide, for, if not mad, she has no other option, because already deprived of identity and a life of her own worth living. It is not by chance that Hetty, in contemplating and projecting her own receding image into its bleak future, thinks sanely for the last time in terms of employment: 'What was before her? A new place somewhere ... wages ... exactitude ... the employer and employed. What else?' (20, ellipses in original). In so closing, 'Alone' glances proleptically at what the present chapter considers the most important causal explanation of the conditions depicted in *Sister Woman*: its insistent and persistent economic contextualizing of the lives of working women.

I have dwelt at length on this opening story because Sime herself does such an economical job of setting forth the subject and themes of her story cycle (in a manner that recalls *Viger's* opening paragraph in 'The Little Milliner'). 'Adrift,' the second story, ups the ante immediately, so to speak, by repeating the themes of 'Alone' with regard to the life of a prostitute. The narrative point of view changes from the third-person subjective of 'Alone' to a first-person narrator who sounds identical with the prologue narrator. This narrator becomes the touchstone of the majority of the ensuing stories. Reminiscent of Leacock's narrator in *Sunshine Sketches*, she is changeable, chameleon-like in her ability to close with her subjects, to assume the high-ironic style of the opening paragraph of 'Art' (transcribed above), to exploit her position as an insider or outsider as either point of view suits her purposes. In other words, Sime has no problem with creating a narrator who transgresses the artificial (and Modern/New Critical) edicts regarding a singular and consistent point of view.

'Adrift' is the story of a French immigrant seamstress who earns the better part of her living as a prostitute. It begins with something of a narrative trick (and not only because readers do not yet know they are being introduced to a prostitute): 'She came in to sew for me, but she wasn't that awful infliction – the woman who comes in to sew by the day. I liked her and I liked to have her. There was something about her blue eyes that it gave me pleasure to look at; and she had that most charming and rarest thing in woman – a merry laugh' (22). If readers don't presume they are listening to what will soon reveal itself to be a female narrator – and a pattern has not yet been established – they should be assuming that this narrator is male. The suggestive sexual possessiveness of the second sentence would support the supposition, as would the condescension that recalls the prologue male, as would the objectification of the female subject, as would the infantalizing of that subject. In a story whose purpose is to decry the objectification, the commodification, of the female subject for the purpose of paid sex in a market economy – 'Her young body was for sale to any man that cared to buy' (22) – what might Sime be doing with this sleight-of-voice beginning? If as Dean argues (after Foucault, who does so for the whole of Western civilization), women writers in agreeing to explain themselves to patriarchy are complicit in reinserting a redefined 'femininity' into the gender hierarchy (60–1), what indeed is Sime doing assuming the role of the male listener-gazer? The answer, I think, is that she is performing one of those subtle narrative, self-reflexive, and subversive turns that recur occasionally in *Sister Woman*. ('When I began,' observes the wry narrator of 'Art' [231], 'I thought there was a story, but it seems there isn't.')[17] Here, she deprives the prologue's male interlocutor of his privileged position and figuratively interposes herself between her vulnerable female subject and that judgmental male gaze. And with this little performance of narratological transvestism, she prevents the patriarchal objectification of the prostitute for further vicarious consumption and is able to reposition the subject for a sympathetic female listener-companion: 'At lunch-time we dropped work and came together into my little kitchen' (24), the room of their own which is often the site in these stories for many a non-judgmental sororal tête-à-tête.

In her occupation as seamstress, the young prostitute of 'Adrift' is also presented as an artist, already recalling the servant girl of 'Alone' who showed her 'artistry' (15) in devotion to domestic work for her lover-employer. The seamstress's work is a natural art: 'she created her little wares as a poet creates his; half-unconsciously, as a thrush throws out its notes' (23; later [30], the seamstress is compared to a sculptor). At one point the prostitute-seamstress distinguishes the motivations of the so-called professional from those of the literal amateur, asking the narrator, '"Do you know, madame ... the way it feels to love to do a thing? Not for what you get from it – not to gain anything – just to love to do it?"' (29). And the narrator, who is virtually identical with the prologue narrator, and at least continuous with Sime the writer, answers simply, '"Yes."' This valorization of women's work as/and art, of domestic service and sewing, is not for the unintentional purpose of making the essential new woman comfortably accommodated within patriarchy (as Dean would have it). It is a validation and valuing of women's work as art, period, which becomes one of the most repeated themes of the story cycle. It may come trailing the haze of the domestic mythology of the nineteenth century (but why should that myth be cavalierly dismissable, as the blanketing word 'Victorian' too often disguises?), yet it does so in a modern context and patently wants to be taken at face value. As shown, this valorization-as-art of women's skilled work most likely derives from Sime's experiences of William Morris's arts and crafts movement, while the sympathetic view of an economic necessity that makes prostitution understandable was probably influenced by Bernard Shaw's strident feminism, and both come generally from the Fabian Socialism that Morris and Shaw espoused throughout their lives.

In its presentation of prostitution as an economic, if nonetheless morally evil necessity, 'Adrift' powerfully repeats the theme of the status of women's work that 'Alone' introduced in its presentation of the serving girl's perception of her bleak future as repetitions of demeaning employer-employee relations. The seamstress-artist prefers her sewing work – '"I loved the work, madame, believe me ... and yet – and yet – I gained so little. They pay so very, very little"'(30) – but opts for prostitution out of an admirable need to ease the financial burden on her family, which was permanently straitened by a useless father. However, Sime the realist also presents the pre-prostitute seamstress as motivated by envy of her well-off clients, especially of one who had gained her comfortable position from prostitution. '"I, too, had things to sell,"' she realized, neatly commodifying herself in admitting complicity (32). The harder economic-realistic line of 'Adrift' also anticipates the thirteenth story, 'The Wrestler,' where a dying mother confesses to having prostituted herself for the sake of her family. There, though, in story cycle fashion the theme is developed within the context of a harsher patriarchal world of demanding bosses and bleak economic necessity in a travelling sideshow for which the word 'exploitative' would be a tautology. So the prostitution is more excusable there than in 'Adrift,' as well as also being in the past of a dying woman and forlorn mother.

But the most interesting recurrence of the prostitution theme is the twentieth story, 'A Woman of Business,' which, in repeating it for the third time, also now treats the subject unapologetically, implicitly justifying a mother-prostitute's profession as the means of ensuring an only daughter's economic and social well-being. In 'Adrift' the normalizing narrator finally loses patience with the self-justifying young prostitute: "'Émilie ... you have sold yourself into slavery, my dear'" (33). And Émilie, assisting Sime's continual problematizing of words such as 'work,' 'art,' and here 'prostitution,'[18] responds, "'What is that word?'" When Émilie comprehends the narrator's comparison, she has the audacity to suggest a defiantly abnormal comparison: "'Yet," she said, "always to see those things [finery]. Always to wish and wish – and gain so little. No change – no chance. Marry – and lead a life like Maman? Esclavage, ça! No ..."' (33–4, ellipsis in original). The narrator offers to find more sewing work for the prostitute, but Émilie refuses. 'Adrift' ends with an image of falling snow and the suggestion of an analogous (Joycean) moral death: 'The snow came drifting up against the window pane' (34). But the figurative censure does not diminish the shocking *Shavian* analogy uniting prostitution and marriages that are bad either in themselves or when entered into for economic convenience. It is this aspect of 'Adrift' that recurs and is developed in 'A Woman of Business,' where conveniently the prostitute is again older and about to retire from the trade.

It may be that Madame Sloyovska is not, technically speaking, a prostitute, but more a 'gold-digger' like Eloise Ruelle of *Viger*. Here, though, definition walks a dotted line: 'She had had many lovers and she had made them all pay – according to their means; and I daresay she had given them honest value for their money' (203–4). Whatever the precise term for Madame's practice, her favours are dispensed as a simple business transaction in a capitalist economy (we might even wonder if the witty Sime has ironically alluded to the Marxist dictum: 'from each according to his abilities, to each according to his needs!' [*Gotha*, 10]).[19] As Campbell has recognized, 'A Woman of Business' apparently owes something to arch-Fabianist Shaw's play on the same subject in *Mrs. Warren's Profession* (Introduction, xx–xxi). Consider Shaw's remarks on the subject of his play, as quoted from letters in Weintraub's cleverly titled *Fabian Feminist*:[20] 'It is easy to ask a woman to be virtuous; but it is not reasonable if the penalty of virtue be starvation, and the reward of vice immediate relief' (Weintraub, 4); or Shaw's observation that gender relations in capitalism leave a woman with the decision whether 'to sell herself to a gentleman for pleasure rather than to an employer for profit' (in Weintraub, 5).

Compare the equivocating Sime narrator on Madame Sloyovska, the aging woman of disrepute:

> Madame Sloyovska has led what we call a bad life. She is thoroughly disreputable from head to heel. She has walked in the shadiest paths, and there are few dirty tricks that her hands haven't dabbled in. The snatches of her life, as she gave them to me hurriedly in the glare of that unprotected light, sounded like something you might read in a dime novelette. They were bald and bad and low and mean and unspeakably sordid – they were the life of a loose woman from her own lips. Madame Sloyovska had had lovers galore, and when she had had one lover's money she had gone on to the next one and she had had his money. Could there be anything more definitely against the moral code? And yet – explain it how you will – I felt no rancour against Madame Sloyovska as she told me – things. I felt even that no special blame attached to her.   (204)

Although she cannot remove Madame from 'the glare of that unprotected light' – legitimate social mores and judgment – Sime shades her with a protective maternal motive, a move that recalls the narrator's interposing herself between the young prostitute of 'Adrift' and the implicitly ever-present male interlocutor of the prologue. When Madame talks about her daughter, 'a lovely maternity settle[s] on her,' and she is, because of her self-sacrifice for her daughter's sake, 'beautiful' (205). Towards the end of this story, the narrator says she 'knew why Madame had worked or sinned or whatever name you like to put it to it,' but that she 'had sold over and over again the only thing she had to sell – her body' (206). In a manner that again recalls her association of Morris's Fabian socialism and 'the early Christians' (*Brave*, 12), Sime concludes this story with an apt allusion to the story of Christ saving the adulterous woman from a stoning (John 8:7): 'And when she gets to the next world,' the unrepentant narrator says of Madame Sloyovska, 'I think she will find a place prepared for her – but which of us shall say where?' (206). Doubtless a part of Sime's didactic purpose with such a story even this far along in the cycle is still to shock, or at least to discomfort, the complacent bourgeoisie, as was Shaw's stated purpose with Mrs Warren.[21]

'Munitions,' the third story, plays on its title by exploding, with help from the First World War, the subservient patriarchal worlds of the first two stories. Unfortunately, the sister-women who find war-time work in a factory are liberated into an identity where freedom licenses them mainly to act like boorish men, chewing tobacco, taking snuff, spitting, telling bawdy jokes. Perhaps Sime viewed this sort of 'masculinization' as a necessary stage towards women's equality. In any case, the women of 'Munitions' are introduced in a way that again recalls the opening narrative trick of 'Adrift.' Readers might mistakenly think them prostitutes or drunks, a misperception which the narrator corrects: 'It wasn't in the least that they were what is technically known as "bad women." Oh no – no! If you thought that, you would mistake them utterly' (35). The implication is clear: for the sake of women's advancement, sometimes good new women must act like the old 'bad' women. 'They had spent their lives caged, most of them in shop or house, and now they were drunk with the open air and the greater freedom and the sudden liberty to do as they liked and damn whoever stopped them' (35). Observe how the narrator adopts the rough language of her labouring women, thereby making her sympathies, perhaps her identification with them, apparent.

It would be a mistake, though, to underestimate the function of 'Munitions' in either the movement of the story cycle or the real progress of women that these boisterous 'working girls' represent. The significantly named heroine, Bertha, is freed from a domestic service that recalls Hetty Grayson's demeaning occupation in the first story, 'Alone,' a service which here is more infantalizing than figuratively prostituting, if yet funereal in its description of Bertha's former death-in-life existence. The point is that these women are the real thing for the first time in the story cycle, 'working women,' women working for themselves, achieving a measure of the economic independence and much of the self-esteem that are central to women's progress in *Sister Woman*, if not its ultimate goal. Nor is the sheer exuberance displayed by these sister-women to be undervalued, following as it does the morbidly restricted lives of the women in the first two stories. Here, the women are 'fellow-workers out in the world together ... Free!' (40). Bertha is 'earning money – good money – she was capable and strong.' And not least, they are openly expressing sexual desire for the first time: 'Nellie flushed, with shining eyes' (41), experiencing a desire (not romantic love) that 'touched the spring of life in her' (42). Equally exciting, though, these women are talking, *articulating* one to the other, as the prologue narrator is asked to do by her male interlocutor: 'Here and there was a pretty, young, flushed face, talking – talking – trying to express something it felt inside and couldn't get out' (36). What is left unarticulated in 'Munitions' is that other, more obvious referent for its title: namely, that it is man's war that occasions these women's new-found freedom, and that these women are making weapons for men to blow each other up, and other women, and children. But Sime does nothing with this paradox. It's not the thing to get about 'Munitions.'

The reiteration with a difference of the working prostitute motif that describes the movement from 'Adrift' to 'The Wrestler' to the most obviously Shavian 'A Woman of Business' must serve to typify the cyclical dynamic at work in the twenty-eight stories of *Sister Woman*, which pick up the subject and various themes of the introductory story 'Alone' and develop them in the rhythm of recurrent development that is definitive of the movement of short story cycles. For the sake of space, it can also be observed that all the stories of *Sister Woman* address one of three principle themes or problems, which give rise to at least three corresponding questions, with each theme's question sometimes eliciting in practice – that is, as read out of the stories – a real and an idealistic response. The predominant theme is, as Sime's few critics have observed, the circumstances of women's lives in a world dominated by men, their lives as wives and mothers, and especially as the latter. With the concomitant question: What is enduringly (or essentially) female? And the unequivocal answer: 'Motherhood' (the title of story 8), maternal love, and idealized love itself in the safe-keeping of women. The second theme is the relentlessly implied critique of the economic system of consumer-capitalism in which women must participate in the movement towards a hoped-for equality, as seamstresses, prostitutes, cleaning women, salesgirls, and more recently as office and factory workers (and perhaps as writers, as the ever-present narrator of the stories, the prologue, and epilogue implies). This theme gives rise to the related questions: What price women's freedom in such a system? Must women become more like men? Live without men? What does women's freedom mean realistically and ideally? The third theme is immigration, a subject of apparently much less interest, until it is remembered that Sime saw the immigrant's situation as similar to the modern woman's in that both temporarily occupy a liminal space of divided lives and loyalties, whether between the Old World and the New or the older patriarchal dispensation and the modern. This third theme gives rise to a question that can be phrased in the colloquial expression, What is the (New) World coming to? That question is the one that remains least answered, by definition so. But one thing the modern New World must and will come to according to *Sister Woman* is a redefinition of such 'Old-World' words as 'woman,' 'work,' 'family' (as does *Viger*'s 'Paul Farlotte'), and 'love.' In a number of the stories of *Sister Woman*, women are presented in the act of choosing to redefine what these words mean for them. For instance, what 'family' might mean in the modern world: for Madame L'Espérance of 'Jacquot and Pierre' it is mothering the eponymous boys as if they were her own (113–14); as for 'The Charlady,' the Scottish woman who made a bad marriage and lost both her children in the Old World to similarly bad circumstances, it is mothering the wayward children of the New World in lieu of her own: "'it's my ain bairns that seems born again in ilka ane o' them'" (261).

These three thematic categories – the feminist, economic, and modern – can fairly be subsumed under the banner of women's freedom, which is centrally involved in them all. That is why the last two stories of the cycle, 'The Bachelor Girl' and 'Divorced,' return to the theme of women's freedom and schematize the questions associated with it in ways both ludicrous and sublime. Consider their beginnings: 'A bachelor girl! What visions of cigarettes and latch-keys – and liberty!' (272); and the three-word opening sentence of 'Divorced': 'She was free' (282). But what a difference between the two in the ways they address the chosen freedom of the bachelor girl – as meaningful farce – and the divorced woman's sombre decisions, whose outcome brings the cycle to something of a mystical close. With these two stories Sime wants to leave her sister-women with a clear sense of difficult choices to make.

'The Bachelor Girl' follows 'Polly,' a story about yet another seamstress who is going blind and so facing a future of poverty. The primary interest of 'Polly' is inarguably economic, but its villains, its capitalist exploiters, are not men but other women, nuns to be precise, women who have chosen celibacy, that exclusive sisterhood, and devotion to a religious ideal over the traditional female struggles in a patriarchal world. Nuns figure intermittently in *Sister Woman* (for example, in the sentimental 'A Page from Life' as the shadowy keepers of an orphanage), enough so to suggest that Sime may even have been punning in the title of her story cycle, and there is always implied criticism in their presentation. This may be Sime's Presbyterian reflex, or it may be racially-politically motivated (anti-French, or in response to the Conscription crisis of the First World War), but it is also in its implied derisiveness a use of the exclusively women's world of nuns to criticize any notion of a modern world in which sister-women would live without men. In 'Polly,' in any case, the association is at its most decidedly unfavourable, as the nuns have exploited Polly's art (her fine sewing being another instance of Morris's influence on Sime) for monetary gain and then put her out the door when she came of age. In the penultimate story of the cycle, 'The Bachelor Girl,' the well-named Tryphena (a 'labourer in the Lord' commended by St Paul to the Romans [Rom. 16:12]) has a lifelong relationship with nuns, and her radical feminist independence is supported by the convent in farcical fashion.

It is the sardonically comic treatment of this bachelor girl that signals Sime's unwillingness to take seriously what Tryphena would represent: a definition of women's freedom exclusively in economic terms and exclusive of men: '... liberty! Yes. But if it be a professional bachelor girl the liberty is restricted by the necessity to go on earning money to be free with' (272). Despite the mistaken definition of freedom in economic terms, and the dark implications of women's freedom in a radical sorority – Tryphena and the nuns – Tryphena is at once redeemed somewhat (like Madame Sloyovska and others) and made more ludicrous by an enduring maternal desire: Tryphena wants nothing to do with men, Tryphena wants a baby. Tryphena arranges to buy a baby from the nuns (Sime doesn't suggest the orphanage baby has been fathered by a priest). For the bachelor girl who defines freedom in economic terms in a world without men, motherhood itself is, *quid pro quo*, a legal and capitalistic arrangement. Sime underscores her clubbing criticisms of this radical sorority by having Tryphena insist that her adopted baby be a girl (279). The story, and what serious critique it makes in caricaturing, achieves a state of Leacockian nonsense when the narrator learns that Tryphena is not even going to get the baby she pays for: the nuns will keep it and raise it until she is more financially able to look after it herself, or to pay someone else for its care, thereby rearing another Tryphena. Tryphena is a silly woman. The nuns are more coven than convent. 'The Bachelor Girl' seriously travesties those feminist transgressions which themselves travesty what is most dear to Sime's heart: women's authentic freedom with men, in motherhood and family, and in the community of sister-women.

It is something of an aesthetic speed bump to move from the comic treatment of the extremes of feminist freedom and ridiculous sororal motherhood in 'The Bachelor Girl' to the sombre tone of 'Divorced.' That movement has, though, the head-clearing effect of jolting readers with the force of contrast. Here, the issue of women's freedom within patriarchy takes precedence over even the preceding recurring treatments and idealizations of motherhood itself, and this sharp (re)turn has the effect of asking readers to reconsider the preceding stories under that unifying banner of women's freedom – which is the kind of work performed by the best return stories. This is not to say that there are no exceptions to the priorization of motherhood in the preceding stories; the sixteenth story, 'Union,' most anticipates 'Divorced' both in their paired titles and in the hard-won vision of love which their heroines win through to. In 'Union,' however, this complexly figured love is sexually complementary in the equal-but-different gender mythology that best describes Sime's view of spousal love in *Sister Woman*: 'And sometimes she felt herself his counterpart – his other half – he was the thing she needed, and she was what he required; and these times were the best of all' (173). This kind of love anticipates the return story's mystical construction when towards the end of 'Union' the woman is described as feeling 'that she embraced the world – that everything in it was dear and precious to her. And she felt that she could pack the whole world into her love and make it a part of it – that her love was so big that it could hold everything, even what is base and defiled. She felt that she had slipped out of the narrowness of self and become a part of life' (176). And in case matters are rising too near the mystifyingly abstract, Sime immediately follows this passage, and ends 'Union,' with the woman expressing sexual desire: 'the longing to be united with it [her husband's soul] by means of the flesh sent a sharp pain through her body, and she seemed to feel her soul throb in her' (176). In 'Divorced,' the protagonist must create her mystical vision of love apart from while yet a part of her despised ex-husband. Still, as to the priorization of motherhood, Sime is not dogmatic; in 'Union' connubial love is made permanent in the absence of children: 'Alison Jeffrey had recognised that life is many-sided, that there are infinite views and infinite possibilities in it – that a woman is a woman even if she is barren and childless ... yes, she had even recognised, at moments, that life may be better so' (168, ellipsis in original). I can only say: so much for those critics who would stamp and shelve Sime as a conventional maternal feminist. Her feminist vision is, like Scott's view of modernism, more complex than any one label can encompass.

As shown, 'Divorced' begins 'She was free' (287), a pointed sentence which functions first in this return story as a declaration for all the trapped women of the preceding stories. But the word 'free' is immediately problematized, or highly ironized. As 'The Bachelor Girl' has just made comically clear, for Sime the idea of women choosing on principle to live apart from men is a laughable understanding of freedom, figured best by the shadowy lives led inside a convent, and never a state seriously to be desired except in abusive circumstances. At first Ella Hume, the divorced woman, does not want to be free of her husband because to be free is to be alone, even though her husband, Jay (a generic male name, diminution of John and Jack), was an abusive philanderer. Recalling the first story of the cycle, 'Alone,' where Hetty contemplates a suggestively 'romantic' suicide (16), here bad romance is again implicated in Ella's mistaken marriage to the wrong man: 'Ella Hume remembered him as she saw him first, handsome and full of life and overpowering; the very thing to carry a woman off her feet and swing her into matrimony' (283). Recalling the 'The Bachelor Girl' (and 'An Irregular Union'), the divorced Ella now 'worked for her money, and what she earned she lived on. She earned enough to have a tiny bachelor flat to come home to. When she put her key in the door there was no one on the other side – no man – no marriage to be free of any more – just loneliness' (284–5).

'Divorced' presents an impressively realistic portrayal of a divorced woman, her emotional vacillations, her lingering desire even to consider reclaiming the only painful identity she has known. Readers of this study might well want to think, 'And divorced men too.' But not Sime: she distinguishes essentially between men and women with regard to their acceptance of divorce, and does so with a perfect simile:

> [Jay] had chucked [Ella] away as a boy throws a stone into the distance, and he would think of her as much as the boy thinks of his stone. She knew it. She knew it and she had a passionate feeling that it wasn't fair that Jay should have this advantage too. Why should he have the privilege of forgetting, while she had to feel his hands on her for evermore? Sometimes she felt inclined to argue with God about the way He had made woman – to argue with Him and to show Him how unfair it was. Jay could go on to other women – and enjoy them. He had enjoyed them even while she was there. But she ... she didn't want other men.   (286–7, ellipsis in original)

Of course these are individualized characters, and of course there is a lot of angry presumption about men's love on Ella's part, and perhaps some ignorance as to the cultural construction of sexual mores. But this return story carries a great deal of meaning, and its particulars must also bear the weight of generalizations as the story and Ella move towards a consolation that is a mystical idealization of love. Ella's and Sime's complaint, if it may be so attributed, is against the systemic patriarchy of their day regarding marriage and divorce, and a complaint that implicates the God of Genesis, definitely a 'Him' who has created gender unequally and apparently given men the disposition to enjoy the garden of earthly delights more freely than women can. This is not only a maternal feminism now, though it is yet a form of biological determinism, and an essentialist view of gender, but also what might be termed a spiritual feminism in that it implicates women's souls. It is a feminism too that ultimately allows women a freedom that would seem to be unavailable to men, whose freedom here is only physical and material, and a more meaningful freedom than men's. Finally, I don't think it far-fetched to suggest that for Sime 'God,' with pronoun referent 'Him,' could well be a code word signalling her awareness of the social construction of gender roles.

But for Sime the drag of the mundane institution of marriage cannot be bypassed: Ella may be 'done with matrimony, but matrimony was not done with her' (284). Women can make the decision to be free of a bad marriage, but it is made yet more painful if done with mistaken notions about the force of hundreds of years of social convention. Such is the caveat of the realist Sime. Doubtless more shocking for its time, Ella, like Alison at the end of 'Union,' also still wants her former husband physically, and is almost as driven by this sexual desire as by the need for companionship and an identity within socially sanctioned marriage: 'She wanted him. She wanted the feel of his hands on her; she wanted to hear his voice. She wanted the physical joys he had taught her and given her – she who had only longed for freedom! – and she wanted them from him' (287). 'How inexplicable!' she marvels at her own vacillation. '"Are all women made like this?" she asked herself. "Are we all cursed with this foolishness? Must we all be bound to one man – and to him only?"' (287). The answer provided by 'Divorced' is a surprising Yes, but not, trickily enough, a necessarily dismaying affirmative in the context of the material world. Obviously not, as the woman is divorced from the man. And it is in this sense that the title becomes a pun, for 'Divorced' finally is a story about love surviving divorced from union in its narrow sense, outside the material presence of the other.

Conflicted as she is a year after the divorce from Jay, Ella Hume resolutely decides, 'No. She wouldn't go back' (288), and this is more of a genuine clarion call than the opening naïve declaration of freedom. There will be no going back, no retrogression. Progress towards independence and equality is the goal, not abstract freedom. Most significantly, though, Ella does not regret the trial of her marriage; she recognizes its value, apart from its former physical pleasures, in a complex vision of love that sees the trial of a bad marriage as tempering the soul in life experience. In the following, Sime writes realistically to what she will call in her book on Hardy 'the order of life itself' (45):

She had escaped from him, feeling as one would feel escaping from a shower of offal. She had shaken off his name – the ring he had given her – she had refused his money, everything that was him. And she knew that she had always loved him. She knew that nothing he ever had done or ever could do would make any difference. She knew that she always would love him. She felt as if her love was in every separate cell of her body and as if they must vivisect her to get it away from her – and if they vivisected her she knew she would escape from them with her love still in her soul. 'How *can* I love him?' she asked herself. Her reason told her she loved a scoundrel – worse than that. Her reason told her she was a fool. But she knew that if she could save him from death she would throw her body between him and danger. (289)

Here, Love itself in the upper case (*pace* the narrator of 'Art') is the ideal. The repeated implied contradiction of what 'her reason told her' suggests a reason why Ella's married name was Hume. It may be a reference to the philosopher David Hume, whom Bertrand Russell described as the 'dead end' of 'empirical philosophy' (659), in that Hume represented 'the bankruptcy of eighteenth-century reasonableness' (672) by demonstrating that everything and so nothing could be rationally proven. What Russell observes of Hume's philosophy and the consequent Romanticism that came to force with Rousseau is true also of the direction Sime's Ella Hume takes: 'It was inevitable,' Russell writes, 'that such a self-refutation of rationality should be followed by a great outburst of irrational faith' (673). Ella Hume's outburst of faith in idealized love is the opposite of rationalized freedom. It wins her to an irrational liberation from her despairing isolation: 'The old feeling of – of entirety – came sweeping over her. She felt this single life, that she had struggled so to get back again, falling away from her. She knew that just as she had once belonged – and she rejoiced in the word "belonged" – to her husband, so she belonged to him now. She felt that rather than belong to any other man she would destroy herself ... and it came over her as the wind comes curling and twisting over the plains that she was – bound' (290, ellipsis in original). That is a mystical vision of Love indeed, one that comes complete with the inspiring breath of the deity Herself: 'And in her – was it in her soul? – she deified her love' (290). The repetition of 'belong' and the final word 'bound' compound the complexity of a vision of love that bears comparison with the Christian legend of being freed within a cell. Finally, though, God is scarcely gendered at all, or is so only in the matrimonial edict that opposes 'man' to God: '"Whom God has joined together let no man put asunder." "God is love," she said to herself. "Love joined us – we are one"' (290). The sense of 'entirety' and oneness supports the reading that this is Sime's vision of a mystical moment involving an idealization of a Love that is in woman's keeping: 'The thought came to her that she was the keeper of their love and that, in that day to come, she would have his share to hand back to Jay' (290). Such a vision of Love has no time for the mundane notional liberty valued by the sororally exclusive Tryphenas of the world.

At least a dozen other stories of *Sister Woman* are deserving of close readings, both for their imaginative and compelling variations on the theme of woman's freedom in the modern world of consumer capitalism and for their function in the story cycle. But this chapter has tried the reader's patience for too long as it is, and my only excuse is that it had more contextualizing and recuperative work to do than any of the others. That said, I must beg the reader's indulgence a while longer, because I want to close as I began, by redirecting what would be the natural course of this conclusion to another essay from *Brave Spirits,* which will serve to leave *Sister Woman* in as revealing a light as the opening paragraph from 'Art' forecast Sime's writerly excellence.

In 'Six Red Roses,' Sime writes about six Asian women she met over the course of her life, the first of whom is Shushama. Sime discourses generally on the predicament of modern Western women in comparison with the perceived 'completeness' of Asian women:

> I wondered if in the past Western women too had been complete, not of course in all cases but in some, and if their present incompleteness is due to an education that they have, so far, found to be a little indigestible. Shushama, I would say, had not a great deal of knowledge but what she did know she knew. Are you acquainted with many Western women of whom you could say so much? I am not. They have broken through the fenced area within which they once found themselves confined, and now that they are outside they are uncertain and distressed.   (123)

The idea here of an essential 'completeness' recalls the experience of well-being and 'entirety' (290) experienced by Ella Hume in her mystical vision of love at the end of 'Divorced.' Sime's memoir of the Asian women achieves completeness itself with Mrs Funk, the enterprising wife of an unworldly Chinese businessman sent by his government to Canada to study the railway system. Mrs Funk invites Sime to a tea which is really something of a mid-twentieth-century Tupperware party for two (Mrs Funk hopes to become an importer-exporter and she is obviously soliciting Sime to spread the word). Mrs Funk declares that, on returning to China,

'I want our home to be happy and comfortable, and if I have children I shall want them to be well educated; and that is not done without money. I shall earn it, and my husband will be free to find out things and become famous' (144). Sime's reflections on the realistic, economically grounded ambitions of this last of her 'six red roses' are worth quoting at length as an indirect authorial commentary on her own intentions with *Sister Woman*:

> Wife, mother, sister and fellow human being all spoke in her tone. I thought to myself, 'You are a very happy woman, and long may you remain so! ...' In India no less than in China and Japan the yeast that works in women and sets them in a kind of ferment to become a little different from what they have been, had been active for quite a long time. It had been at work all over the East and indeed one might say all over the world. I suppose it was poor Mary Wollstonecraft (whom Horace Walpole called 'a hyena in petticoats') who set the ball a-rolling almost a century and a half ago with her *Vindication of the Rights of Woman*, a book that after all only asked that women should be granted a little more education as something they were entitled to. (144)

This passage succinctly displays Sime's empathy for her feminist predecessors and her expectation of patriarchal derision as well as nicely serving her vision of a global sorority making its way by the classical Fabian means of gradualism and permeation through education towards the entitlements of equality in difference.

Sime proceeds:

> The mention of that book [Wollstonecraft's] makes me think of a piece of greenery that I have in my room – I am told it is called 'huckleberry foliage.' I have had it for some months now and all the time it has been growing and throwing out new shoots, becoming more and more like a Japanese picture every day. It came to me originally with some roses and I placed it and them in water which I always kept fresh; and when the roses had fallen and were thrown away I let the huckleberry foliage stay. Somehow I thought it looked intelligent, and evidently it *was* intelligent; it knew what it wanted and it is doing everything it can to get it. Women, I think, were like this piece of greenery. Suddenly, for no very obvious reason, they felt that they wanted to grow, to send out new shoots, to take up more room, in fact to have a more definite place in the world. And no one can deny that they *have* made a fresh place for themselves. They have grown taller in their minds; they have thrown out what were, for women, new ideas. They were not specially

encouraged any more than my huckleberry was but you can't stop things from growing when they grow from the inside.   (144–5)

Sime provides here the best interpretation of her organic-vitalist meta-phor, but it might not be overdetermining its many meanings to suggest that the shedding of the roses – image of romantic love traditionally as well as the emblem of her six Asian acquaintances – is instructively liber-ating. For Sime, women's growth is, like the plant's, constrained by sys-temic, patriarchal mythology, its assumptions and impositions, prime among which would seem to be the idea and effects of romantic love and what that illusion has done to her Asian acquaintances and 'Western women.' But as *Sister Woman* stories such as 'The Bachelor Girl' show, simplifications and damaging ideas can come as well from women who consider themselves the liberated ideal.

At the conclusion of her lengthy essay, Sime strengthens the connection between women's suppression and romance:

[her Asian acquaintances] were all of them ... making their way *out* of the romantic era in which I myself and my contemporaries grew up and in which all my feminine forbears had both grown up and died. And even of the lady-in-waiting [to the Dowager Empress of China] one might say that though she was not herself 'romantic,' she was a part of the romantic era just by virtue of being alive in it. In the course of the dinner at which she and I foregathered the talk at the other end of the table from where we sat turned on the subject of dancing and very naturally so, for Argentina, the then famous dancer, was one of our guests of honour. In order, I suppose, to illustrate something she had been saying Argentina at one point in the conversation lifted her arm and moved her shoulders in a dancing posture, and the lady-in-waiting, observing the gesture, remarked – was it to herself or was it to the world in general? – '*I* can dance *too*.' In these four words, with the emphasis put, as it was, on the first and the last of them, lay the germ of 'And I have the right to dance.' The lady-in-waiting was like the rest of her sister-women; we all feel that we have a right to grow.   (145–6)

Apart from its skilful return to the organic metaphor evocative of roses and their meanings, and of much else that requires no gloss, this passage provides, and nowhere more explicitly than in the closing sentence, a direct and articulate answer of the sort Sime would not allow in her fic-tion to the somewhat thick male interlocutor of *Sister Woman*'s framing prologue and epilogue.

Misao Dean reads the close of *Sister Woman*'s epilogue as a triumph of patriarchy in reintegrating the new woman into her age-old subservient position in the gender hierarchy: 'The "Epilogue" expresses the male hearer's "relief" that the women's desire "sounds simple" (292); the act of articulating the feminine self has allowed the male hearer to objectify and contain women's desire in predictable and traditional forms. While the narrator attempts to evade this containment by protesting, "I'm not even started yet" (292), the collection ends here; though the last words of the "Epilogue" describe an action performed by the narrator, in a sense, the man has had the last word' (75). But the male has the last word only in so far as he speaks the last piece of dialogue, an objection which doubtless is what Dean's 'in a sense' is meant to hedge against. Regardless, it is the narrator, the author of these stories, who has the last word, and that word is a thought and a gesture clearly signalling her intention to continue her campaign to make a great variety of her sister-woman stories known to the world. By reading the close of *Sister Woman* to make it consistent with her enlightening readings of other New Woman novels of the turn of the twentieth century, Dean is actually reading the story cycle unhistorically and paying too much attention herself to 'traditional forms.' Campbell better describes the determined and hopeful close of the story cycle when she says that 'Sime subverts the conventional "happy ending" of romance with an ending that emphasizes quest. The woman writer embraces not the man, but her typewriter, her real companion in the quest for a better world for women' (Introduction, xxvi). Dean might have avoided her misreading had she taken notice, as Campbell does (xvii), of the generic fact that *Sister Woman* is not a novel but a story cycle. Not only does the form of the story cycle enable Sime to refuse to conform to the compromising closures of the New Woman novels surveyed by Dean (via Gerson, Macmillan, and others), but formally it also rejects them and all they concedingly imply. The fictional facts are that very few of the stories of *Sister Woman* achieve happy endings; and that in its epilogue the cycle itself arrives at an open closure with the breakdown of what began in the prologue as an amicable relationship between a fairly sympathetic man and a new woman, and with the female narrator caressing her typewriter keys in a determined and conspiratorial manner. For its time (and as Sime observes in the final passage above, we are all ideologically part of an 'era just by virtue of being alive in it'), *Sister Woman* makes a realistic, idealistic, and courageously uncompromising feminist argument in fiction for women's equality and freedom.

Finally, the maternal feminism that constitutes the central myth of

Sister Woman, or more directly Sime's valorization of a broadly under-stood 'Motherhood,' is more often expressed in the stories as a form of communal maternalism in the adopting and mothering of others' children as if they were everyone's than as the deterministic biological expression of an essential maternal feminism. And it is in this way that the seemingly maverick *Sister Woman* ultimately shows its ideological investment in the very Canadian myth of community – here, a community of disparate sis-ter-women in an urban place. Of course, Scott's Viger and Leacock's Mariposa were ideological and somewhat exclusivist too. But remember-ing those earlier fictional communities shows the way that *Sister Woman* is yet situated in the continuum of those Canadian short story cycles that figure place as creative of identity, whether individual, national, or gen-dered. When we turn from *Sister Woman* in 1919 to *Over Prairie Trails* in 1922, that *annus mirabilis* of Modernism, we see a very good writer, Fred-erick Philip Grove, employing the story cycle to focus inwardly on the psychological growth of the individual. In comparison with such contem-porary Modern company as Grove offers, J.G. Sime can indeed be seen to have much in common with Scott and Leacock, even to being more 'at home' in Viger and Mariposa.

3

Fabulous Selves: Two Modern Short Story Cycles

To turn from J.G. Sime's *Sister Woman* in 1919 to Frederick Philip Grove's *Over Prairie Trails*, published only three years afterwards, is first of all to return via the short story cycle to a rural-wilderness space much less populated even than the semi-rural community of Scott's *In the Village of Viger* published some quarter-century before *Trails*. The obvious reason for this return is the change in setting from the much longer settled Montreal fictionalized in *Sister Woman* to the Manitoba of the early decades of the twentieth century. Ironically, though, with Grove the short story cycle moves 'forward' most fully into the traditionally construed Modern period of Canadian literature (roughly 1920–60).[1] In complementary fashion, *Trails* itself can be seen broadly to describe its narrated persona's transition from a Romantic to a more Modern-realistic sensibility in Grove's figuring of his conceiving and perceiving self in nature at that time.[2] To make this textual move from *Sister Woman* to *Trails* is also in a sense to push furthest to the generic limits of what can usefully be called a short story cycle, both for Grove's *Trails* and perhaps more so for the other primary text under consideration in the present chapter, Emily Carr's *Klee Wyck* (1941), because the genre of the prose pieces in these two story cycles cannot clearly be designated short *fictional* narratives.

But investigating where fact ends and fiction begins for the changeable Grove and the reminiscing Carr is an exercise outside the province of the present study, though there are a few relevant comparative biographical-bibliographical facts worth noting. *Trails* and *Klee Wyck* were both first books by writers working outside their usual media – the novel and poetry (at the time, and first English book) for Grove, and of course painting for Carr. Both Grove and Carr wrote their first books from distant reflective perspectives on earlier versions of themselves (only a few years away for Grove, decades for Carr), or as what Doris Shadbolt calls for Carr 'episodes recalled in nostalgic or revisionary retrospect' (Introduction, 5). So both would be creating, revealing, and justifying that earlier developing version of their searching selves – as is often the case with first books – more than chronicling or transcribing from purported factual records such as notebooks and journals.[3] For the ways in which they shape the early development of their artist-selves, *Trails* and *Klee Wyck* are also first instances of the Canadian short story cycle as künstlerroman, a use of the genre which will be developed in the contemporary period by Margaret Laurence in *A Bird in the House* (1970), Alice Munro in *Who Do You Think You Are?* (1978), and Thomas King in *Medicine River* (1989). In this respect, Sherrill Grace accurately observes, if with foreshortened view, that the story cycle form is 'usually concerned with the progression through time of an individual who is often an artist in the making' (440).

Most pertinently for present purposes, though, both *Trails* and *Klee Wyck* are story cycles representing the Modern period in the continuum of the Canadian short story cycle. Both texts are composed of stories that have their own integrity and yet are best appreciated in the context of the whole cycle. The individual stories achieve cyclical coherence through the unifying presence of a character, a narrated 'I.' That persona achieves definition in close relation to a particular place (though *territory* might be the better word for the miles of sparsely populated ground over which Grove repetitively travels in search of himself, and for the maritime area of the dispersed West Coast Island/Northern British Columbia Indian villages Carr visits). Both books exhibit the characteristic cyclical dynamic of recurrent development, and both conclude with pieces that function as return stories. Given such a catalogue of shared story cycle family features, it could be said that *Over Prairie Trails* and *Klee Wyck* not only are prime instances of the Modern short story cycle but also illustrate the genre's plasticity, its adaptability to various purposes, changing times and places.[4]

It might seem, too, that with the obsessively individualistic Grove of *Trails* we have, in opposition to the communally interested Sime of *Sister Woman*, a neat gender difference in the uses of the story cycle genre in the Modern period. As the preceding chapter shows, Sime employs the story cycle to present a sororal community of individuals who figure as criticisms of a patriarchal-capitalistic system that objectifies and commodifies women, and that would stubbornly maintain the supremacy of men over women in the gender hierarchy. Grove's focus throughout *Trails* is the ego sublime of his very male narrated persona alone in the natural world, in an evolving relationship with that world, acting, acted upon, reacting – extravagantly exhibiting at all times what K.P. Stich has described as 'the narcissism in his self-representations' ('Narcissism,' 31). But of course the pre-Modern Duncan Campbell Scott was, like Sime, more interested in the welfare of the community than in the individual, or in the individual within a community, as was Leacock in *Sunshine Sketches*; and twenty years after *Trails* in Carr's *Klee Wyck* we have a female artist's story cycle whose true subject is, much indeed like Grove's, the delineation and pres-ervation of a developing narrated persona, of a self, in league with her Native subjects (totem poles and peoples) against the wasting threat of the natural world (time, forest, and ocean) and (non-Native) civilization. So it is not simply a gender difference, this perceived shift in attention from the communal to the individual in the history of the Canadian short story cycle, but is more attributable to the change from nineteenth-century/ Victorian to twentieth-century/Modern times (though I do not discount the broader role gender played in the aesthetic preferences and canon for-mations of Modernism).

What remains unchanged from Scott to Leacock to Sime to Grove and Carr – what appears to become more pronounced through the middle decades of the twentieth century, as we shall see in George Elliott's *The Kissing Man* (1962), Munro's *Who Do You Think You Are?* (1978), and briefly in Thomas King's *Medicine River* (1989) – is the relation among self-identity, community, and place in the Canadian short story cycle. And, to conclude this bridging discussion, it needs to be said that the geo-graphic movement westward, especially with Grove's *Trails* but also with Carr's *Klee Wyck*, into the frontier ethos of individualism that was as nec-essary to success in Canada as in the United States, may be coequal with the modern interest in individual psychology as a cause of the shift from communal to individualistic matters. Interestingly, in *Trails* Grove feels driven repeatedly to state, if increasingly with something of a doth-protest air, that the end of his man-alone-in-nature quests is that first unit of community – family, his wife and child and home. It is unthink-able that Huck Finn or Nick Adams would ever feel the need to justify his adventures so.

Where Sime returned to the story as exemplum for her feminist and Fabian-socialist didactic-illustrative purposes, Grove's stories in *Over Prairie Trails* derive from an array of earlier shorter and longer prose forms and fictional modes. They have had a number of descriptives attached to them: 'the familiar nature essay' (Spettigue, 199), 'nature writing' (Keith, 'Grove's,' 77), 'linked meditative essays' (Gadpaille, 30), 'seven autobiographical essays' (Lane, 160), while Rudy Wiebe prefers 'fictional autobiographical picaresque' (Afterword, 355) to describe *Trails*, and the term 'chronicles' (353) to describe the form and purpose of Grove's entire fictional project.[5] Frank Davey has remarked the generic contrariness of the stories in *Trails*, suggesting an intriguing relation to Grove's immigrant and alias-assuming identity: 'Once again we have texts that refuse to separate themselves from signs that mark writings allegedly "lower" than the Modern short story – specifically from the signs of the anecdote or the informal essay. Marked as informal essays, these texts also ask the reader to deal with the double fictionality created by the signs now posed by Grove's Canadian and German author-name' (146–7).[6] But there are a number of other genres on which the stories of *Trails* draw: memoir, confessional, spiritual autobiography, anecdote, personal and nature essay, and nature sketch, even critical essay, scientific report, and field notes, none of which need be considered as generically inferior to the Modern short story. These forms comprise enough of a mélange in *Trails*, I think, to obviate the need to coin a term that works better than the generically adaptable 'stories.' It should be remembered, too, that the personal nature essay, the label that probably comes closest to fixing one genre to the stories of *Trails*, was very popular in the early decades of the twentieth century in North America, and was practised with much success by Bliss Carman in such collections as *The Kinship of Nature* (1903; and see New ['Geography,' 54], who talks of Charles G.D. Roberts's realistic animal stories in connection with *Trails*). Associating Carman and Roberts, the 'post-romantics' (McLeod), with the acclaimed first practitioner of naturalism in Canada, Frederick Philip Grove, is not so far-fetched as it must appear, as I hope to show.

Like Sime's *Sister Woman* with its twenty-eight stories, prologue, and epilogue, Carr's *Klee Wyck* contains perhaps too many stories, twenty-one, for it to avoid the charge of repetitiveness, if not of self-indulgence (and unlike the gyno-lunar possibilities of the number twenty-eight, there is no apparent rationale for the number twenty-one in *Klee Wyck*).[7] Although most of the descriptives applied to the stories of *Trails* could as justifiably be applied to the individual pieces of *Klee Wyck*, the latter are more accurately described as sketches, and appropriately so as they would recreate the aging and ailing painter's actual sketching expeditions some decades earlier. Carole Gerson and Kathy Mezei's definition of the literary sketch as 'an apparently personal anecdote or memoir which focuses on one particular place, person, or experience' (Introduction, 2) neatly describes the form of the pieces that comprise *Klee Wyck*. Still, Carr insisted on calling her prose pieces 'stories,' and Doris Shadbolt, her most informed biographer, is illuminating in this regard: 'Her very term "stories" for the short pieces that make up most of the books – really sketches, vignettes or anecdotes ... – implies objectification and shaping' (Introduction, 6). Like Grove, who is forever returning and retelling in the stories of *Trails* – to home, over and over roughly the same prairie trail – Carr in *Klee Wyck* is returning to and retelling the scenes and stories of her inspired youth, when she found her subject(s), including her self, and sometimes attempting also to return in a later story, such as 'Salt Water,' to the very sites she had visited not only earlier in life but already again in preceding stories of *Klee Wyck*. Both Grove and Carr enact 'the performance of identity as iteration,' which Homi Bhabha sees as a response to cultural displacement. In their story cycles they do so quite literally pursuing, in Bhabha's phrase, 'the re-creation of the self in the world of travel' (9). Both *Trails* and *Klee Wyck* evince this compulsion to trace and retrace, and trace again, the figure of the younger artist in the defining landscape, as if their author-artists are anxious about the possibility opposite to self-definition: self-erasure. As one consequence of this repetitiveness, the twenty-one stories of *Klee Wyck* – some of them very sketchy sketches indeed of only a couple of pages – can make its shape as a story cycle difficult to recognize.

The Fabulous Self: Frederick Philip Grove's *Over Prairie Trails*

The seven stories of *Trails* present no such obstacle to recognizing the definitive cyclical pattern of recurrence and development: the repeated trips home, Grove's (the narrated persona's) responses to the varied challenges he encounters, and the incremental changes in his view of himself – his self-reliance – in nature. To call the final story of *Trails* a return story is almost to be as repetitive as the stories are themselves, because, with the exception of the fifth story, which describes the only setting out from home with the town as destination, the other six stories of *Trails* all describe a return, and a return home. As stated above, Grove is at pains repeatedly to convince his readers not only that wife and child and home are the goal of his trips – 'My goal was my "home"' (48) – but that his small family as future readers is the purpose of his putting pen to paper (57, 70). He will contradict both pleas, frequently addressing a broader readership in assuming what it has seen or may already know, and right from the introduction placing the very word 'home' in quotation marks

(11). Perhaps the peripatetic Grove means only to signal the provisional status of his residence at that time, the domestic situation of *Trails* being a make-do arrangement, with Grove teaching in town and his wife teaching in a country schoolhouse some forty miles to the north. Nonetheless, the repeated quotation marks have the effect of making readers wonder what 'home' means for this assertively confused narrator; as Stich ('Narcissism,' 34) observes based on his knowledge of German, 'the [quotation marks] could be for emphasis as much as for ironic retraction, since [Grove] is both attracted and repelled by domesticity.' Similarly in 'L'Envoi: The Train to Mariposa,' Leacock repeatedly places quotation marks around the word 'home' (*Sunshine Sketches*, 141), but there the intention is clearly to ironize and criticize, to make the silent auditor (and readers) wonder what Mariposa and its values can still mean as 'home' – a word and idea that centred Leacock's Tory-humanist vision – in the coming modern world. In *Trails*, it is as if Grove would intermittently have his readers imagine him as one who has just missed the last train to Mariposa and is forever chasing the caboose in his horse and buggy. He wants his wider readership to think him so traditionally home-bent, yet contrarily he also would have them see him as a romantic figure forever alone in a hostile and beautiful world. But no one who reads *Trails* can doubt that for Grove the challenge of the trip quickly becomes far more interesting than the desire to arrive home (see Keith, 'Grove's' 79). Already in the second paragraph of the introduction, following immediately on his nod to wife and home, he states somewhat startlingly that the trips themselves 'soon became what made my life worth living' (11), an admittance which must surely have disquieted further his Penelope-like wife. But Grove is right, of course: the interest of this story cycle resides not in the return home, but in Grove's pursuing an image of himself – and he *is* a man who has left behind a whole Old-World identity – over landscapes that reshape his idea of himself despite himself, so to speak. As he remarks in 'Snow,' if not as I turn his expression, for Grove *Over Prairie Trails* is very much 'the narrative of my drives' (92).[8] Grove alone in a hostile and beautiful natural world is the only dominant image of *Trails*. And, ironically, paradoxically, this is the stylized pseudo-romantic image of himself that he must leave behind. In other words, the mystery of the Grove persona's conflicted self is the wrapped enigma that *Trails* resolves, though not comfortably or absolutely.

This unresolved 'dualism,' which Margaret Stobie concludes was ingrained in the duplicitous Grove (189), is first and most clearly expressed by him in English in the story cycle that is *Over Prairie Trails*, the form that lends itself so admirably to the figuration and exploration of fragmented entities. The cyclical form is nicely adaptable to what Stich calls 'Grove's contradictory penchants for repetitiveness and sameness' ('Narcissism,' 36), though recurrence with a difference better describes the story cycle dynamic and Grove's use of it in *Trails*.[9] But the Grove persona that emerges in *Trails* is very much a divided writer-persona, at least as much of two minds about the domestic scene versus hinter-landscapes as was Charles G.D. Roberts (Bentley, 'Poetics'). As with the Roberts of such poems as 'The Tantramar Revisited' and 'Two Rivers,' for the Grove of *Trails* 'home' persists as a word in enclosing quotation marks that shimmer with their anxious offer of security that is also entrapment. In the first three stories of *Trails* especially, Grove presents himself as a self-sufficient and exceptionally resourceful man in love with freedom and the open road. The first image of the narrated 'I' is of a lone man purchasing a horse, and of a man who knows horse flesh, so a proto-typical western man who would represent the North American type of rugged cowboy idealized still, and perhaps made most movingly iconic for Canadians in such a poem as Al Purdy's 'The Cariboo Horses,' where 'On the high prairie / are only horse and rider' (*Being*, 72). But more than Roberts or a Purdy cowboy, the early (if forty-year-old) Grove can be understood as presenting himself after the self-stylings of Roberts's cousin, Bliss Carman, in accordance with the whole vogue of romantic wanderlust that Carman (with Richard Hovey) had widely popularized in three Vagabondia volumes (1894–1900) not long before Grove himself would be bumming about North America.

In his introduction Grove wants readers to know, 'I am naturally an outdoor creature – I have lived for several years "on the tramp" – I love Nature more than Man' (11). In the first story, 'Farms and Roads,' he continues to press the image of himself as riding out on the open road: 'I had torn up my roots, as it were, I felt detached and free. ... neither by temperament nor by profession had I ever been given to the accumulation of the wealth of this world' (16). In 'Dawn and Diamonds,' the third story, he muses on the alluring effect of a crisp December morning: 'These days seem to waken in me every wander instinct that lay asleep. There is nothing definite, nothing that seems to be emphasized – some-thing seems to beckon to me and to invite me to take to my wings and just glide along' (63). Doubtless there is much of Goethe's Young Werther in this pose, of Byron, of Baudelaire and Rimbaud, of the self-willed Nietzschean hero (Knönagel, 88–91), and of the English Decadents gener-ally, but there is at least as much of Carman, the popularity and influence of whose Vagabondia volumes cannot be overstated because it has been so often undervalued.[10] To take but one well-known verse, compare the following from Carman's much-anthologized 'A Vagabond Song' with Grove's declaration immediately above: 'There is something in October sets the gypsy blood astir; / We must rise and follow her, / When from every hill of flame / She calls and calls each vagabond by name' (68). Along with the similarity of sense in the two passages, there is the key similarity of the oft-criticized vagueness of Carman's style (the 'some-things').[11] And as is well known now, thanks to the work of Douglas Spettigue, not only the alias Grove of the passage above but also Felix Paul Greve had answered the call of the open road, Grove for literary reasons in his searches for America and himself on his tramps, Greve for escape from embezzlement charges (Spettigue, 165–8).

Or Grove may more accurately be said to be fashioning for himself a broadly romantic and rebel's cloth which is a pinkish combination of the Goethean figure, the Byronic-Nietzschean hero, the French *symboliste* poets, the Decadent man of letters (after Wilde, one of his literary heroes), and Carman. Like Byron's Manfred or even the Shelley persona of 'Ode to the West Wind,' the Grove persona of the first half of *Trails* repeatedly breasts bad weather, feels fellowship with a literal lone wolf (21), and reads natural events anthropocentrically for ill – 'All nature was weeping' (51) – and good: 'But as if to reassure me once more and still further of the absolute friendliness of all creation for myself' (27). Into, or onto, this combination he would stitch the dominant colouring of the scientific naturalist, of the field worker taking his observations and recording them with objective fidelity, somewhat slavishly after another model, the American naturalist John Burroughs (Stobie, 53–4). This way, Grove sometimes inadvertently presents himself as a figure not unlike the character who would be mocked twenty-five years later by fellow Manitoban Paul Hiebert in the person of the pseudo-scientific literary critic of *Sarah Binks*, Doctor Taj Mahal. Consider the twisting paradox of the following incident: after repeatedly having practised the pathetic fallacy himself over his endless trails (see Keith, 'Grove's,' 81–2), Grove can actually digress ironically on John Ruskin's coinage of the term itself: 'Yes, the snow, as figured in the waves, *crawled* over the ground. There was in the image that engraved itself on my memory something cruel – I could not help thinking of the "cruel, crawling foam" and the ruminating pedant Ruskin, and I laughed. "The cruel, crawling snow!" Yes, and in spite of Ruskin and his "Pathetic Fallacy," there it was! Of course, the snow is not cruel. Of course, it merely is propelled by something which, according to

Karl Pearson, I do not even with a good scientific conscience dare to call a "force" any longer. But nevertheless ...' (115). And off he rides, madly in opposite directions, spurred here by a Schadenfreude that is the only instance of laughter in *Over Prairie Trails*. That Grove would call anyone a 'ruminating pedant' following a chapter 4 that outdoes any mythic Eskimo in its attentiveness to varieties of snow, let alone the supremely stylish Ruskin, and in a book as pedantically exhaustive and exhausting as *Over Prairie Trails*, is perhaps one of the more charming instances of his ego sublime. (Not to be outdone by either Grove or Dr Mahal, I counted: in the average-size opening paragraph of the second story, 'Fog' [33], there are twenty-one instances of the first-person pronoun, thirteen of which are first-person singular, as witness the following boast: 'But when I look back at that winter, I cannot but say that again I chose well.')[12]

Grove's way of seeing nature is not only romantic and post-romantic (that is, Darwinian) but also pre-romantic, or neoclassical. His ideas on landscaping would be at home with Alexander Pope at Twickenham or Thomas Jefferson at Monticello. He envisions an ideal of a prairie farm that would suitably accommodate a member of the eighteenth-century gentry: 'In my mental vision I saw beeches and elms and walnut trees around a squire's place in the old country' (18). His perceptions of the natural world are usually organized with reference to the picturesque and the sublime, two of three predominantly eighteenth-century aesthetic categories (with the third being the beautiful). The following pictorial observations illustrate the preceptor's desire for such a bucolic scene of gentle variety divided into the picturesque arrangement of background, midground, and foreground: 'The straight line is a flaw where we try to blend the work of our hands with Nature. They [local farmers] also as a rule neglect shrubs that would help to furnish a foreground for their trees; and, worst of all, they are given to importing, instead of utilising our native forest growth' (23).[13] (As will be shown, he also adroitly employs the conventions of the sublime in the pivotal fourth chapter, 'Snow.') Grove can be resolutely anti-modern, as when he snootily assesses a farm's house for being 'so new and up-to-date, that it verily seemed to turn up its nose to the traveller. I am sure it had a bathroom without a bathtub and various similar modern inconveniences. The barn was of the Agricultural-College type – it may be good, scientific, and all that, but it seems to crush everything else around out of existence; and it surely is not picturesque' (22). In short, the one conclusion about the Grove persona that emerges from an attentive reading of *Over Prairie Trails* is that the narrated 'I' is at best an eclectic mismatch of attitudes and philosophies, and at worst a mishmash of posturing and contradictory self-promotion. I cannot say which version is dominant or more impressive, only that the more romantic figure gives way to the more realistic one in the course of the cycle.[14] And Grove does skilfully employ the dynamics of the story cycle form to show his persona moving at least somewhat closer to the modern, unromantic principles that he intermittently expresses and aspires to: those being associated with the domestic communal realm and a conventionally realistic understanding of nature as indifferent to human idealizations of it and humankind's relation to it. So it must remain a possibility that Grove has purposely constructed this somewhat maudlin figure of Grove in order to show himself developing the more modern attitudes for which Frederick Philip Grove himself is rightly celebrated in Canadian literary history.[15]

As remarked, *Over Prairie Trails* hardly requires evidence of cyclical unity other than what it displays through the Grove persona and the persistence of place in the repeated trips themselves. And of course the episodic cyclical structure, as opposed to what would be gained through a continuous narrative, also destabilizes those essentialist figures of coherence (as the introduction of the present study has argued). But the seven sketches also achieve coherence and a cyclical shape by being arranged chronologically, organized on a seasonal model, even on the school year, beginning in the early fall and closing towards the end of winter when Grove submits his resignation to the school board (144; the time here is not given exactly).[16] And doubtless, given the Manitoban climate, it is no accident that the more romantic view of nature infuses the first three stories and that the more realistic (Darwinian-modern) view dominates the final four. Also structurally there are some observable arrangements of sketches: the third sketch, 'Dawn and Diamonds,' visually answers the second, 'Fog'; and the fifth, 'Wind and Waves,' establishes narrative coherence with the fourth, 'Snow,' beginning where it ends. The cycle also achieves coherence rhetorically by means of prolepsis primarily (see for example 20, 25, 60, 78, 83, 84, 89), by anticipation, and in the final three sketches by what might be termed backglance. These devices, interestingly enough, are the real skills that allow the intrepid Grove to survive his adventures on the trail: anticipating obstacles and challenges, knowing beforehand what the weather will bring, remembering what the road and weather have already delivered.[17] The fact alone that these seven trips have been selected from among seventy-two (12) speaks to the matter of careful structuring, to say nothing of fictional conflation of the real trips, and to design with a purpose (see Keith, 'Grove's' 83). And I would add, given such novels as *Fruits of the Earth* (1933) and *The Master of the Mill* (1944), and Grove's penchant for planning grand fictional projects in trilogies (Stobie, 188–9), that one of the enduring rewards of reading Grove is his architectonic skill as his well as his architectural interests.

In the careful structure that is *Over Prairie Trails*, the fourth story, 'Snow,' is, as I've been hinting, pivotal both formally and thematically. It functions as a form of death and rebirth through which the problematically romantic Grove persona passes. Its overriding importance in the story cycle is signalled perhaps by the fact that it is not only the middle but the longest of the seven. In more than the obvious way, the first three lead up to the fourth in terms of the repeated challenges and pleasures they offer the resourceful Grove persona both physically and with regard to his romantic idealizations of nature. Even here, though, the second story, 'Fog,' anticipates the fourth. There is the obvious meteorological similarity between the obfuscating fog and mountainously drifting snow, both of which threaten to keep Grove from attaining his ostensible goal, 'home,' and to leave him wrapped (perhaps rapt, given the death-wishing aspect of his kind of worry-free vagabondage) in splendid isolation. Just what the dense fog is is a mystery Grove ponders obsessively through the beginning of the second story. Finally, in an empirical process of observation and reasoning that is reminiscent most of that earlier western explorer David Thompson taking the measure of a prairie mirage (99–100), Grove determines that he is dealing with a suggestively biblical pillar of fog that, in collapsing to the earth, spreads densely from a centre point. But Grove also wants the fog to be metaphoric, a kind of death: 'The stillness of the grave enveloped me' (41); 'But then I reflected again that this silence of the grave was still more perfect, still more uncanny and ghostly, because it left the imagination entirely free, without limiting it by even as much as a suggestion' (46; see also 45). Not only is the fog a death, but also here an occasion for the undisciplined play of imagination, the perhaps too free fancy of pure romantic inspiration. But if death primarily, then the death of what? The senses, certainly, which link the romantic Grove directly to nature, and the sense of sight mainly, so that he has to rely shakily on hearing and touch (with his horses). But also, I think, it is the death of that more romantic, excessively self-reliant 'I' who so colours the first three sketches of *Trails* and runs rampant in first-person pronouns in the opening paragraph of the adumbrating 'Fog.' It is in 'Fog' that the Grove persona declares, in comparing Old-World mythologies with New, that the European is 'not half as weird ... as some realities are in the land which I love' (39). It is in the midst of this fog that Grove reminds himself as much as the reader, 'My goal was my home' (48). And it is in emerging from this real and metaphoric fog that he is greeted by his wife holding aloft a lamp (54–5), presenting an icon of domestic wisdom.

The contrasting third story, 'Dawn and Diamonds,' is then a happy Christmas story, and here Grove reverts to, or reasserts, the radically romantic side of his persona, expressing himself in those previously quoted terms that seem clearly to echo Carman's (and Hovey's) preference for the open road of vagabondia. Not only does the third story contrast with the second in terms of the visual imagery of clarity versus obscurity, it also anticipates the climactic and mystical moment in the fourth. In 'Dawn and Diamonds,' Grove observes the permeating quality of the light that surrounds him: 'I could not cease to marvel at this light which seemed to be without a source – like the halo around the Saviour's face. The eye as yet did not reach very far, and wherever I looked, I found but one word to describe it: impalpable – and that is saying what it was not rather than what it was. As I said, there was no sunshine, but the light was there, omnipresent, diffused, coming mildly, softly, but from all sides, and out of all things as well as into them' (62).

In the pivotal 'Snow' Grove indulges in something of an orgy of death-wishing, frolicking madly through and over gargantuan drifts of that traditional symbol of death and coming out alive after all (to borrow from the epigraph to fellow Manitoban novelist Margaret Laurence's *A Jest of God*). Like numerous 'Canadian' writers before him (for instance, Frances Brooke, Catharine Parr Traill, Susanna Moodie), Grove draws on the conventions of the sublime (as codified by Edmund Burke) to conceive of more than to see Canadian wilderness in its mightiest, most terrifying, and simultaneously most awe-inspiring and humbling aspect. The story is structured around his encounter with three snowdrifts: a big one (82–3), a bigger one (87), and the, as it were, mother of all drifts (96–9). Even before encountering the first snowdrift, there 'was an impression of barren, wild, bitter-cold windiness about the aspect that did not fail to awe my mind; it looked inhospitable, merciless, and cruelly playful' (80), which expresses the radical emotional response the sublime conventionally elicits, and employs the key verbal marker of an imminent sublime experience, 'awe.' In further taking the measure of the snowy trail/trial that lies ahead, Grove makes clear that readers are aboard for the sublimely (and note again the set-apart 'awe') climactic experience of *Trails*: 'I still remember with particular distinctiveness the slight dizziness that overcame me, the sinking feeling in my heart, the awe, and the foreboding that I had challenged a force in Nature which might defy all tireless effort and the most fearless heart' (85). Nature is no longer the idealized entity to be pictured, worshipped, and bonded with; rather, Grove now 'stud[ies] the mentality of [his] enemy' (91).

'Snow' and *Trails* achieves its climactic moment, then, when Grove and his horses and cutter rest atop that biggest snowdrift in the world:

> I shall never forget the weird kind of astonishment when the fact came home to me that what snapped and crackled in the snow under the horses' hoofs, were the tops of trees. Nor shall the feeling of estrangement, as it were – as if I were not myself, but looking on from the outside at the adventure of somebody who yet was I – the feeling of other-worldliness, if you will pardon the word, ever fade from my memory – a feeling of having been carried beyond my depth where I could not swim – which came over me when with two quick glances to right and left I took in the fact that there were no longer any trees to either side, that I was above that forest world which had so often engulfed me.   (98)

This is patently a mystical experience for the Grove persona: metaphorically as well as literally transported now, enraptured and ecstatic not at high noon in summer but in the dead of a northerly Canadian late-winter's day, amazed and amazingly triumphant in and over nature and death. As much as having driven his horses in this 'narrative of his drives,' Grove has driven himself to this peak experience, to the fullest expression of his sublime romantic ego in the only context that can match and satisfy it, above a Bunyanesque forest world that has entangled and would continue to entangle him, even somewhat out of himself, on top of all things wild and beautiful.[18] But of course the ecstatic moment can't last – 'Then I drew my lines in' – for it is also a death of a kind. As he writes towards the end of 'Snow,' 'It seemed a lifetime since I had started out. I seemed to be a different man' (101). And as he says mournfully to his wife at the end, 'with as much cheer as [he] could muster, "I have seen sights to-day that I did not expect to see before my dying day"' (102). Grove has seen many strange northern sights to this point in *Trails*, and it is metaphorically true that the weirdest he ever did see was the figurative death of the radically romantic Grove atop his snowy pyre. And so 'Snow' ends as it must, with the day dying and the domestic goal still deferred: 'And taking her arm, I looked at the westering sun and turned toward the house' (102).

Structurally, the effect of this figurative death of the romantic man and projected birth of the domestic man is immediately apparent. In the fifth story, 'Wind and Waves,' the Grove persona now sets out from home with the town as his destination. On this trip thoughts of home cling to him in a way they had not earlier, making him 'soft' (110), and the manly Grove is literally freezing, hardening, as he puts distance between himself and home.[19] Now the arrival at his goal, the place at the other pole from 'home' on these trips, is anti-climactic, without reward. Of course, as Grove observed of the period following his encounter with the biggest drift: 'The anti-climax had set in' (100). And in the sixth story, 'A Call for Speed,' with a sick child to hurry home to and doctor, Grove's thoughts are at home before he actually is. The sublime ego is still evident in 'Speed,' but now the braggadocio has a decidedly domestic reference: 'I was enough of a doctor to trust my ability to diagnose. I knew that my wife would in that respect rather rely on me than on the average country-town practitioner. All the greater was my responsibility' (130; throughout *Trails*, as here, Grove puts his boasts in the mouths of others, magnifying his impressive accomplishments by having others warn him that what he intends cannot be done [see 35]). Grove's unattractive narcissism, too, is still amply on display, as he burdens his daughter with the responsibility of redeeming what he considers his wasted life.[20] My intention here is not to bury Grove in tainted snow but to show the ways in which the stories following 'Snow' are more nostalgic, regretful, and backglancing, and their design in leading to the final story, the return story, which portrays a renovated Grove.

The first evidence of a changed Grove is his willingness at the beginning of 'Skies and Scares' to take advice and change his mind about which trail he will take home (143). Later, he confesses that he has 'often observed how easily my own judgment was deluded' (153), when, of course, he has never before genuinely observed any such thing. If anything, such a decision and concession recall his somewhat smug contrariness in earlier stories of the cycle and thus point up the tempering throughout the seventh story of his excessive self-reliance. There are numerous other and direct markers that this seventh is a return story: backglancing, Grove directs the reader to an incident 'on the last described drive' (148); and, almost wearily, he expects the reader to save him the trouble of repeating the descriptive work of preceding stories – 'of which I have spoken in a former paper' (150), 'as perhaps the reader remembers' (152), 'You will remember ...' (154). He also makes summary statements in the context of the whole cycle: 'the drive was one of the most marvellously beautiful ones that I had had during that winter of marvellous sights' (146). Versions of backglancing are of course characteristic of the return stories of cycles, which contain, as one of their functions as peroration, the essentials of the preceding stories. And as stated earlier, the weary backglancing of the final three sketches of *Trails*, and especially of 'Skies and Scares,' is in marked contrast rhetorically to the exuberant prolepsis of the first three stories.

In keeping with its function as return story, 'Skies and Scares' revisits with a difference what I think is the climactic image of *Trails*, the snowdrift, which Grove now refers to proleptically as 'the first disaster' (144), preparing the reader for his final defeat. Here again the recurrence of snowdrift is most significant for its difference from earlier instances. Grove describes his encounter with it momentously: 'And suddenly the world seemed to fall to pieces. The horses disappeared in the snow, the cutter settled down, there was a snap, I fell back – the lines had broken.' Not only has Grove's mistaken reading of the way over this drift separated him for the first time from his horses and control over them, but the horses emerge from the drift in a comic tableau, with Peter standing on top of Dan who is lying on his side (145). This scene, which might be seen to parody surrealistically Grove's ecstatic moment in the climactic 'Snow,' also anticipates the more truly parodic incident later when the cutter sits on top of a lowly fence post (157). This, the third of three mishaps on the final trip, is anticipated again as 'the certainty of impending disaster' (156) and it brings *Trails* to a close. 'Holding the horses back with [his] last ounce of strength,' Grove mistakenly urges them on too gently, panicked they bolt, he again loses control of them, and eventually concedes that 'this incident, for the time being at least, had completely broken [his] nerve' (158). Earlier he has prepared for the significance of this final trial, stating that he 'had never yet given in when [he] had made up [his] mind to make the trip, and it was hard to do so for the first time' (155). No longer the excessively self-reliant romantic, the Grove persona admits at last the figure of his dependent humanity. Having in his view failed a numerologically significant three final trials (the second is skidding off an icy bridge because Grove, 'through overconfidence ... was caught napping' [153]), he 'drove into the yard of a farm where [he] had seen the light, knocked at the house, and asked for and obtained the night's accommodation for [him]self and for [his] horses.' Perhaps it is overstating my case to suggest that in seeing the light, as well as in the New Testament allusion to knocking and entering (Matt. 7:8), Grove humbly signals his conversion from a neo-romantic-Nietzschean world view of ego and might to a Christian-humanist view of fallibility and communal interdependence.

As was remarked earlier with regard to the cycle's coherence, Grove also completes *Trails* with a cyclical-seasonal, and what sounds a mocking, anticipation of the promise of spring on the wind – 'There was a promise in it, as of a time, not too far distant, when the sap would rise again in the trees and when tender leaflets would begin to stir in delicate buds' (152) – which is qualified by the realistic/Canadian expectation of more snow: 'So far, however, its more immediate promise probably was snow.' This tempering of what in shorthand might be called the romantic-sentimental view (and there may well be some Grovean fun here at the expense of Shelley's 'Ode to the West Wind') with a more modern-realistic and nordic Canadian view is representative of the shift in the Grove persona's conception of nature and his relation to it. In the first place, the wind that brings him this promise of spring is associated not with the open road of *wanderungen*, as it would have been in the earlier stories, but with 'the homely and human' (151). When he looks 'way down in the north, at the edge of the world' (147), the goal presumably of all wanderers-by-choice, he sees a cloud formation in the shape of a fist. He then imposes a pastoral image on this formation, seeing it as 'a strip of flocculent, sheepy-looking, little cloudlets that suggested curliness and innocence. And the moon stood in between like a goodnatured shepherd in the stories of old' (148). But the stories of old no longer hold for Grove, for the clouds are immediately seen in a martial metaphor, as 'soldiers drilling in times of peace, to be reviewed, maybe, by some great general' (148). This martial metaphor is the one that persists, the shepherd becomes a general, though the fist relaxes into less threatening 'unseen hands' (149) at work behind the clouds. Nature is no longer a romantically beneficent or Darwinian-Nietzschean malignant phenomenon/force that can be bonded with or bested. Rather, nature keeps its distant mystery in a suggestively Platonic-Naturalistic conception that considers humankind as the shadowy subject of some cosmic experiment: 'And so I watched that insensible, silent, and yet swift shifting of things in the heavens that seemed so orderly, pre-ordained, and as if regulated by silent signals' (148). No mere snowdrift, it is this repeated intimation of a great presence behind and ordering things that defeats/transforms the Grove who had been going either to battle with/frolic in/penetrate nature (and sometimes all three simultaneously) through the preceding six stories: 'To this very hour I am convinced that the skies broke my nerve that night' (158), which 'skies' Stich ('Narcissism,' 38) reliably interprets as 'heaven, the All.' To the end an ego, however humbled, of celestial dimension and design.

Writing in 1928 – that is, after the Grove novels *Settlers of the Marsh* (1925), *A Search for America* (1927), and *Our Daily Bread* (1928), and the nature essays of *The Turn of the Year* (1923) – Raymond Knister chose *Over Prairie Trails* as Grove's 'most satisfactory book' ('A Canadian,' 15).[21] I don't know of course whether any subsequent novel would have caused the ill-fated Knister to alter his appraisal, but I doubt it, and do so in light of Grove's oeuvre. For all its irksomeness of ego, there is yet something aesthetically most satisfactory about *Over Prairie Trails*, a completeness and charm that is lacking in the novels (with the possible exception of the ant book, *Consider Her Ways* [1947]), and I would attribute its achievements in large part to its form as a short story cycle.[22] Grove didn't quite 'discover the new form' with which Robert Kroetsch credits him (*Lovely*, 62), but he did show in *Trails* an innovative way in which the form of the story cycle could be employed – for the delineation of the developing psychology of a single character. And that was making it new.

Fables of Identity: Emily Carr's *Klee Wyck*

As Stephanie Kirkwood Walker writes in her study of Carr as a test-case subject of the art of biography, 'few women artists and few Canadians have received as much biographical attention' (13). Contextualizing information can almost always illuminate particular texts, but part of the challenge in reading *Klee Wyck* as a story cycle is to resist colouring the text and its persona's actions within wilderness nature with the image of the artist Carr as a kind of fully formed and feminist idolater of Nature and Native civilization. Hilda Thomas has cautioned something similar (paralleling my own wish to expand the exclusively feminist readings of Sime's *Sister Woman*): 'There is a real danger, however, of romanticizing Carr's attitude towards both the native peoples and women, of appropriating her text by means of insufficiently grounded notions of "the goddess," or unsubstantiated dreams of matriarchal power' (5). By writing herself as Klee Wyck within the text, Carr is signalling us to read the story cycle as the portrayal of a process of growth and accommodation, and as fiction. So when Roxanne Rimstead writes that 'the loosely arranged sketches of *Klee Wyck* share with totem art a loose but coherent, associational arrangement of meaning (as opposed to linear story)' (40), she is both right in recognizing the importance of form in the book and wrong in viewing it as a loose arrangement and as somehow in the tradition of totemic art. Like Thomas King's *Medicine River* after it (discussed in the conclusion), *Klee Wyck* is well-made fiction in the tradition of the

English-Canadian short story cycle. In her journal entry for 16 September 1933, Carr articulated a theory of art composition that is Modern and organicist, reminiscent even of Poe's short story theory and the hermeneutic circle of story cycle reading: 'I begin to see that everything is perfectly balanced so that what one borrows one must pay back in some form or another, that everything has its own place but is interdependent on the rest, that a picture, like life, must also have perfect balance. Every part of it also is dependent on the whole and the whole is dependent on every part' (*Complete Writings*, 697). When, drawing on Annis Pratt's essay on Canadian female protagonists in wilderness settings, Rimstead writes 'that when female heroes feel a close affinity with nature and native animism it is often because, from their marginal position, they see society as the engulfing monster which threatens to enclose them in restrictive roles (unlike Frye's male hero who fears being engulfed by nature)' (37), she is both mistakenly radicalizing reading options along gender lines and misprisioning Frye. What Klee Wyck experiences in nature is not a female exception to Frye's admittedly selective and tendentious reading but another specific instance of it. I would go so far as to suggest that there is no great difference between Klee Wyck's response to natural wilderness and, say, the Susanna Moodie persona in *Roughing It in the Bush* – even as between Klee Wyck and Moodie as famously figured (if similarly misprisioned) by Margaret Atwood in *The Journals of Susanna Moodie*. Though, of course, Klee Wyck and the Moodie persona move towards very different accommodations.

Where Grove's *Trails* deposits him on top of the biggest snowdrift in the world, which puts him momentarily above 'that forest world which had so often engulfed [him],' Emily Carr in *Klee Wyck* wants 'to get into' the trees that represent a nature everywhere unconsciously bent on obliterating her sense of self. This getting into the trees involves a process – a cyclically repetitive process – of discovering the power of the trees in their totemic form and of identifying herself with the Indians who created the totems. My reading here may indeed be reminiscent of the grand thematic criticism of such works as Frye's *The Bush Garden* and Atwood's *Survival*, but this apparent retrograde approach will prove, I hope, illuminating.[23] *Klee Wyck* is a story cycle that anticipates by some thirty years D.J. Jones's admonition in *Butterfly on Rock* to 'let the wilderness in' (8). It expresses as it critiques by turns the 'garrison mentality' of imperialist civilization and its fear of that 'something' in nature which Frye imputed to Canadian poets. 'I have long been impressed in Canadian poetry,' he expressed famously in his conclusion to the first edition of the *Literary*

History of Canada, 'by a tone of deep terror in regard to nature ... It is not a terror of the dangers or discomforts or even the mysteries of nature, but a terror of the soul at something that these things manifest.' When critics quote this passage, they stop there. But Frye's continuing gloss on his own remarks is most relevant to Carr's project/process in *Klee Wyck*: 'The human mind has nothing but human and moral values to cling to if it is to preserve its integrity or even its sanity, yet the vast unconsciousness of nature in front of it seems an unanswerable denial of those values' (225). Understood so – as anxious about self-annihilation in wilderness space, and as searching for appeasement of and accommodation within that threat – the reminiscing Carr can be seen in *Klee Wyck* to be recreating the cyclical story of her developing self.

The framing structure of *Klee Wyck* communicates much about the development of the narrated 'I,' the eponymous Klee Wyck, of these twenty-one stories/sketches (and like Carr herself, I am simply going to call them stories, because that is what they are). The first story, 'Ucluelet,' introduces the scene of a girl, a 'fifteen-year-old school girl' (3), left alone in strange territory to the care of unknown missionaries. Such a *mise en scène* supports my suggestion that *Klee Wyck* is indeed the first use of the short story cycle as bildungsroman-künstlerroman. Readers are never told where this suggestively figured orphan came from or even why she is there. The first readers of the book would have known something of the painter's legend (see, for example, Clay's and Garfield's book reviews), as present-day readers are familiar with the various profiles and biographies and television documentaries, so all have tended to bring an over-informed response to their readings of *Klee Wyck*. But the text tells us only that the unnamed narrator is delivered to the mission by 'an enormous Irishman in a tiny canoe,' and that, in fetching her, 'The Irishman did not have any trouble deciding which was I.' That is all in the first typically spare paragraph of *Klee Wyck*, and its stiltedly correct closing sentence underscores that the true subject of this story cycle will be, as it is in Grove's *Trails*, the self-formation of reiterated identity in a marginal wilderness setting. The 'which' where 'who' is called for as the correct form of the first-person pronoun helps the presentation of the narrated 'I' as unformed, if not as dehumanized. (And one thing that becomes immediately apparent in *Klee Wyck* is that Carr is a fine and precise writer; the book did win the Governor-General's Award.) The repetition of her canoeist's nationality suggests that she is delivered to this place of threat and redemptive potentiality by a representative of the Old World, by European civilization, and that it has delivered her up in a state of some anxiety. Furthermore, if the narrated 'I' of *Klee Wyck* is supposed to be identical with the author, then Carr is falsifying her actual age here by half. Shadbolt reminds us that Carr must have been about twenty-eight years old at the time of her first visit to 'Ucluelet' (*Emily Carr*, 87). I can think of no other reason why such a precise writer (Carr) would falsify her age other than that she is intent on writing fiction, a short story cycle künstlerroman, not a loose memoir circumscribed by actuality. Moreover, she is obviously exploiting the conventions of certain kinds of stories, such as those determining reader response to tales of orphan children delivered up to crusty old maids and self-defining adventures (*Anne of Green Gables*): such a fictional strategy would immediately gain the reader's sympathy, as does the device of a first-person narrator, at least initially.

The final story of the cycle, 'Canoe,' by its simple title alone recalls the opening paragraph of the first story and shows thereby that the primary structuring element of *Klee Wyck* is indeed framing – which comes as no surprise from the pen of a painter. In this return story, the Carr persona is paddled away in another canoe, returned whence she came. This time the canoe is occupied by three generations of an Indian family, with whom Klee Wyck is clearly at home. As much as she was figuratively an orphan in the first story, by the last she is an honorary member of an Indian family. The Carr persona ensconced comfortably in the family canoe in the return story has secured an identity from and within wilderness space. It is this emphasis on the status of Klee Wyck's self-possession, which is pointed up by the framing structure of the story cycle, along with the recurrence of threats to literal self-possession in cyclical variations on the theme, that most makes *Klee Wyck* a story cycle, 'Canoe' the return story that closes the frame, and the eighteenth story, 'Salt Water,' the climactic figuring of the theme of identity in relation to place.

The self-possession of the narrated 'I' is initially and repeatedly under stress from the natural environment, which is another reason why the persona of 'Ucluelet' must be young and unnamed. The first story proceeds to key scenes both of naming and unnaming, thereby introducing the dominant theme of the cycle. 'Ucluelet' also introduces the key symbol of *Klee Wyck*: the tree. For the Carr persona, the tall standing-alone tree serves a totemic function even before it is recognized as totem pole. She first takes particular notice of such a tree upon arrival at the mission: 'Outside the kitchen window, just a few feet away at the edge of the forest, stood a grand balsam pine tree. It was very tall and straight' (23). And when that night she tries uneasily to sleep in a room associated verbally with death and the death-life of the forest, she is comforted by this emissary tree: 'The room was deathly still. Outside, the black forest was still too, but with a vibrant stillness tense with life. From my bed I could look one storey higher into the balsam pine. Because of his closeness to me, the pine towered above his fellows, his top tapering to heaven' (26). The male-gendered tree functions totemically, spiritually, with obvious associations of phallic power, but most truly in a fusion of these three. If ever there was a writer for whom a tree is not just a tree, she is Carr.

Three events which will be repeated with variation in the story cycle are first enacted in 'Ucluelet': the anonymous persona is named by Indians; she then enters a kind of liminal wilderness space which figures the threat of self-annihilation, or unnaming; she is rescued by an Indian from the forest that presents one of the two (with the ocean) predominant representations of that natural threat. She is of course named Klee Wyck, Laughing One (25–6), by the Indians, which names the narrated 'I' as identical with the book being read. Like *Jane Eyre* and *Anne of Green Gables*, *Klee Wyck* is eponymous fiction. That we are dealing with carefully shaped autobiographical fiction is shown further in this first story in the scene of a religious service where Indian and white cultures clash to the uneasy bemusement of all (26–7). There is clear indication here that Carr is looking for something calamitously climactic with which to justify her first story. As will often prove to be her writerly strategy, she deflects attention from her shaping of herself and onto the subject most definitive of that self-shaping: Indian culture, and Indian life in opposition to a life-suppressing non-Native civilization/religion (see Rimstead, 33–5). No sooner has this scene of local colour concluded than Klee Wyck finds herself walking along the beach 'upon a strip of land that belonged to nothing,' then 'in this place belonging neither to sea nor to land' (27). She is delivered from this no-self's land by an old Indian man, stripped himself and stripping a fallen tree, with whom she communicates without benefit of words. Leaving him, she is about to head into 'the forest so that [she] could round his great fallen tree,' when he pulls her back: 'The Indians forbade their children to go into the forest, not even into its edge. I was to them a child, ignorant about the wild things which they knew so well.' Thus 'Ucluelet' establishes the pattern of naming, threatened unnaming, and rescue by Indians with trees/totems that recurs and develops throughout the short story cycle that is *Klee Wyck*. As is well known and oft quoted, Carr once wrote, 'often I wished I had been born an Indian' ('Modern,' 20). In the first story of *Klee Wyck*, and *in* Klee Wyck, she (re)writes her autobiography and achieves fictional rebirth as an Indian (see H. Thomas, 13, 19).

The forces that threaten selfhood are as relentless in *Klee Wyck* as the pounding surf, and so the function of re-establishing identity *as* Klee Wyck must be repeated and strengthened. Obviously, the story cycle with its dynamic of recurrent development is ideally suited to such a task. The most interesting event that is repeated and varied is the threatened unnaming, partly because the occurrences are so subtly startling in the context of stories whose purpose is less dramatically to sketch places and Native subjects, but also because they immediately evoke the totemic-talismanic response. These recurrent events are remarkably similar to the few that occur in the companion story cycle of this chapter, *Over Prairie Trails*, those lost moments of the Grove persona in the liminal time-spaces of 'Fog' and in and atop the drifting snow of 'Snow,' wherein he is losing a version of himself as he recreates himself above the 'forest world which had so often engulfed' him. Both the trails of *Trails* and the reinscriptions of a totemic 'Indian' identity in *Klee Wyck* illustrate the need for reiteration, for endlessly encoring performance of identity. And this endless cycling around the elusive/fictive essential self illustrates the Modern interest in the psychology of consciousness as well as Grove's and Carr's awareness of just how tentative and tested *self*-consciousness is alone in the great unconsciousness of nature.

Immediately in the second story, 'Tanoo,' which takes its title from an Indian village of a Southern Queen Charlotte island, Klee Wyck again encounters this symbolic dead zone of identity, the space 'so still and solemn' (28). Significantly she enters this space after parting from an Indian couple on their boat, the Native boat community which becomes a version of the ship trope in *Klee Wyck*. When her Indian friends return for her, 'this feeling went away.' But when the canoe departs again for the anchored boat, once more 'there [is] nothing but wide black space' (29). And when Klee Wyck departs Tanoo, she 'le[aves] the silence to heal itself,' with 'the totem poles staring, staring out over the sea' (30). These first totems of the second story of *Klee Wyck* pick up the tall tree image of the opening story, and recall its function as comforting guard, which function is unnecessary already for Carr to remark. After the eponymous heroine, totem poles provide one of the prime elements of coherence in *Klee Wyck* (with the place or territory, Indians generally, particularly Jimmie and Louise, the boat-owners and guides). What is somewhat surprising is the appropriative talismanic function of the totem poles for Klee Wyck. It is as if Carr has her Klee Wyck make a very personal deal with the totems: she will preserve them in art if they will preserve her in her newly named persona.[24] This implied bargain is sealed when Klee Wyck meets with the D'Sonoqua pole.

If 'Ucluelet' begins by drawing on the conventions of orphan stories, 'D'Sonoqua' begins like a love story: 'I was sketching in a remote Indian village when I first saw her' (40). 'Her' is the most mysterious totem pole of all: wrapped in mist and the mystery of the forest wilderness itself. 'Who understands the mysteries behind the forest' (42), Carr wonders: not *of* the forest, note, but romantically-idealizingly 'behind' it. D'Sonoqua represents one way of approaching that mystery, and of placating its threat. The remnant Indian village where Klee Wyck first encounters D'Sonoqua is surrounded on three sides by ocean, 'with the forest threatening to gobble it up on the fourth' (43). Departing from this first meeting, Klee Wyck again enters the strange space of symbolic unnaming, or threat of self-annihilation. Here the experience takes place on water: 'the edge of the boat lay level with the black slithering horror below. It was like being swallowed again and again by some terrible monster, but never going down' (43). Forest wilderness and ocean soon come to represent those consuming forces of unconscious nature set relentlessly upon devouring civilized land and the ground of selfhood, those powers which Hilda Thomas (18) calls 'the engulfing power of undifferentiated nature.' Only a totemic power taken *from* that power can resist the all-unconscious, potentially nihilistic force of nature. Only such a totemic bargain of preservation and self-preservation can allow the goodness and beauty of nature – which is there also for Carr, if surprisingly very little remarked in *Klee Wyck* – to emerge.[25] As she was to say in a 1913 lecture (which is early in her late-blooming career) on the artifacts of Indian civilization: 'Only a few years and they will be gone forever into silent nothingness and I would gather my collection together before they are forever past' (in Shadbolt, *Emily Carr*, 104).

Carr uses the same 'behind' metaphor suggestive of a romantic noumenal view of phenomenal nature when presenting Klee Wyck's confrontation with the D'Sonoqua totem: 'I went back, and sitting in front of the image, gave stare for stare. But her stare so over-powered mine, that I could scarcely wrench my eyes away from the clutch of those empty sockets. The power that I felt was not in the thing itself, but in some tremendous force behind it, that the carver had believed in' (42). Shadbolt states generally that Carr's view of the totem poles is a self-projecting one: 'when she speaks (mistakenly) of the native artist's "deep desire" for self-expression it is quite clear that it is her own desire which she is reading into his attitude' (Introduction, 12). But of course that is the point. The stare into empty sockets suggests conventionally a meeting of souls, though here initially of soul and soullessness, this stare-down that is also love at first sight. Or rather, the eyeless object of the lover's gaze may be possessed of soul in a radically different and inhuman way, which accords well with Carr's presentation of wilderness nature in *Klee Wyck*. The passage ends by turning attention away from the totem to its creator, 'the carver,' and makes the totem the art of a believer in that 'tremendous force' which the totem both represents and placates. The real discovery here is not the impressive totem of D'Sonoqua in itself, possessed of 'power, weight, domination' (41), which Hilda Thomas somewhat mistakenly views as 'a figure of psychic wholeness' signalling the 'end of alienation' (14); it is rather finding the artistic means of connecting totem-ically-placatingly with what this figure represents of nature's dual aspect as malevolent soul-destroyer and solicitous beneficent mother.

Those three nouns above – power, weight, domination – might seem to point up again a phallocentric reading of the D'Sonoqua totem on Klee Wyck's part, but D'Sonoqua is a natural goddess, 'the wild woman of the woods' (42). After her totemic function as intermediary, this is the second most important aspect of D'Sonoqua: she is a she, strangely feminine certainly, as her myth makes her (like fairies and gypsies and other such woodland folk) a child-snatcher too. Nonetheless, D'Sonoqua is no ugly witch, but 'graciously feminine' (44).[26] *Klee Wyck* confirms her relationship to the female totem by subsequently demonstrating mysterious knowledge of where totems of D'Sonoqua will appear before she actually sees them: 'To myself I said, "There is D'Sonoqua"' (43). This place where a D'Sonoqua totem is next discovered is presented as very much a feminized space; her wilderness temple guards are cats who give a 'thin feminine cry' to signal Klee Wyck's arrival. Across D'Sonoqua's 'forehead her creator had fashioned the Sistheutl, or mythical two-headed sea-serpent' (44). The Sistheutl, like the twining serpents of the caduceus with its message that the cause of disease can be the cure, cleverly suggests the duality of D'Sonoqua and the wilderness-nature she figures. By the conclusion of 'D'Sonoqua,' Klee Wyck is comfortably ensconced in a wholly feminine and protective space, sketching among a dozen rubbing and purring cats; now D'Sonoqua 'summed up the depth and charm of the whole forest, driving away its menace' (44). In short, D'Sonoqua provides Klee Wyck with both her first female-gendered totem and her initial conception of her role as an artist working a bargain with the forces of duplicitous nature that lie behind the totem.

This moment of comfort is temporary, transient. The securing of self is an act that must be repeated, developed, strengthened in the course of the story cycle that is *Klee Wyck*, because the assaults on self are, as I've repeated myself, relentless. These experiences of threatened unnaming are always signalled by Klee Wyck's finding herself in the potentially destructive liminal space. In the ninth story, 'Greenville,' a brief one-sentence paragraph describes this space-time as 'between lights, neither day nor dark' (47). In opposition to the feminized cats of the secure space that ends 'D'Sonoqua,' this threatening space is accompanied by 'skulking shadow-dogs following' Klee Wyck. Suggesting that she is experiencing a hysterical reaction, 'Emptiness glared from windows and shouted up dead chimneys, weighted emptiness, that crushed the breath back into your lungs and chilled the heart in your sweating body' (48). Even 'the match the Indian struck refused to live.' Recalling her first night's sleep in the missionaries' house in 'Ucluelet,' here she finds herself 'lying in that smothering darkness and not knowing what was near [her]' (49), not daring to 'raise [her] veil ... Mosquitoes would have filled [her] mouth' (52). In the twelfth story, 'Sailing to Yan,' she says possessively, figuring the opposition between malevolent nature and the 'art' that placates it, that mist 'stole my totem poles' (56). In the thirteenth story, 'Cha-atl,' she describes her approach to the surf-booming west side of a Queen Charlotte island 'as if you were coming into the jaws of something too big and awful even to have a name' (57). The unnamer denies naming of itself. Here she encounters ample evidence of nature's destructive effects on the Indians' habitation: 'Trees had pushed off the roof and burst the sides. Under the hot sun the lush growth smelt rank ... While I stood there that awful boom, boom, seemed to drown out every other thing' (58). As was the case with Grove in 'Snow,' here the repetition of the word 'awful' (filled with awe) suggests that Carr, the painter, is drawing on the language of sublime description to convey the experience of self humbled in the presence of an inconceivable power not especially disposed to the care of fragile, individuated humanity. And as always when confronted by this unnaming, Klee Wyck has recourse to *her* talismanic totems: 'By and by the roar got fainter and fainter and the silence stronger. The shadows of the totem poles across the beach seemed as real as the poles themselves' (59). Recalling the old Indian man of 'Ucluelet,' the first story of the cycle, who saved her from the threat of forest wilderness, in 'Greenville' it is 'the womanliness of the old squaw' that comforts her through another dark night of the soul: 'All night long I was glad of that woman in Greenville' (49). The recurrent development dynamic operative in *Klee Wyck* as a story cycle is admirably exercised in the movement from an opening story that figures its tree phallically and has Klee Wyck saved by an Indian man to where, in 'D'Sonoqua,' 'Greenville,' and 'Cha-atl' sequentially, the totem pole has been feminized, she receives comforting rescue from an Indian woman, and the pines are like 'little ladies' (57).

The suggestively Gothic threat-rescue pattern of *Klee Wyck* reaches a climax in the eighteenth story, 'Salt Water.' By far the longest of the stories, 'Salt Water' draws on the genre of the shipwreck adventure. It opens with Klee Wyck enjoying a rare mystical moment with a suggestively feminine nature which, in the preceding stories in its ungendered state, most often has threatened her individualized identity: 'There was neither horizon, cloud, nor sound; of that pink, spread silence even I had become part, belonging as much to sky as to earth' (66). Significantly here, she claims sisterhood with neither the ocean nor the forest, the two figures of greatest threat in the preceding stories; nonetheless, the loss of identity is clearly mystical, ecstatically pleasurable, and the liminal space of unnaming has become an undifferentiated womb of a kind. Here, Carr is for once using one of those '"female metaphors"' that Hilda Thomas (6) mistakenly perceives throughout *Klee Wyck* and defines as 'submerged metaphors of engulfment, absorption, assimilation in which the boundaries between inside and outside are nearly obliterated.' Here too, signalling the cumulative function of story cycles and enacting their swerve towards return, a lotus-landed Klee Wyck plans to revisit Tanoo, Skedans, and Cumshewa, sites of three earlier visits and the titles of stories 2, 3, and 4. However, the rosy/pink view changes when Klee Wyck encounters the parallel recurrence of the old threat, assisted now by non-Native civilization, in those Indian places: 'Civilization crept nearer and the Indian went to meet it, abandoning his old haunts. Then the rush of wild growth swooped and gobbled up all that was foreign to it. Rapidly it was obliterating every trace of man' (66–7). Not only Native or non-Native, note, but generic man.

The intrepid and unflinching Klee Wyck makes it only as far as Skedans, which is described as having been assaulted by 'some monster' who left 'deep bare scars' on the island (67). A series of mishaps leaves her abandoned to her own devices until she is rescued and returned to civilization by non-Native men on a fishing barge. Unsurprisingly, it is not a happy event. A climactic panic sets in when, asked simply to climb a wharf ladder, she finds herself being forced into that unnaming space of nothingness: 'I could not ... could not mount into that giddy blackness'; 'to abandon [her rescuer] for a vague black ascent into ... nothingness' (74, ellipses in original). Keep in mind: here Klee Wyck is climbing an iron wharf ladder, which needs to be said, as it could hardly be deduced, even from the words 'rung' and 'wharf':

I grasped the cold slimy rung. My feet slithered and scrunched on stranded things. Next rung ... the next and next ... endless horrible rungs, hissing and smells belching from under the wharf. These things at least were half tangible. Empty nothingness, behind, around; hanging in the void, clinging to slipperiness, was horrible – horrible beyond words! ... (75, ellipses in original)

Readers must wonder: What is going on here? Clearly more than the mundane action being described. Is it a rare instance of situational, verbal-rhetorical humour in *Klee Wyck*? No. But even if it were, what would that humour be doing/hiding? Rather, what we have on display here is panic preceding the forced entrance into the familiar unnaming space, and it has many causes. The return to non-Native civilization follows a drawn-out, calamitous excursion. The first sign of impending disaster was the failure to return to those defining moments of her fictionalized 'youth' in Skedans, Tanoo, and Cumshewa. Klee Wyck is being forced back into non-Native civilization, and, recalling the Irishman and his canoe of the first story of the cycle, she is being delivered up again into the unknown from another non-Native's boat. She would be, in this last regard, as understandably disappointed as Anne Shirley being taken away from Green Gables and back to the abusive orphanage. Furthermore, Klee Wyck's hysterical reaction follows her most recent and powerful confrontation with evidence that nature is a monstrous devourer of all things human – now particularly and personally connected to scenes of her earlier self-realizing trips. Thus a seemingly inexplicable reaction to an everyday occurrence (climbing a wharf ladder) presents a dramatic, even a highly melo-dramatized, final instance of what is most threatened: Klee Wyck's literal self-possession in her newer identity. Although Shadbolt is always insightful in her observations of the ways Carr fictionalized herself in her autobiographical writings,[27] she (Shadbolt) is mistaken, at least as regards *Klee Wyck*, when she asserts that 'the sense of her "I", the unshakeable certainty of her own being, is there from her birth' (Introduction, 7). Risky as it is to project the teller from the tale, I must say: that cannot be true. *Klee Wyck* repeatedly explores the opposite possibility: the evanescence of self or, put positively, the self as process. And it does so within a short story cycle whose pretext is the artist's sketching expeditions and whose subtext is the künstlerroman.

The final three stories of the cycle depict the anti-climactic movement away from the unnaming nothingness of 'Salt Water.' In doing so, they function like the last three, if much longer, stories of *Over Prairie Trails* following the climactic 'Snow.' The nineteenth story, 'Century Time,' is set in an Indian cemetery (75–7): that's where the reader finds Klee Wyck after the dead-zone conclusion of 'Salt Water.' She emerges reborn yet again (and again much like the Grove persona after 'Snow') into the twentieth, 'Kitwancool,' where she passes through a kind of natural hell of synesthesia: 'the scrub growth at the road-side smelt red hot' (78). She is figuratively reconceived, reborn, and reconfirmed as Klee Wyck in the titular Indian village where 'black and clear against the sky stood the old totem poles of Kitwancool' (79). There is much self-dramatization and gnomic utterance here:

'My heart said into the thick dark, "Why did I come?"
'And the dark answered, "You Know."' (79)

The image of Klee Wyck trying to fall asleep in such a spooky darkness again recalls the opening story of the cycle as well as a number of similar scenes of abandonment throughout. Here in the penultimate story, intent upon reclaiming her self and her purpose, she is reconfirmed in her mission by darkness itself, which reminds her of what I have called her bargain with the totems and the Native culture that produced them. It's a kind of benediction, to be blessed with the confirmation of why you are here.

The next morning, like a prophet come from meeting with her god, she must go and tell her purpose to an Indian mother, who asks her pointedly: '"What do you want our totem poles for?"'

'Because they are beautiful. They are getting old now, and your people make very few new ones. The young people do not value the poles as the old ones did. By and by there will be no more poles. I want to make pictures of them, so that your young people as well as the white people will see how fine your totem poles used to be.' (80)

This elegiac declaration scene performs at least three functions. It is a powerful statement, an explicit iteration, of purpose – the preservation/self-preservation bargain. It shows *Klee Wyck* to be also in the tradition of the pastoral elegy whose consolation is achieved through art.[28] And it recalls positively the scene from the first story, 'Ucluelet,' where the sketching girl Klee Wyck provokes a somewhat violent reaction from an Indian who does not want his soul-stealing likeness drawn. Further, the relationship with the interrogating Indian mother re-establishes the recently threatened Klee Wyck in secure matriarchal domain: 'Woman-hood was strong in Kitwancool' (80). In yet further confirmation of this maternalization of place and the phallic totems themselves, which began with 'D'Sonoqua,' in the village of Kitwancool the totems present 'several times the figure of a woman that held a child.' These nurturing icons both repeat and develop the encounter with D'Sonoqua, who was, recall, a stealer of children, and it might even be said, *improves* upon D'Sonoqua functionally. Finally, in what is one of the most obvious manipulations of events for fictional purposes, Carr conjures up a storm that accosts Klee Wyck with a final unnaming nihilistic instance of neither this nor that: 'the totem poles went black, flashed vividly white and then went black again.' Overdoing it somewhat, she has Klee Wyck crawl for shelter onto the roofed grave of a medicine man. Of course Klee Wyck emerges alive after all to say in the story's closing one-sentence paragraph, with literal reference to a recently jailed Indian but with loud bio-fictional signifi-cance: 'Now I knew who the hero was' (83). The educated imagination of short story cycle readers will hear in this Janus-like assertion (with regard to subject and time) an echoing answer to the equally odd sentence in the story cycle's first paragraph, where the 'the Irishman did not have any trouble deciding which was I.'

In the penultimate story, 'Kitwancool,' Klee Wyck remarks, speaking doubtless for her author, 'When the Indians accepted me as one of them-selves, I was very grateful' (81). Like Grey Owl and in illustration of the title of Robert Kroetsch's novel, by the end of *Klee Wyck* the Carr per-sona has 'gone Indian.' She wants to identify herself with Indian life, I believe, not only because Native culture has created the totems that func-tion talismanically with reference to that Frygean 'something' in nature which threatens her soul, but also because Indians, as she perceives and presents them, live half in that liminal space that Klee Wyck herself always enters as prelude to the threat of unnaming. In 'Cumshewa' she observes that 'Indians are comfortable everywhere' (33). In 'Sleep,' a fam-ily of Indians camping on the beach exists in marked contrast to her own discomfort: 'These children belonged to the beach, and were as much a part of it as the drift-logs and the stones' (54). The Indian way of life pre-sents Carr with an example of living that turns the threatening space into the kind of potentially creative, or at least accommodating, personal ver-sion of the 'interstitial space' that Homi Bhabha describes (3), and to which I had recourse earlier to elaborate Duncan Campbell Scott's fasci-nation with transitional times and liminal spaces. Shadbolt has written, perhaps more accurately than she may have intended, of Carr's 'simply interpreting her contacts [with Indians] according to her own romantic constructs' (11). I am not sure what Shadbolt means by 'romantic,' but I suspect she is using the word in its popular sense of ennobling the savage. Carr's vision *is* romantic, but it definitely does not valorize Indians as Rousseauesque noble savages. Rather, she expresses in her view of Native life a powerfully attractive (for Klee Wyck) alternate way of living with/in nature, if a way that primarily contributes most substantially to her own romantic and self-creating myth.

One of the defining characteristics of this potentially accommodating space is a form of timelessness, which for Carr is a defining feature of Indians themselves in their relation to non-Native notions of time. In 'Greenville,' Indians live 'as if time did not exist' (47). Or more accurately, they are governed temporally by natural markers: 'Indians slip in and out of their places like animals. Tides and seasons are the things that rule their lives: domestic arrangements are mere incidentals' (49). Rather than finish building a house, Indians will 'lie around in the sun for days doing nothing' (50). And at her most insensitive: 'Perhaps in a way dogs are more domestic and more responsive than Indians' (52). As Robert Fulford has observed in a cleverly reactionary apology for Carr's appropriation of Native culture, such views are decidedly politically incorrect. I don't think, though, that correctness ever bothered Emily Carr, or it did so only to the degree that she deplored the Victorian correctness of her childhood home in Victoria. Racist as the expression of many of these features of Native life must sound to contemporary ears, Indian ways of living are mostly appreciated by Carr, and her racism is without ugly intent, obviously. But to recap what I've been suggesting here: Carr always presents the threat of unnaming as emanating from nature as ocean and forest; a defining feature of that annihilating power is its strange anti-mystical timelessness; she discovers the feminized totems as powerfully talismanic in negotiating accommodation with the annihilating threat; she admires the culture of the creators of those totems, and admires further the Indians' ability to live practically in a timeless way.[29] For Carr, Indian atemporality is to living what the totem pole is to wilderness threat, because, of course, the natural progression of linear time, terminating in death, is the essential aspect of nature that threatens individualized identity.

Klee Wyck's return story, 'Canoe,' requires no extensive commentary. Perhaps it functions more as a closing frame story than as a return story proper. Perhaps the three stories that precede it constitute a type of conglomerate return story to the places and people that contribute to the cycle's dominant theme of self-identity and its preservation. Or perhaps the final four stories can be seen together to constitute the return movement of the whole cycle. Still, in 'Canoe' Klee Wyck is comfortably returning to the place whence she came. She is being delivered by an Indian family comprising three generations, in a cedar canoe where 'the mother in the stern held a sleeping child under her shawl and grasped the steering paddle' (85). It is something of an iconic image, or at least a tableau vivant, of her new-found family, and the canoe an Ark trope indeed. More impressively, it is also a cleverly disguised version of the totem pole. In a very real sense, Klee Wyck is inside one of those trees that, as forest wilderness, have threatened throughout; in a figurative sense Carr has made her Klee Wyck part of a totem of Indian family:

> As the canoe glided on, her human cargo was as silent as the cedar-life that once had filled her. She had done with the forest now; when they shoved her into the sea they had dug out her heart. Submissively she accepted the new element, going with the tide. When tide or wind crossed her she became fractious. Some still element of the forest clung yet to the cedar's hollow rind which resented the restless push of waves.

One of many a remarkable passage of fiction-writing in this painter's book (and one, note, that wittily breathes new life into the 'going with the tide' cliché). The tree, like the totem poles of the cycle, is here feminized. In the transformation to canoe the tree has relinquished the forest's glooming stillness and her cedar heart for human cargo and become, like the totems, a nature-human collaboration negotiating a half-and-half existence. If this canoe could literally speak – it certainly does figuratively – I suspect it would do so much like its shapely sister in Isabella Valancy Crawford's 'Said the Canoe,' in subtly subversive condemnation of the imperialistic non-Native males who violate nature with no thought for the necessity of accommodation within her (both nature and canoe), cavalierly ignorant of the threat which they paradoxically create and invite, as is signalled at the end of Crawford's poem: 'The darkness built its wigwam walls / Close round the camp, and at its curtain / Pressed shapes, thin, woven and uncertain' (70).

Secure in the maternal bosom of such a feminine and familial mode of conveyance, Klee Wyck experiences no anxiety now when she enters the familiar space of unnaming: 'Time and texture faded ... ceased to exist ... day was gone, yet it was not night. Water was not wet nor deep, just smoothness spread with light' (ellipses in original). Given the cyclical repetitiveness of *Klee Wyck*, the art of self-definition is doubtless intended to be viewed as a continuing process.[30] As for reaching a lasting accommodation with nature, what W.H. New has said about the relation of self and nature in *Swamp Angel*, by Carr's fellow west-coast writer Ethel Wilson, applies equally to conditions at the end of *Klee Wyck*, and brings us back to those garrison mentality thematic critics (Frye, Atwood, Jones) of the mid-1960s and early 1970s: *Klee Wyck* argues (I substitute freely) 'not for resistance to the natural wilderness, but for a sympathy between wilderness and the innermost self. "Innermost," however, creates a problem, for it suggests an absolute condition, whereas [*Klee Wyck*'s] narrative rejects absolutes as being contrary to the process of living. Yet the [story cycle] permits an *absolute* "innermost" to at least be conceptualized if never quite defined' (*Land Sliding*, 154–5). As chapter 5 of the present study will show, something very like this could be said of Rose at the end of Alice Munro's *Who Do You Think You Are?*

Repetition, reiteration, rehearsal of the performance of identity: *Over Prairie Trails* and *Klee Wyck* evince the compulsion always to go again to confront and find accommodation with and within a nature that – whether deep sea, forest, or outer space – appears in its vast unconsciousness inimical to individuated human consciousness. The form of the short story cycle, the genre that best speaks to the destabilization of essentialist concepts, that formally features recurrence and development, repetition and variation, is admirably written in these two books showing the Modern Canadian adaptation of story cycle form in the exploration of individual psychology. Over and over his prairie trails, Grove will sign himself on the prairie landscape like a stylus tracing and retracing his own profile as he impresses the new image himself, and Carr will repetitively sketch her Klee Wyck sketching her talismanic totem poles from morning till night in ambivalent nature, until like Klein's vanishing poet 'they map, / not the world's, but [their] own body's chart' (104).

4

'To keep what was good and pass it on': George Elliott's *The Kissing Man*

George Elliott's *The Kissing Man* has remained, since Dennis Duffy's observation in one of only two critical articles devoted solely to the book (published in *Canadian Literature* over a quarter-century ago), an 'underground classic' (52).[1] Elliott's virtual silence for more than three decades after *The Kissing Man*'s appearance in 1962 may partly explain the scarcity of published criticism,[2] as may the book's unconventional form, the short story cycle. But Elliott began publishing books of fiction again in the mid-1990s towards the end of his life, and story cycles had long since become more fashionable, yet little is said now of *The Kissing Man* and less written. To borrow from Sarah Binks, the underground classic is in danger of going down to the magma. Consequently this chapter has a threefold purpose: to direct overdue critical attention to this remarkable story cycle, which W.H. New described in the second edition of the *Literary History of Canada* as 'deceptively simple' ('Fiction,' 259); to contextualize *The Kissing Man* in the continuum of the Canadian short story cycle and the tradition of magic realism; and to offer a close reading of some key stories of the cycle, showing the ways they repeatedly create symbols and rituals that enable the memories and create the meanings that Elliott envisioned as definitive of life in an unnamed southwestern Ontario town at the middle of the twentieth century.[3]

Returning via the story cycle from the open spaces of the West to a central Canada setting only some half-century after *Viger* and *Sunshine Sketches*, we find place as small town presented still in tones of nostalgic longing and confused regret. It is as if Elliott writes in fulfilment of Scott's and Leacock's fictional warnings of what was passing, especially with respect to the relation between place and identity, and in response to his predecessors' urgings of the necessity to remember forward the values of small-town community. Such are the workings of Bakhtinian genre memory and the Frygean imaginative continuum in the Canadian short story cycle. Duffy (54–5) has reported, somewhat provokingly, that 'Southwestern Ontario has produced some fair literature of this sort ... George Elliott has speculated in conversation that perhaps because Western Ontario "peaked" in the [18]90s and has gone nowhere since, ... its liveliest spirits migrating West or to the cities, the place provides that sense of a golden age gone bust ... that good writing thrives on.' Although there is productive as well as provocative observation in Duffy's and Elliott's speculations, it is worth noting that, with respect to the present study of Canadian short story cycles, of the two writers who 'migrated' West, Grove and Carr, one of them, Carr, found similar subjects of human folly in the artifacts of various Native communities older than any dreamt of in the philosophies of longer-civilized Easterners. Facetiousness aside, at times the setting of *The Kissing Man* does feel eerily like a ghost town whose living residents behave as if haunted (*pace* Birney) by a wealth of historied apparitions.

The Kissing Man, very much in the tradition of *In the Village of Viger* and *Sunshine Sketches of a Little Town*, is distinctively a contemporary short story cycle of place as small town. It fictionally anatomizes a semi-rural community, the unnamed town, looking at the characters, institutions, traditions, mores, and rituals that give that place coherence over time, again as did its predecessors. In effect, *The Kissing Man* analyses what makes a physical place a human community, for good and ill, and signals what threatens the continuance of small-town life and communal values. Following also from Grove's *Over Prairie Trails* and Carr's *Klee Wyck*, *The Kissing Man* figures its prime threat as coming from within human nature as well as abstractly from without in the passage of time and fashions. The short story cycle form, especially in its cross-sectional technique, continues to be ideally suited to such an anatomy of place. The story cycle of place, whether rural or urban place, written here by Elliott at the beginning of the contemporary period in Canadian literature and subsequently by such others as Hood in *Around the Mountain* (1967), Richler in *The Street* (1969), Hodgins in *Spit Delaney's Island* (1976), Mistry in *Tales from Firozsha Baag* (1987), and King in *Medicine River* (1989), proves to be generically continuous with the likes of *Viger*, *Sunshine Sketches*, *Sister Woman*, *Trails*, and *Klee Wyck* (the latter two for their evocation of territorial place; and of course Hodgins, broadly considered, shares his place, Vancouver Island, with Carr). Reminiscent of Scott's insistence on spatial and temporal setting in the first paragraph of

Viger and of Leacock's opening guided tour of Mariposa – 'In point of geography ...' (see 1–5) – *The Kissing Man* is self-consciously a story cycle of place; the opening of its first story, 'An act of piety,' locates the community and town cartographically, with reference to compass points: 'She looked to the east and named off the neighbours ... She looked to the west and saw ...' (1).

Such story cycles of place likely have their antecedents in the subgenre of the village poem, which begins in Canada with Oliver Goldsmith's *The Rising Village* in 1825, and has origins in such eighteenth-century village novels as his great-uncle's, the Anglo-Irish Goldsmith's, *The Vicar of Wakefield* in 1766. Village fiction became mostly a North American phenomenon encouraged by the American writer and editor William Dean Howells, and such stories of the regional place reached a high popularity in the late nineteenth-century vogue of local-colour fiction.[4] In Canada the tradition of small-town fictions, the novel form of which is epitomized early in Sara Jeannette Duncan's *The Imperialist* in 1904 (set in a fictionalized Brantford, Ontario), continued through the twentieth century, finding anxious voice in the self-reflexive musing on the genre that begins Robertson Davies' *Fifth Business* in 1970 (self-reflexive in that the novel's opening appears to be written under the influence of Leacock's Mariposa; interestingly, its later portrayal of the small-town saint-whore seems to provide the target for Munro's feminist critique of such wish-fulfilling types in *Who Do You Think You Are?* [26; and see Mathews, 181]). But rightly bypassing the many worthy novels of small-town Canada and lighting on short story cycles, Clara Thomas has observed that 'after *Sunshine Sketches, The Kissing Man* is the next landmark in our small-town literature' (101). I agree, and would add only that Elliott's *The Kissing Man* may also mark a terminal point, or at least signals the start of a long period of inactivity, in the continuum of Canadian story cycles whose subject is place as small town exclusive of extensive character development.

The Kissing Man differs most noticeably from its literary and generic predecessors in style: it is neither local colour, nor humour, nor naturalism, nor social or psychological realism. *The Kissing Man* draws more obviously on the styles and techniques of myth, parable, fable, tale, folk tale, and legend, mixing the mundane and marvellous in an unapologetic manner which by 1962 had already long been termed 'magical realism' (Flores, 188), the term which Peter Hinchcliffe and Ed Jewinski call a 'complex and unstable critical concept,' an 'oxymoronic phrase' (5–6). Regardless of such taxonomic difficulties, Angel Flores could nonetheless have been predicting *The Kissing Man* when as long ago as 1955 he described the magical realism of South American fiction writers generally as evincing 'the same preoccupation with style and also the same transformation of the common and the everyday into the awesome and unreal' (190), and characterized their prose style as one that 'seeks precision and leanness' (191).

But if *The Kissing Man* anticipates Canadian uses of magic realist techniques and some of the dominant stratagems of postmodern fiction (as in, for example, the short stories of such writers as Jack Hodgins, Matt Cohen, and Eric McCormack), it is also true that in terms of deep-structuring subtexts it relies respectfully, in high Modern manner, on older stories drawn from a variety of sources ranging from the biblical account of Jacob and Esau ('When Jacob Fletcher was a boy') to Irish legend ('A leaf for everything good') to various North American folk tales ('The commonplace'). With the notable exceptions of Howard O'Hagan's *Tay John* (1939) and Sheila Watson's *The Double Hook* (1959), it remains true that *The Kissing Man* was unique in the world of Canadian fiction for an elliptical prose style that can make Norman Levine's look florid and for a mundanely marvellous presentation of fictional events. However, as in *The Double Hook* (which is deeply structured on the *Oresteia* of Aeschylus and reaffirming of the values of family and community), the avant-garde techniques of *The Kissing Man*'s stories – temporal disruptions and compressions, narrative lacunae, a general making strange – serve a decidedly conservative and characteristically Canadian vision of the importance of family and community. Of course, both the form and subject of story cycles of place – the connecting of discrete sections, the absence of a protagonist, the return story – already express a conservative-communal, as opposed to a liberal-individualist, vision. Although it can appear every bit as strange, *The Kissing Man* is no *Beautiful Losers*; and if at times as fictionally adventurous, it is not ideologically postmodern in its relation to such a central construct as authority, whether the normalizing communal or the implied authorial. In the context of the continuum of Canadian short story cycles of place, Hood's *Around the Mountain* and Richler's *The Street* are chronologically the works that follow *The Kissing Man*, and they are conventional in form and style, being more of a return to the sketch-book form of the nineteenth century than an advancement in the use of cyclical story form.[5] Even Hodgins's *Spit Delaney's Island*, though certainly innovative stylistically in places, is tame by comparison with *The Kissing Man*. And those comparisons should serve to highlight again the extent to which *The Kissing Man* was both technically innovative and the mid-century's most interesting instance of one of the two major categories of Canadian short story cycle.

The marvellous aspect of *The Kissing Man*, which involves the figuring of what amounts really to the repressed or denied spiritual and emotional dimension of small town life, provides a way of representing the intangible – what Duffy calls 'another dimension of existence' (55) – concretely in fiction. Marvellous occurrences also contribute to the means by which communal value and truth can continue to be expressed across generations. Though unremarkable when labelled the emotional and spiritual life, in *The Kissing Man* this aspect of town life is presented startlingly as an other-worldly realm that pervades the daily lives of the residents, sometimes violating everyday reality in a materially and emotionally disruptive fashion. Such destabilizations are best exemplified by the compassionate Kissing Man of the title story, a magical figure, perhaps a projection or eruption of suppressed female desires, who literally appears out of thin air in the middle story of the book both to commiserate with the dowdy women of a very ordinary dry-goods store and to figure the maturing of a young woman. The Kissing Man simply appears, unexplained in any literal sense of the word, if suggestively in answer to individual and communal needs. In their function as a coded literary-aesthetic answering to suppressed or denied needs, such fictional techniques of *The Kissing Man* share something with – offer a Canadian parallel to – the political-cultural *raison d'être* of South American magic realism.

Generally the workings of magic realism are usefully described by Robert R. Wilson, who explains and emphasizes the nature of hybridity in the magic realist world:

> On the one hand, the hybrid constructions of magic realism arise ... when something different, even inconsistent, arrives. It comes from outside an already established world ... and informs it temporarily. On the other hand, one world may lie hidden within another. Then the hybrid construction emerges from a secret already contained within, forming an occulted and latent aspect of the surface world. (72; see also Hancock, 36; and Patterson, 29)

Whereas fictional magic was used to destabilize the postcolonial reality – the politically useful illusions conjured by officialdom – of various South American authoritarian states, Elliott uses it in *The Kissing Man* as a means to concretize the ways in which Canadian communal continuities are effected and small town life is endured. But like South American magic realism itself in its reactionary formation, Elliott's magic realism can also be understood as partaking of the surrealist reaction against nine-teenth-century realism and naturalism, and so indebted as much to André Breton as to Alejo Carpentier.[6] It is not true, as Carpentier asserted, that 'the marvellous is not universal, but exclusively Latin American' (in Han-cock, 36; cf. Iftekharuddin interviewing Robert Coover, 93). That is a rather limiting and unliterary view of what is, even in its South American origins and context, a literary technique of Modernism (consider the Night Town scene of Joyce's *Ulysses*). Such an exclusive view is also igno-rant, if understandably so, of what many Canadian critics, from A.J.M. Smith to David Bentley, have recognized as the definitive Canadian liter-ary attitude, which devolves from the privileged position of writers who can choose eclectically from among innovations arising elsewhere and adapt those styles, techniques, and poetics to a Canadian environment.[7] Elliott himself has explained his use of magic realism as not a political weapon but a 'coping mechanism': 'I contend that magic realism is a thing that happens between a writer and a reader in which the reader who can-not cope with reality with the tools he has, is given an extra invisible tool to cope with reality' ('Concluding Panel,' 124). He means 'coping' as in managing what one of his characters calls 'the fraileries of mankind' (92), not as in tossing a fictional Molotov cocktail.

Of equal relevance to Elliott's adaptation of surrealist and magic realist techniques is the recognition of how little has changed in the idea (as opposed to the representation) of small towns in Canadian short story cycles from Scott's Viger to Munro's Hanratty. Elliott's vision of small-town community life is still essentially conservative, and no more radically Tory than was Leacock's (which was radical only in that it criticized a crassly materialistic view of human affairs). That conservative-humanistic vision is clearly signalled early in *The Kissing Man*, in its epigraph taken from arch-conservative T.S. Eliot's *Notes towards the Definition of Cul-ture*: 'But when I speak of the family, I have in mind a bond which embraces ... a piety towards the dead, however obscure, and a solicitude for the unborn, however remote' (n.p.; see Eliot, *Notes*, 42). In a number of ways, this epigraph can be seen to predict the themes and cyclical shape of *The Kissing Man*, whose first story, 'An act of piety,' obviously echoes it, and whose last, 'The way back,' makes a fictional argument for 'a solic-itude for the unborn.' All of the stories of this cycle repeatedly and vari-ously portray attempts to create personal and public symbols and rituals which enable such cultural continuities and bear witness to what Leacock himself called 'all less tangible and provable forms of human merit, and less tangible aspirations of the human mind' (*Essays*, 77).

I will have cause to return to some of this contextualizing background for *The Kissing Man*, but it is past time for turning to the stories themselves.

Readers of *The Kissing Man* must often feel about its enigmatic fictions as the boy Finn feels about the gnomic old man in the seventh story, 'A leaf for everything good' (the story I use as a kind of pivot for my discussion): puzzled, wary, toyed with, impatient, and ultimately perhaps, satisfied, if inexplicably so. The consistent third-person narrator of *The Kissing Man*, like that story's old man sitting by the pond, talks cryptically as if in possession of secret knowledge and wisdom that he wishes to impart to readers, information that cannot be conveyed by conventional means, such as in an algebraic equation or the representational techniques of realistic fiction. As Geoff Hancock has observed of magic realist fictions, 'the narrator ... is a reminder of the deep faith of an oral culture, presupposing a belief shared by hearers and tellers ... Magic realists affirm the art of making fiction at the same time that they connect their marvellous tales to the roots of society' (44). Readers, like the boy Finn, may find themselves attracted to these puzzling stories and their taciturn narrator; and readers must exercise, as fishing Finn does, receptive forbearance if they are to hook and reel in meaning from Elliott's elusive collection. Much will remain of puzzle and enigma, and living with irresolution and mystery is apparently a large part of the meanings of *The Kissing Man*. Perhaps readers can learn, as Finn discovers, only that what initially appeared transparent, still, and shallow is actually murky, dynamic, and unfathomable. Indeed, Elliott has said of *The Kissing Man* that 'if themes and passions in various of the stories in the collection remain unresolved, it is because nothing in life is ever resolved' (in Duffy, 52).

Like a great-grandchild uncannily born with its ancestor's features, *The Kissing Man* also closely resembles the first Canadian short story cycle, *In the Village of Viger*, in subject, style, and purpose. It is a cycle about a central Canadian small town under various pressures from within and without. It is organized on the framing principle, with key introductory and return stories, and with the interior stories repeating and developing its dominant theme of memorial transference. In style it can be seen to share with *Viger* the influences of the tale and folk tale tradition, whose conventions would also have been the largest of the tributaries that contributed to magic realism.[8] Recalling the opening of *Viger* with its dual temporal focus and introduction of the theme of transition, the first sentence of 'A leaf for everything good,' the seventh story, observes that, since the incidents to be related in the story, the town pond has been converted into a bowling green (75). Linear time is relentlessly threatening throughout *The Kissing Man*, and this *ubi sunt* trope contributes largely to making the unvarying tone of the cycle sombre and elegiac, and its dominant emotion nostalgia. Here, the loss of the pond, like Daigneau's pit in Viger, gains a regrettable significance in light of its importance in the transference to Finn, a troubled boy, of what the old man knows of the submerged emotional life of the town. But change is an inevitable consequence of the passage of time, which would seem to be one of the lessons that Finn learns while fishing (84). Change as inevitably destructive of what *The Kissing Man* repeatedly calls the 'good' is what the more favourably portrayed characters and the created symbols and rituals of *The Kissing Man* struggle to counter and accommodate.

The one ineluctable consequence of linear time brings about the death of Mayhew and Tessie Salkald in the opening story, 'An act of piety,' placing the pioneer and patriarchal Salkald farm in a kind of temporal suspension. Their passing forces Honey Salkald 'to remember all he could about Mayhew and Tessie' (10) in order to effect the transition of the Salkald legacy to himself. Honey manages this transition through a ritualistic act of piety – tending Tessie's grave (9) – and a reluctant confrontation with the past in the person of the gossipy Mrs Palson. Readers can only presume that Honey learns from Mrs Palson about Tessie's intolerance of the infected Irish family some fifty years earlier (see C. Thomas, 103). Tessie's intolerance put considerable strain on the bond of unspoken understanding that existed between herself and Mayhew (3). Her exclusionary attitude may also have had ill effects on her children, because, though none of the stories deals with the second generation of Salkalds (which in itself says much unfavourably), Johnson Mender in 'What do the children mean?,' the ninth story, observes that Honey's dad 'never came around' (103–4). While tending Tessie's grave, Honey remembers what was fine and grand about Mayhew (11), not, note, the intolerant Tessie. It is from his subsequent talk with Mrs Palson that he learns, presumably, what was amiss in so-called 'Proud Tessie's' life. After his talk with Mrs Palson, Honey 'knew enough, now, about Tessie to make the old truth fresh and almost complete' (12). Although time destroys and causes the forgetting of much, Honey, at the conclusion of the first story, 'wanted only to keep what was good and pass it on' (12). Here, the 'good' is aligned with first-settler farming in the community, with largesse and humble pride, and with Honey's inclination to stand on the shoulders of those traditions, while by implication the 'bad' is the sort of communal intolerance that reeks of racism and was present too in Viger and Mariposa.[9]

Honey knows only 'enough' because no character (or reader) can know all; apparently, action (and meaning) must also sometimes be taken on faith. The first story ignores the actual information Honey receives from Mrs Palson in favour of attending to the occasion and agency of its transference: the ritual of tending the grave and the unreported talk with the community gossip (who serves here a useful communal function reminiscent of Madame Laroque in *Viger*). Honey's observance at the graveside is the titular act of piety, an action which, as previously noted, illustrates the book's epigraph from T.S. Eliot's *Notes towards the Definition of Culture* ('a piety towards the dead'). The passage from Eliot defines family as 'a bond which embraces' the dead, the living, and the unborn; and earlier in his *Notes* Eliot has described family as 'the primary channel of transmission of culture' (41). A number of other characters in *The Kissing Man* attempt to create symbols, to establish or to continue rituals and traditions that forge and fortify such culturally embracing familial bonds. And not only 'The way back' but also 'What do the children mean?' illustrates from the epigraph Eliot's notion of 'a solicitude for the unborn.' Such stories, like Eliot's broad understanding of 'family' within culture, focus on the two-way traffic along these invisible channels that reach across generations, from the dead to the living, to the newborn and even the unborn. It could be said that *The Kissing Man* variously figures, in a manner that parallels the argument of T.S. Eliot's 'Tradition and the Individual Talent,' a kind of community and the individual life. (And recall how apt indeed was Scott's making fractured family the sounding board of the anti-modernist-metropolitan theme of *Viger*; and that the newly formed Pepperleigh family unit constitutes the saving grace of Mariposa in the three romance stories of *Sunshine Sketches*; and even that Grove makes home and family the goal of his trips.)

Other literary texts also leave traces in *The Kissing Man*, providing guidance and revelation for characters and readers alike. In the first story, Honey's uncle, Dan Salkald, reads William Cullen Bryant's popular 'Thanatopsis' at Mayhew Salkald's funeral, and the reading changes Honey's understanding of his grandfather's life and death (10). Typical of Elliott's reticent style, no lines from the poem are given, but Bryant's poem would have suggested to Honey that death is not an end – a nothingness – but rather a 'lying down to pleasant dreams' (l. 81). Also, the lines 'Earth, that nourished thee, shall claim / Thy growth, to be resolved to earth again' (ll. 22–3) anticipate Doctor Fletcher's private ritualistic eulogies in 'You'll get the rest of him soon,' the fourth story: 'Nourish him,' the Doctor prays, 'be patient with him because you'll get the rest of him soon' (44). It is, presumably, death understood as in 'Thanatopsis' that allows Mayhew Salkald to die defiantly (10) – to Honey's initial perplexity – and later causes characters such as Doctor Fletcher fiercely to guard their privacy for the sake of personal ritual. Such an understanding of death also foregrounds the disparity between, and the necessary distinguishing of, the public man and the private in such as Mayhew and Fletcher. As Robert Kroetsch observes generally in the passage quoted in the introduction of the present study, 'In Canadian writing, and perhaps in Canadian life, there is an exceptional pressure placed on the individual and the self by the community or society. The self is not in any way Romantic or privileged. The small town remains the ruling paradigm, with its laws and familiarity and conformity. Self and community almost fight to a draw' (*Lovely*, 51). This struggle for balance between the individual and the communal is evident also in *Viger* and *Sunshine Sketches*, though there 'the small town remains the ruling paradigm' unequivocally. As Frye observed, 'a good deal of what goes on in Mariposa may look ridiculous, but the norms or standards against which it looks ridiculous are provided by Mariposa itself' (Conclusion, 237). Although *The Kissing Man* is a story cycle of place as small town in the tradition of the *Sketches* and *Viger*, by the beginning of the contemporary period the individual's right to privacy and personal meaning is accorded equal status. Which is not to say that *Viger* and the *Sketches* dismiss the importance of the private and personal, as witness the scenes of the Little Milliner alone in her room (14) and the pathetic Dean Drone shunned and worrying the meaning of the epithet 'mugwump' (63) for his communally and self-constructed identity.

Another text referred to in *The Kissing Man* is Ecclesiastes, a book which Doctor Fletcher knows 'by heart' (13). It provides yet another way of understanding the view of life and its magical dimension portrayed in the story cycle (and to this purpose, the more the better). Ecclesiastes (the narrator) repeatedly insists in exhaustive ways that man's works are a 'vanity of vanities' (1:2), especially if those works are intended in defiance of individual limitations as regards consciousness of mortality and of the necessity for community under the mysterious ways of God. Thus do 'Thanatopsis' and Ecclesiastes offer, from within the fictional world of *The Kissing Man*, illuminating commentary from older traditions on the fiction's presentation of various modern presumptions, thereby enacting intertextually one important theme of the story cycle itself.

Or perhaps Elliott's vision of the reality of this audacious aspect of *The Kissing Man* – the magical dimension, the spiritual and emotional – can helpfully be glossed with the comment of a later Canadian patriarch of prophetic mien and nineteenth-century sympathies, Robertson Davies, another of Elliott's fellow chroniclers of small Ontario towns and magical dimensions:

> I feel now that I am a person of strongly religious temperament, but when I say 'religious' I mean immensely conscious of powers of which I can have only the dimmest apprehension, which operate by means that I cannot fathom, in directions which I would be a fool to call either good or bad. Now that seems hideously funny, but it isn't really; it is, I think, a recognition of one's position in an inexplicable universe, in which it is not wholly impossible for you to ally yourself with, let us say, positive rather than negative forces, but in which anything that you do in that direction must be done with a strong recognition that you may be very, very gravely mistaken.   (Cameron, 'Robertson Davies,' 41)

Throughout the eleven stories of *The Kissing Man*, characters are shown coming to awareness of a numinous realm (location of those 'powers' of which Davies speaks) that interpenetrates the mundanely material world. In the sixth story, 'The kissing man,' the concretely realized, staid and suffocating environment of Geddes's dry-goods store is disrupted by the spontaneous appearances of the compassionate Kissing Man. But the empathy experienced by the women who contact the Kissing Man is sug-gestively contingent on their awareness of the need for such communally necessary virtues as sympathy, empathy, and compassion.

Initially, 'The Kissing Man' presents adolescent Froody as a cool spec-tator of the faceless customers, her neighbours, who pass through Geddes's (68). The arrival of the Kissing Man is concurrent, then, with Froody's refusal to identify her life with the painful lot of the women she daily serves. The subsequent movement within Froody from apathy to empathy is not explained. Presumably, she changes because she must, as Finn moves towards the old man because he must. In both characters there is trepida-tion and resistance as the encounter looms. Froody's awareness of the Kiss-ing Man's presence in the store breaks slowly upon her. She does not witness his meeting with Mrs Muncey, though she does notice Mrs Muncey's pathetic reaction (69). When Froody sees the Kissing Man with Miss Corvill, she wants to scream out, wants to ask Miss Corvill what the Kissing Man had said. Although at this point Froody still believes that she doesn't care, she reacts by reaching 'out for the faces in the crowded store because a change had come over everything' (71). Froody comes to under-stand that life, especially life as a woman, without the compassionate Kissing Man is a 'barren orderliness,' the patriarchal world of Muncey, Weaver, and Sobel (71), the looming and emotionally sterile world of her convenient relationship with Doug Framingham (72), a world further suggestive of the symbolically violent orderliness of the axe-handle factory and the bowling green that displaces the pond in 'A leaf for everything good.'

The Kissing Man thaws Froody's cool and contained sensuality, perhaps even her emotional frigidity, violating her detached complacency and challenging the illusion of exception and exemption she has enjoyed, and she finally recognizes that she too needs the Kissing Man. She makes an overture to him, and his ominous reply – that she doesn't need him 'yet' – causes Froody to shudder (73). The Kissing Man's prediction vanquishes what remains of Froody's self-satisfied vanity of vanities. She sees that she too will grow old, that she too may be left with loneliness after living and loving (to echo the rhetoric of the Kissing Man). This is the painful, mature knowledge that Froody acquires, the increase of knowledge involving an increase of sorrow. But this passage into maturity also connects Froody to her community, and to none more so than her communal sister women. Revealingly, such knowledge appears already to have been part of the older women's lives, for Miss Corvill is not 'shocked, angry or surprised' (71) by the Kissing Man or his summation of her life as forlorn. Froody may not understand so at the time, but her growing awareness of what amounts to her lack of humanity, as it is presented to her incrementally by the compassionate Kissing Man, is compensation for her loss of a distinctiveness based on physical appearance, aloofness, and naïveté. Viewed in Blakean terms as a movement from Thel-like innocence to experience, Froody's hesitant emergence into the mature and sororal life of the community is 'good.' She will not live in a town without pity.

Presumably, Froody is predisposed to recognize the apparitional Kissing Man, which corresponds to her awakening to the need for connection and parallels Finn's surfacing faith in the presence of trout in the pond. Where the Kissing Man is the figure of Froody's passage to maturity within community, 'A leaf for everything good' traces the complicated process by which the wider community's compassion, understanding, and faith become submerged, embodied symbolically in trout, and retrieved by Finn. According to the old man who sits daily by the pond and has 'the shape of the town clear in his heart' (75), the willow under which he sits draws from the earth and air the unspoken feelings and frustrated desires of all the townsfolk who come to grieve by the tree. The old man describes the process whereby the trout become an embodiment of the buried life: 'Yes. A leaf of love, a leaf of loneliness, a leaf of regret, a leaf of remorse, a leaf of compassion, a leaf for everything good and forgotten, for everything bad and always here. They fall into the pond and the trout eat them' (78). Belief in the existence of trout so nourished requires faith indeed; the skill to catch one requires patience and a willingness to acknowledge a shared community of joy and pain. The townsfolk deny the presence of trout in the pond, thereby symbolically repressing further those feelings that the trout embody (78, 84). Contrarily, Finn finds himself drawn to the old man, drawn finally by the lure of the possibility of trout in the pond (79). As was the case with the invasive Kissing Man, it would seem that there are instances when the '[other] dimension of existence,' as Duffy describes it, calls to its potential acolytes, though few are chosen.

The use of trout to embody and symbolize mysterious communal knowledge is not original to Elliott. The fish icon was of course the secret sign of catacomb meeting-place for the persecuted early Christian community, and it continues as an emblem of Christ. The folklore of Ireland contains many instances of sacred trout (and other fish) inhabiting enchanted wells and ponds. One such story recounts a prophecy foretelling that 'a man named Finn would be the first to eat of the salmon of knowledge, which swam in the pool of Linn-Fee' (Wood-Martin, 1:109). Here, the fish is a salmon, probably because in Irish legend trout, considered sacred and not eaten, are confined to holy wells. Elliott seems to have fused the functions of trout and salmon, as can be seen from the following instance of the Irish legend:

> The salmon watched the nuts on the hazel, and when they dropped into the water devoured them greedily. Their bellies became spotted with a ruddy mark for every nut they had eaten; on this account the salmon became an object of eager acquisition, for whoever ate one became, immediately, without the trouble of studying, a learned scholar, or an eloquent poet. (Wood-Martin, 1:108)

The trout in 'A leaf for everything good' are not eaten, though the old man claims they would be the 'best eating in the world' (80), and, in any case, catching one symbolizes a similar possession of its knowledge. In the Irish folk tale concerning Finn and the salmon of knowledge, there is also a boy and an old man, 'a certain old poet.' But this is where the Irish story (like many legends, myths, and fairy tales) becomes, like *The Kissing Man*, confusing because of doubling, mirroring, disguise, and a paucity of narrative detail.

Briefly then, the old poet is *also* named Finn, and he fishes in the pool of

Linn-Fee 'every day from morn till night' until he catches the salmon. Along comes Demna, a boy fleeing his enemies, who is actually the legendary Finn MacCool in disguise. Finn, the old poet, gives the disguised Finn MacCool the promising salmon to cook, charging him not to eat or even to taste it, because the old man knows that the first to do so will be given the power of second sight. As Finn MacCool is broiling the fish, a blister rises on its side. He breaks the blister with his thumb, scalds the thumb and sticks it into his mouth, consequently acquiring his 'tooth of knowledge' and depriving the old poet of the prophetic prize. Thus Finn MacCool acquires the gifts of prophecy and divination, but 'there appears to have been some sort of ceremony used ... and it would seem that the process was attended with pain, so that it was only in very solemn and trying occasions he put his thumb under his tooth of knowledge' (Wood-Martin, 1:109).

Obviously, Elliott has drawn respectfully, in high Modern manner, on the Irish legend for the deep structuring of 'A leaf for everything good' (as, more obviously, he uses the Old Testament story of usurping Jacob and stolid Esau in 'When Doctor Fletcher was a boy'). But he has also altered and adapted the Irish legend to his own purposes. For instance, the old man in Elliott's story is eager to have Finn understand, and to live his life according to, the essence of what the trout embody: that something more important than the practical – the intuitive, the emotional, the spiritual. And the trout in 'A leaf for everything good' are associated with the spiritual-emotional well-being of the community rather than with the prophecy of grand historical events such as the outcome of battles, though both nonetheless share this basic text of the young male hero's initiatory relation to his community. Perhaps what Elliott's Finn learns, what the fish and Finn finally come to embody together, is closer to Finn's meaning in Joyce's use of the legend in *Finnegans Wake*: Finn as the figure of dormant culture, who incorporates and dreams the potential future of his people, involving the possibility of cultural continuance until a greater 'awakening.' As I have remarked earlier in this study, in Canadian literature, A.M. Klein's drowned poet is another such figure, as is Al Purdy's horse and rider in 'The Cariboo Horses' another mythic figure of cultural loss and potential retrieval:

> clopping in silence under toy mountains
> dropping sometimes and
>   lost in the dry grass
>   golden oranges of dung

(Being Alive, 72)

Geoff Hancock has argued that 'magic realists disrupt history ... by placing Biblical myths, timeless myths and pagan allusions at the service of the narrative' (44). And certainly Elliott partakes of magic realist practice in his destabilizing use of elements from myth and fable. But he is not intent on disrupting a Canadian history that he represents neither in nightmarish terms, as in Joyce's vision, nor in politically violent terms, as in the visions of South American magic realists. Rather, in *The Kissing Man* Elliott opens a strange fictional space for the recovery of the repressed emotional and forgotten spiritual dimensions of small town life, without which vital attributes the human community verges on becoming, to borrow Earle Birney's memorable phrase again, a lifeless place haunted by its lack of ghosts. Elliott's strategy is more typically the Canadian way of adapting other cultures' literary techniques to an environment where history and its records are, of necessity, evidence of instructive humanity to be cherished.

Although readers know what Finn MacCool acquires from the fish – the power of prognostication – we do not learn what Elliott's Finn comes to know. We are left finally with our wondering dangling, as it were, into this deceptively simple story. There are nibbles of meaning, certainly, but nothing pendantly paraphrasable (which inability is a literary good). It is possible that Finn, like Honey Salkald before him, learns something about the exclusive, repressive underside of small town life; but unlike Honey, who boldly takes possession of the family farm, Finn, without a caring family, leaves the town. And his departure, taken after painstakingly landing the culturally packed fish, may constitute the story cycle's most unfavourable prophecy for the small town, comparable to the implications of 'No. 68 Rue Alfred de Musset' in *Viger* and the three stories on dispiriting Mariposan religion. Readers must of course make do only with what the narrator tells them in his enigmatic manner, this narrator whom Duffy has described as 'wise and wise-assed' (54). But the lacunal style invites responsive readers to imagine content and meaning into the narrative gaps. To take but one example, we might speculate that Finn achieves what the old man had achieved, 'the shape of the town clear in his heart,' as opposed to muddled in his head. Finn was always more interested in the other dimension of town life – the intangible, the immaterial. He had 'other things' on his mind, things opposed to school, to 'algebra or anything like that' (76). In such an imaginative decoding process, readers of *The Kissing Man* are helped by closely observing the process of Finn learning to fish – by attending to his 'close fishing,' so to speak – first of all by noticing what Finn notices as he angles for the elusive trout (80).

His coming to awareness of the trout's significance recalls Froody's growing consciousness of the Kissing Man's presence in the preceding story. When Finn fishes with a coachman fly, he notices for the first time 'the slight movement of the water in the direction of the dam' (84). He switches to worm bait and perceives that the pond is visually penetrable only to a point. Finn learns that what appears at first to be a shallow, stagnant pond is, upon contemplation, revelatory of a Heraclitian universe in process and, signifiantly, he recognizes this truth while employing the more organic bait. This is perhaps the primary lesson of all small town fictions, from *Viger* to *As for Me and My House* and beyond: pay close attention, there is more here than meets 'the careless eye' (as *Sunshine Sketches* [2] calls it). Later, Finn loses track of linear time while fishing (85), freed momentarily from such temporal traps as school and a future on the linear axe-handle-factory line. These discoveries are not arrived at by a logical process, nor does Finn intellectualize them. He senses in an almost precognitive manner: 'He could feel them [the tree roots] under him and he could feel the process of taking from the earth.' Only then does he begin to make the discovery meaningful, as real to him as the trout are to the old man, as both see with the inner eye: 'He *saw* a girl sitting under the willow, crying, and if he closed his eyes he could *see* her tears falling on the clay. He *looked* up and *saw* the top branches and it came to him. He *heard* a noise behind. He turned and *saw* ...' (85, emphasis added). As many of the other stories show, in *The Kissing Man* the primary sensing organ is the heart, and only after it has been kick-started (as happens in 'What do the children mean?' [106]) can the senses truly perceive the world in that visionary way whereby Blake saw the sun as a singing heavenly host.

With Finn, the process is, as it is with Froody, a gradual discovery and confirmation of the existence of an immaterial, emotionally repressed, sometimes magical dimension to life in the small town. For Froody, the agent of discovery is the Kissing Man; for Finn, the agents are the old man and the trout. In other stories a similar device, or symbol, is used to bring characters into contact with the invisibly spiritual or buried emotional life of the town, thereby strengthening communal bonds across time. The emphasis is usually on remembering (uncovering and recovering), preserving, and passing on. This theme is set forth in the first story of the cycle, 'An act of piety,' in Honey's ability 'to keep what was good and pass it on.' Honey's triumph over time is possible only after a mining of the past to make connection with the pioneer farming tradition figured in Mayhew Salkald and to uncover what in Tessie's life was not right, what was in fact anti-communal. Thus the 'good' that Honey wishes to possess, safeguard, and pass on is not simply the pleasant but also the painful: this is the 'old truth fresh and almost complete' – *almost* because it is always being revisioned in the present for the future. Similarly, the old man by the pond does not instruct Finn to hook only the pleasurable: he wishes him particularly to grasp what is painfully lonely about the lives led by his neighbours. (The epigraph to Sheila Watson's *The Double Hook* comes inevitably to mind: 'when you / fish for the glory / you catch the / darkness too.' And as I have shown, Carr portrays Klee Wyck learning in her quest for totems something very similar about nature's darkness and light.) Hermetic as some of the foregoing must sound at times, Elliott's fiction makes of the mysterious an event to be known: following the teaching of his legendary guiding figure, Finn takes on faith the old man's knowledge of the mysterious trout's presence: 'Believe? I know,' the old man claims (78). And so Finn catches the fish.

In 'A room, a light for love,' the fifth story of the cycle, Alison Kennedy's chandelier is another such symbol of an individual's and a community's need for continuing connection over time (see C. Thomas, 102). The chandelier functions as container and cue for the communal good that should be passed on. It suggests that such memorial objects are not simply invested with symbolic significance: they are extensions in space and time of the spiritual and emotional life that partakes of the mysterious realm inhabited by such as the Kissing Man and Finn's trout. Elliott's conception of the symbolic chandelier of 'A room, a light for love' is in fact ideally, even quite literally, Coleridgean, where 'a Symbol ... is characterized by a translucence of the Special in the Individual or of the General in the Especial or of the Universal in the General. Above all by the translucence of the Eternal through and in the Temporal. It always partakes of the Reality which it renders intelligible; and while it enunciates the whole, abides itself as a living part in that Unity, of which it is representative' (*Collected*, 30). Clearly.

In the first few pages of 'A room, a light for love,' such words as 'new' and 'fresh' are repeated to suggest that there is always need for change for one's own and others' sakes (though not for the sake of change itself), or a need to make new uses of established institutions and traditions. Comments and reflections imply that Alison was not fulfilled in her pre-war relationship with husband Gerry Kennedy, that she was perhaps on her way to becoming like one of the oppressed and disillusioned women of 'The kissing man.' But Alison takes decisive action. She remodels the Queen's Hotel into a place where her wide circle of friends can meet; she buys a new chandelier and transforms it into a symbol of her heart and her community's submerged longings. The chandelier, recalling the willow tree in 'A leaf for everything good,' contains for a spell all the unspoken or seldom mentioned feelings of those who frequent the Kennedys' parties; it is described as 'shining down and drawing to its crystal beads all of what they felt' (63). Also, by remodelling the Queen's, the regal and feminist Alison 'discovered the pride in herself, the confidence, and the idea of control was new and compelling' (53–4).

In remodelling the hotel, Alison renews herself as well as revitalizes the town, because she and her hotel become the hub of a communal social circuit. Hotel and woman are effectively identified as extensions of each other: 'She sort of flowed into the grey doors and they sort of flowed her on into the red wallpaper and the cream ceiling so that it was all of a piece' (56). The parties that she gives at the Queen's function as a communal catalyst, strengthening bonds: families 'who never had anything to do with each other outside' are drawn together; pretentious behaviour and social status are forgotten for the moment (57). Alison makes people such as Doug Framingham and Jeth Geddes feel simultaneously distinctive and bound one to the other through her, her hotel and its chandelier. Doug feels (all innocently) that his love for Alison 'seemed more right because it involved more than two people' (59).

With her hotel and chandelier Alison finds a means of allying herself with the forces for good, which are presented here in opposition to the isolation of small-town repressiveness and, again, the entropic effects of time itself: the story is full of parties and fond nostalgia. Alison fights and wins her personal woman's war against these enemies of community while her husband is off fighting his country's war (in a manner that recalls the empowered women of Sime's 'Munitions'). In the time she has, Alison accomplishes her vaguely stated, but inarguably communal, goal: 'other things, not the private things necessarily, but what stops the loneliness' (57). She fabricates from the material at hand a private ritual that acknowledges the existence and importance of the emotional life of the individuals who make up her community. Each individual in Alison's wide circle of affection (to borrow again the title of Duncan Campbell Scott's last book) is represented by a crystal bead in the chandelier, and she smashes the appropriate bead as each old acquaintance passes on (in this story and cycle the euphemism is apt). The entire chandelier is smashed when Alison dies, and the hotel is in decline, at the mercy of trendy antique dealers. But such material disintegration is inevitable. Through her accommodating spirit and its symbol, the chandelier, Alison achieves a distinctly human victory over time and entropy. Paradoxically (and not so paradoxically, if we think of such rituals as Last Suppers, Communion, or more anciently of gods dismembered), the destruction of the chandelier and hotel is necessary to the connections and continuity Alison forges: 'The chandelier was destroyed, so the thread of memory had been established' (62); or, as Gerry and Doug reminisce after Alison's death, 'each memory began with the chandelier' (62, 64). Their remembering is important not only for their own peace of mind but for future generations, as Doug observes: 'It matters to the new ones coming along to hear our noises' (62) – an observation which works again as both an illustration of the book's epigraph from T.S. Eliot and a gloss on its conservative theme of the implied contract between the dead, the living, and the unborn.

Remembering is accorded priority indeed in *The Kissing Man*, as are the symbols and rituals that facilitate it. The first story, 'An act of piety,' establishes the memorial function of the cycle when Honey Salkald is forced to remember all that he could about his grandparents in order 'to make the old truth fresh and almost complete, ... to keep what was good and pass it on' (12). Towards the end of that story, 'the past was in [Honey], never to be forgotten or ignored' (12). And earlier in the story, when Honey '[crouches] over a deep well, waiting for the water to settle so he could see his reflection,' the past and memory are seen to be constituent and constitutive of self-identity: 'Memories flowed through him, memories of his grandmother' (7). The functioning of memory is the subtext of the third story, 'The listeners.' This story employs the ritual of blowing the contents out of eggs, and then positions the symbol of the blown eggs to convey the emptiness of a marriage and the effects that the ritual, the symbol, and the bad marriage have on the children – particularly on the workings of Young Audie's memory.

Mrs Audie Seaton was once a girl who 'talked with spirit and wondered and asked questions and told how she felt about things' (32). She was once full of vigour, a compassionate girl who, anticipating the gnomic utterances of Finn's wise old man and Froody's Kissing Man (as well as the titular figure in 'The man who lived out loud'), viewed people as 'waiting to die, waiting to be loved, waiting to love, waiting for the loneliness' (32). She was a girl determined not to be a 'lump,' not to marry a lump, and not to raise lumpy children. Yet she ends up surrounded, in her view, by human marble bags and talking to hens – the ostensible 'listeners' of the title – and eventually to her children. By the end of 'The listeners,' Mrs Seaton is herself a blown egg, an emptied shell. She concludes of her desire for intimate connection with her husband, 'It's all gone out of me. All out of me' (39). A blown egg is the perfect symbol for what becomes of the Seaton marriage, and as such the egg functions as something of a negative to Alison's positive chandelier. An intact shell without its meat suggests form without content – *is* form without content – symbolizing the show of a marriage without the emotional sustenance that Mrs Seaton craves. However, she is as much the cause of her situation as are her rural isolation, hard times, and her distracted husband, Big Audie.

As a girl Mrs Seaton had viewed her town as a self-sufficient entity, believing that there was no call for contact with the outside world. This xenophobic inclination leads her to marry Big Audie Seaton (town handyman, something of a *spiritus loci*), hoping to achieve with Big Audie a connubial self-sufficiency similar to her perception of the town's self-contained perfection. But necessity – babies, economic reality – infuses Big Audie with preoccupied determination for material gain, leaving Mrs Seaton waiting for her husband to live up to her ideal of a husband as one who shares with his wife matters of the heart. It could be that the implicit cause of what becomes a failed marriage is Mrs Seaton's exclusive vision of community, family, marriage; if this is the case, her failure is a personal failing which repeats and expands upon Proud Tessie Salkald's racism in the first story, 'An act of piety.' But the key word here is *waiting*. Mrs Seaton's attitude leaves her passive, waiting for her own self-contained and preordained vision of the world to materialize self-satisfyingly. She never acts or interacts in the necessarily creative way demonstrated by such as Alison. She never makes overtures to Big Audie, as did Finn to the old man. She waits: '"I mustn't bother dear Audie now, the way he's so worried over the potatoes. Pretty nearly a year now. The time is long gone and past. Speaking from the heart isn't hard. He can do it. We can. He'll get over the potatoes. He'll be feeling better. I'll wait."' (35). The immediately preceding story, 'When Jacob Fletcher was a boy,' suggests at its conclusion that Big Audie, who seems to have little intrinsic purpose in that story other than to anticipate his important role in 'The listeners,' would have responded to an overture from his wife; there, he comforts Jacob Fletcher, then responds to Jacob's thanks, '"Boy, I always like to stop and talk. You remember that"' (26). His revelation functions as an interpretive cue – as something for readers to remember – for 'The listeners.'

Furthermore, Mrs Seaton's only creative actions and communications involve relations with her hens, which leads to the miscreant ritual of blowing eggs. She pours out her troubles to the hens rather than bothering Big Audie with what she feels are neurotic impracticalities. When she finally resigns herself to her uncommunicative lot with Big Audie, she attempts to ensure that her children will know her situation and, supposedly, benefit from the example of her tribulations. So she opens her disappointed heart to her children as each successively blows the meat from an egg. By this means his blown egg becomes for Young Audie, the eldest boy, the symbol of an emotionally complex experience and, subsequently, the mnemonic cue for his own confused retrieval of what happened.

The mysterious process by which the impressions of disappointment and betrayal in his mother's mind find their way into Young Audie's memory parallels the movement in 'A leaf for everything good' from repressed emotions to tree to leaf to trout to Finn. The hens that are privy to the progress of Mrs Seaton's disillusionment become, like the willow tree, mediums for the retention and transmission of those troubles. The meat in the eggs they eventually lay is, like the leaves of the willow, the substance of Mrs Seaton's disappointment: this, then, is what is blown from the egg and into Young Audie's forming memory. The blown egg, like Finn's trout (and Alison's chandelier), becomes a symbol, an emblem of, and means to, a shared experience. Appropriately, 'The listeners' contains Elliott's most disturbing and haunting metaphor for the process of recollection: a swamp in which memories, 'the bad ones, the unexplained ones, ... pop up to the surface like marsh gas' (29, reminiscent of the bottomless marsh across from the Desjardins in *Viger*). Young Audie's memory of blowing the egg is, for him, 'a pure memory,' recalling an experience he believes he 'really remembered' (29). 'He remembered crying, gasping for air and hiccuping in limp despair. ... That was Young Audie's memory of it' (30). But that is not what happened. Young Audie is actually, strangely enough, an early instance in Canadian fiction of what was to become known in late twentieth-century therapeutic circles and courtrooms as 'false memory syndrome.'

In a kind of memorial transference, Young Audie has confused his reaction at the time of the egg-blowing with that of his youngest brother. At the conclusion of 'The listeners,' the narrator states that, rather than crying, Young Audie had 'smiled a little' as his mother told of her disappointments; that, rather than having trouble blowing the egg, 'it was done quickly' (38). Young Audie has somehow remembered as his own the experience of his youngest brother, who did cry and had trouble blowing the egg (38). The event was markedly traumatic for the child, and Young Audie, who had been waiting and listening nearby – subtly becoming thereby the key titular reference – empathizes with his brother's trauma: 'Young Audie was waiting and he put his arm around the shoulders of the youngest boy for a moment' (38). This simple gesture of sympathy involving physical contact has mysteriously effected – in the way memory works – the memorial transference. Young Audie's smiling during his own participation in the perverse ritual is truly misleading, or rife with anxiety, for he is also absorbing more of his mother's disappointment than he knows. His memory is not a 'pure memory,' but a bubble of marsh gas, versus Alison's bauble of light, haunting him later with an emotional truth truer than any factual account of the incident or of his parents' bad marriage could convey. As this story shows, memory in *The Kissing Man* can be a powerfully creative faculty, and a revisionist one; and even though here the memory is false, it nonetheless has given Young Audie insight to a deeper truth of his family life than his mother had intended. Unlike Honey's ritualistic act of piety, Alison's chandelier, and Finn's trout, the blown egg adds to the pain and confusion of Young Audie's life. As memorial ritual, the blowing of the egg fails to connect Young Audie or his mother to a greater good, whether an enhancing emotional life, familial life, or communal life. As symbol, the blown egg symbolizes failure, even the retributive and revealing failure of manipulated, mistaken memory itself. Equally important, the fact that Young Audie actually recalls his youngest brother's memory as his own argues that the members of a family, and by extension those of the larger community, may be connected in mysterious ways indeed, empathetically, even through a collective unconscious.

Obviously, the fashioning of such symbols and rituals to facilitate memories, to solidify family, community, and continuity is the centre of *The Kissing Man* cycle, which is why the practice is introduced in its first story with respect to a key point of generational transference (at a transitional time, in an interstitial space) in the Salkald family. Every story of the cycle can rewardingly be read for the ways in which it shows various memorial processes at work through ritual and symbol, individually and collectively, for good and ill. But I will look briefly only at one more, 'You'll get the rest of him soon,' before turning to the return story of the cycle, the prototypically titled 'The way back.'

Doctor Fletcher, like Honey, Alison, Finn, and Mrs Seaton, demonstrates strange awareness of a realm beyond the material and practical. He, too, needs to achieve and maintain connection with this dimension through a private and idiosyncratic ritual that simultaneously subsumes the private and personal in the communal and, indeed, connects these to larger Judeo-Christian traditions. Doctor Fletcher, like Honey and Froody a recurrent character in the story cycle, is portrayed as a conservatively proud man, possessing 'pride of origin and unchange' (41), a man whose loyalties are to tradition and his sense of the connectedness of all life in what is essentially an organic vision. His attitude is at once personal and communal, as was Alison's, though there are suggestions that Doctor Fletcher, like Proud Tessie Salkald and Mrs Seaton, guards his privacy too exclusively. His house is walled in and 'he [keeps] to himself.' 'I got a life of my own outside of babying and doctoring, he said, and that life's got to be lived else I'm nobody' (45). But clearly unlike Proud Tessie and Mrs Seaton, he lives close to the body of his community, near the Fair Ground toilets, and he is a small-town doctor – there at birth, there at death. Further, his belief in the reality and importance of life's other dimension is expressed more optimistically than is Mrs Seaton's 'waiting for the loneliness' (32) or the Kissing Man's *'living, loving and loneliness'* (70). In the practice of his private ritual, Doctor Fletcher can also be viewed as a clerical medicine man, this doctor who is described twice as being like an 'Anglican Minister' (44, 46). By means of his ritual, he strives to connect the newborn male members of his community to the vaguely defined entity (a kind of Gaea figure) of his enigmatic addresses. Male members only, because Doctor Fletcher's ritual involves burying a foreskin, that synecdochic figure for 'the rest of him.'[10] Strange as this is, Fletcher nonetheless insists on the value and necessity of his weird practice. He claims that 'boys stand a better chance, ... especially the ones I look after' (43). But in his efforts to maintain this connection, Fletcher is thwarted from within the community by the spitefulness of 'the Lodge' officers, Muncey, Weaver, and Sobel, the three men who later figure as oppressors of women in 'The kissing man' and here harass Doctor Fletcher and undermine his position in the community.

There is in 'You'll get the rest of him soon' an opposition between Doctor Fletcher's personal ritual for communal-spiritual purposes and the social ritual of these Lodge brothers. Similar oppositions – which can most broadly be described as between the material and the spiritual – recur throughout *The Kissing Man*: between Tessie and Mayhew Salkald, between Mrs Seaton and Big Audie, between Alison and entropic time itself, between men and women in 'The kissing man,' between Finn and his father, to mention only those already discussed. In 'You'll get the rest of him soon,' Muncey, Weaver, and Sobel want to initiate Doctor Fletcher into the Lodge, which would be to bring him more fully into the ersatz ritualistic life of the small town. But Fletcher desires only to be left alone to practise his private ritual, initiating newborn boys into his *tempus fugit* vision of the life cycle. He views Mrs Scorrel's baby as 'another chance,

another novice, another initiate' and smiles to himself at the correspondence of terminology between his ritual and the Lodge's initiation rite
(48). When the doctor adamantly refuses the Lodge brothers, they have
him fired from the hospital. Prevented from delivering and circumcising,
removed from his source of foreskins, Doctor Fletcher is himself cut off
from his self-styled ritualistic function and connection with the numinous
dimension. He dies and enters into that other realm, we may suppose.[11]

'You'll get the rest of him soon' concludes with Froody bursting into
clichéd 'terrible tears' upon hearing news of Doctor Fletcher's death (48).
Just why Froody cries remains a mystery, but crying is the common reaction in *The Kissing Man* when characters experience at an (apparently)
non-verbal level a spiritual realm that they had not known about or had
intuited vaguely, or when they confront an emotional dimension that they
had previously denied or suppressed. There is scarcely a story that does
not contain at least one instance of bewildered tears. In 'When Jacob
Fletcher was a boy,' wild Esau cries at the realization that he is losing civilized Jacob to the town from which he is excluded (18; as in the first
story, 'An act of piety,' and the penultimate story, 'The commonplace,'
here prejudicial exclusivity is shown to be the unattractive underside of
community solidarity). Young Audie Seaton believes that he cried when
confronted with his mother's tribulations, though, in fact, he'd not. Alison cries because of the burden of her awareness of the transitory nature
of what she loves most (52). Froody cries again after witnessing the Kissing Man with Miss Corvill and intimating, presumably, her own lack of
compassion. Finn cries when frustrated in his efforts to comprehend what
the old man is trying to show him (81). Spinster Janey, in 'The man who
lived out loud,' cries because she thinks that her private ritual with 'John
something,' a drifter who wants in to town life, has been manipulated by
her brother (98). And Honey Salkald, in 'The commonplace,' cries in isolated impotence when confronted by all that Bertram Sunbird represents
in his role as figurative cuckolder (122). In *The Kissing Man* not-so-idle
tears are the initial and sometimes only response of circumscribed human
intelligence and sensibility when frustrated in its exposure to, and/or
overwhelmed failure to comprehend, the repressed emotional life, the
spiritual, the mysterious.

But, needless to say, this spiritual reality in *The Kissing Man* does much
more than evoke tears, reveal inadequacy and loneliness, permit exclusion
and false memory, and expose ignorance. On the individual level, connection with this mysterious dimension of existence allows Doctor Fletcher
to know, in 'When Jacob Fletcher was a boy,' that the twins he's deliver-

ing will be males, and the old man in 'A leaf for everything good' to know that trout still swim in a supposedly fished-out pond; it allows Alison in 'A room, a light for love' to anticipate when an old acquaintance is about to pass on. Collectively experienced, this other dimension makes possible the changing cohesiveness of the small town over time: it makes of place a human community. In fictionalizing such a vision, Elliott set himself a huge task indeed in *The Kissing Man*. Such a grand ambition helps explain and excuse the story cycle's determinedly minimalist, annoyingly gestural, unrelievedly enigmatic, maddeningly lacunal, strange style. The stories do show clearly, however, the *modus operandi* between the mundane and the numinous dimension: ritual, symbol, memory, and imagination, working through the senses to the heart. These means are seen operating in patiently fishing and observing Finn; and again when Johnson Mender in 'What do the children mean?' envisions his son's emotional awakening through the agency of a child 'tugging at his ear and lifting up his eyelids and kicking him where his heart is to make it go' (106). For that matter, the other dimension's anti-rationalist nature bestows real presence on a Kissing Man in a dry-goods store and an apparitional Johnson Mender strolling into town to requisition newborns at the baby agent's. In the final story of the cycle, the return story 'The way back,' this mysterious, numinous realm makes possible the seemingly ageless 'grinder man,' the blade sharpener who was 'a gnarled, brown old man' (126) when Dan was born and is still vigorously plying his trade at the weaning of Dan's third child (134).

The theme of the necessity of ritual, symbol, and memory for maintaining contact with the spiritual and emotional dimension receives cumulative treatment in *The Kissing Man*'s return story. Well titled as a return story, 'The way back' also functions within the cycle in typical return-story manner, including in its narrative references to many of the preceding stories' key symbols, rituals, and characters: Doctor Fletcher delivers Dan; a blown ostrich egg helps illustrate Dan's alienation as a result of his father's dismissal of the grinder man ritual (127); Dan's father recalls Finn's hard father in the former's belief that 'work's what matters nowadays. Nothing else' (128); Dan avoids the old man who sits by the pond because the old man knows too much; Dan marries Mayhew Salkald's granddaughter; and it is Mayhew, the good patriarch, who returns in this return story to insist that 'there is always hope of return' (132). By recalling preceding stories, the return stories of cycles suggest that 'the way back' is accomplished not only by an individual's decision and actions but by the co-operation of the entire community. Closing its version of the hermeneutic circle, the cycle's return story positions us to read its images, symbols, and rituals for their cumulative value in the context of the whole story cycle, to read (or reread) each story in the context of the completed cycle, and to consider the whole cycle in terms of each reconsidered preceding story.

Here, 'The way back' recounts Dan's struggle to find a way to reconnect with the small-town community of *The Kissing Man*. His father had severed the connection by ignoring the local tradition of having the grinder man stand outside the house where a birth is taking place. Dan's father did so because he was an overly practical man, bluntly cutting (without the blade-sharpener's assistance) his family off from the community. He dismissed his wife's warning that this ritual practice is for the benefit of the father (presumably the mother's connection is primarily biological – birthing, nursing, weaning – a suggestion which helps explain Doctor Fletcher's focus on boys in 'You'll get the rest of him soon'), knowing she is right, yet holding to his rationalist belief that 'it was a story, mystery, something concealed, a feeling. That was bad' (128). Of course, these are precisely the intangible – and here suggestively self-reflexive – markers of *The Kissing Man*'s exploration of, and hope for, a meaningful personal and communal life: that is, for the way to the good.

The result of the father's wilful denial was that his son, Dan, grew up a weird and alienated boy, one who selfishly hoarded the potentially rich gift of a blown egg, dangled a spider over his bed (thereby constructing an exclusionary parody of Alison's chandelier) and screamed when his father attempted to take it down (127). Regardless of damage done, grown Dan somehow wins through to the realization that his father's break with tradition was not, as his father had insisted, 'a question of fashion or times changing' (130). Dan understands, as his father would not, the gestural momentousness of the grinder man's presence and the reasons for his own alienation: 'Thing like that,' he reflects, 'if you don't have a feeling for it, it'll separate you from the kids in school' (129). Here again, 'feeling,' as opposed to rationalizing, is priorized. Dan realizes, too, that his father's attitude is 'the difference between the life of [his] father and the life of the heart,' the heart which is the chief sensing organ in *The Kissing Man*. Dan resolves: 'I want the life of the heart and Mr. Salkald says there is hope, there is a way back. This is the connection' (134).

Dan re-establishes connection with his town by choosing to participate in communal life as it is ritualized in the inexplicable grinder man tradition. By so choosing he contributes to the strength of his family and the whole community, town and farming districts alike. He has the grinder man sharpen some tools, a few of which once belonged to region patriarch Mayhew Salkald. Dan's wife then places Mayhew's scythe under the bed of the baby she is weaning, thereby suggesting through this temporal symbol the continuity of birth, life and death, and connection across the generations. As T.S. Eliot states in *Notes towards the Definition of Culture*, 'Unless this reverence for past and future is cultivated in the home, it can never be more than a verbal convention in the community' (42). In a sense, it is the baby who accomplishes the reconciliation between Dan and his community, and between Dan and the timeless, mysterious realm. Interestingly, this baby also bears witness to Johnson Mender's belief, in the third to last story, 'What do the children mean?,' that children are another means to the way back – perhaps because they are the living way ahead in this book where 'time future [is] contained in time past' (Eliot, *Complete*, 117).[12] The grinder man ritual – like all ritual – connects, here enabling necessary rites of passage and communal coherence.

For all its strangeness, the grinder man tradition also constitutes a simple ritual, as simple as tending a grave, blowing an egg, catching a fish, or, for that matter, as quotidian as eating bread and drinking wine. In *The Kissing Man*'s return story, it is the implications of the quite conscious decision to participate that gesture towards a complex communal unconsciousness (and towards unabashed metaphysical signification). The result of Dan's reverential participation in the domestic grinder man ritual is the re-establishment of familial harmony, the ascription of primary importance to the emotional and the intuitive, and the recognition of a nurturing interdependence of the individual and the community. By recalling various key elements of preceding stories, this return story argues fictionally that the individual's fuller life is only possible within the cohesive community, albeit a community whose cohesiveness is at times double-hooked by an unattractive exclusivity and repressiveness. This fictional argument for an essentially conservative and humanist vision of independent interdependence is made, too, by those earlier Canadian story cycles of place, Scott's *In the Village of Viger* and Leacock's *Sunshine Sketches of a Little Town*. Despite its late-Modernist and proleptically postmodernist panache, *The Kissing Man* – perhaps the last Canadian story cycle focused exclusively on place as small town – continues into the contemporary period the Canadian vision of social organization that priorizes the community over the individual, explores the relationship between individual identity and place, and recovers the value of the individual's place within community.

Thus the eleven stories of *The Kissing Man* present a vision of Canadian (Ontario) small-town life at mid-century that is stroboscopic and fragmentary in its perception of what is passing and lost, a vision that is uncompromising in its perception of life's pain and tragedy. But the book as a whole, employing to masterful advantage the recursive dynamics of the short story cycle, insists fictionally on the reality of a spiritual dimension, a numinous realm that, when acknowledged and experienced, bestows a sense of continuity and a shared community of pain and evanescent joy. Despite its focus on the pain of frustration and denial, despite its elegiac tone, *The Kissing Man* is a work of affirmation. It holds against its *tempus fugit* perceptions a steady vision of meaningful continuity, of time past and time future as ever-present in the rituals and bloodlines of a community. There are characters in these stories (Tessie Salkald, Muncey, Weaver, Sobel, Finn's father, Dan's father) whose attitude is exemplified in Dan's father's view of the grinder man's significance as 'a story, mystery, something concealed, a feeling. That was bad.' But there are also characters in these stories who recognize and honour, as does *The Kissing Man* short story cycle itself, an implied contract between the dead, the living, and the unborn. Mayhew Salkald, his grandson Honey, Doctor Fletcher, Alison, Dan, and others affirm the mystery in the mundane, the importance of ritual and symbol, and the primacy of informed memory for keeping and passing on the good.

5

No Honey, I'm Home: Alice Munro's *Who Do You Think You Are?*

Helen Hoy's account of Alice Munro's revisions to what would become *Who Do You Think You Are?* instantly achieved something of legendary status in Canadian publishing lore. The revision's chief features, earlier recounted by Munro to J.R. (Tim) Struthers, are the eleventh-hour radical transformation from a book of stories variously divided between the characters Rose and Janet to a book about Rose only; the rapid translation of Janet stories into Rose stories; and, not least to a professional writer, the monetary expense to Munro of making extensive changes to a book in galley proofs ('Material,' 29–32).[1] As Walter Martin observes, 'these changes and revisions ... bear witness to Alice Munro's exacting artistic conscience and her devoted commitment to her work' (101). Certainly they do, and it is worth adding that this literary artist's devoted attention to the final form of *Who Do You Think You Are?* occurred with the only fully formed short story cycle she has written.[2] In this last chapter, I want briefly to contextualize the masterful *Who Do You Think You Are?* in the continuum of Canadian short story cycles, to provide a fuller description of its complex form as story cycle, and finally to offer a reading that addresses the question of selfhood and identity aggressively posed in the book's riddling title. In doing so, I will pay closest attention to two stories: the second, 'Privilege,' and the last, 'Who Do You Think You Are?,' because 'Privilege' fictionally analyses the beginning of romantic-sexual love in Rose, and because the title story takes her home. In imagining a contemporary solution to the endemically Canadian riddle of identity, *Who Do You Think You Are?* argues fictionally for the potentially definitive importance of love and for the abiding residence of affirmation in the place of origin.

As I suggested in the introduction to the present study, there will always be overlap in story cycles belonging to either of the two categories of place and character, especially in the contemporary period with cycles of character, such as Richler's *The Street* and Laurence's *A Bird in the House*. *Who Do You Think You Are?* is in fact a supreme example of a contemporary story cycle of character wherein place as small town, Hanratty, is recovered to play a definitive role in the formation of character and, later, the affirmation of identity. Somewhat fortuitously, then, the final short story cycle discussed at length in this study of Canadian short story cycles brings together most unifyingly the subject's two main categories of place and character. *Who* remains, though, like *Klee Wyck*, the story cycle's version of female künstlerroman, being about the growth of Rose the actress, and not about Hanratty per se. The stories are about Hanratty secondarily and only in so far as that place is germane to understanding the development and maturity of Rose. In the context of Canadian short story cycles of character, *Who* can be seen as part of a tradition that begins with Grove's *Over Prairie Trails*, and includes such other works as *Klee Wyck*, Laurence's *A Bird in the House*, Clark Blaise's *A North American Education*, and King's *Medicine River*. Like Grove's and Carr's personas, Rose travels from home in quest of herself, is tested, experiences failure, loss, ultimately enjoys some success, and temporarily returns to her place of origin in something of a compromised and compromising frame of mind. In doing so, the Grove persona, Klee Wyck, and Rose can be viewed as expressing their authors' variously contingent answers to the key modern question of self-identity contained in *Who*'s titular riddle, as well as illustrating the traditionally Canadian engagement with the question of individual and national identity in relation to place.[3]

The question posed in the title must of course be squarely addressed in any serious discussion of *Who Do You Think You Are?* Although the cycle is also about representation in art and literature (see Heble, 105), Munro's fiction is not only, or even chiefly, metafiction, that self-reflexive trope, indulgence in which the reactionary John Gardner dismissed as 'jazzing around' (82). Alice Munro's fiction is so overwhelmingly realistic and representational that its questions about the presence of a centred self in the fictional Rose should make us wonder, surely, about the same in ourselves. Is Rose presented finally by Munro as having won through to a stable sense of self? (Is stability of self-identity a thing to be desired? Robert Kroetsch's essay, 'No Name Is My Name,' offers one interesting answer in the negative.) But if the answer is yes to the first question, how does Rose manage it? Or does Rose *manage* it? Is fictional selfhood not perhaps the mystery gift of her providential author, a compensatory send-off, something like the surprising bounty of silver that pours forth from a pay-phone slot on the fairy-tale mountain in the aptly titled 'Providence' (149)?[4] Or is Rose at the end of the story cycle the self-deluding figure representative of those who hold similarly essentialist notions of autonomous selfhood? In its recurrent use of acting and imitation as a metaphor of self-construction (to say nothing more, as the present chapter does not, of the question of representation as theme [see Mathews]), *Who Do You Think You Are?* does tend to present characters who are reflections of reflections of reflections, as Rose imitating Milton Homer in the title story is actually imitating Ralph Gillespie imitating Milton Homer, that 'mimic of ferocious gifts and terrible energy' (192), who is himself something of a reflecting emanation of old Hanratty itself. In the mirror in a mirror image, as in the *regressus ad infinitum* and the literary *mise en abîme*, Munro recognizes the difficulties of ultimately condensing, grounding, and centring an ideal of self. And again as I have argued earlier, the short story cycle form, with its various strategies of fragmented coherence, has shown itself well suited to the Modern and postmodern representation of selfhood as a vaporous filter of various internal and external stimuli rather than as the metaphysical ground of presence and meaning – or better suited than the conventional novel, with its implications of continuity, coherence, and totality. As Ajay Heble has observed (though without giving its due to the story cycle form of *Who*), Rose's story is a 'kind of discontinuous history with its own missing chunks of information. By refusing to fill in gaps in time, by leaving out whole sections in the chapters that constitute Rose's life, Munro leaves much unexplained' (117). And further:

> The text is marked by an absence that encompasses worlds of meaning, an absence that – like Munro's rhetoric of supposition and her use of the acting metaphor – lends thematic and structural instability to the stories in the collection. The instability in this instance serves once again to complicate the ontological problem. By refusing to construct narratives of continuity, by, as it were, letting the absences speak, Munro reformulates the volume's central question: just what or who is real? (117–18; see also Blodgett, 94)

Despite the compelling logic of such deconstructive considerations, I will argue and conclude below that Munro in *Who* does present the mature Rose as having achieved more of a stable sense of identity than Heble allows; and, what is as remarkable, Rose does so in relation to place and not to the ideal of a reifying love that she chases around most of the stories of this cycle.

Who Do You Think You Are? is a wonderfully well wrought short story cycle, arguably Munro's best book (*pace* Martin [98–101], who fails to appreciate the purpose of the middle stories). With the exception of Leacock's *Sunshine Sketches*, I can think of no other story cycle so carefully shaped to its purposes. Most obviously, the stories follow Rose's growth from childhood to adolescence to middle age, though there are temporal gaps, slippages, and recurrences which readers would not expect to find in the conventional bildungsroman but which are typical of the story cycle's destabilizing strategies. Martin has described the other obvious feature of the book's structure: its ten stories are divided so as to comprise a beginning, a middle, and an end. The first four stories focus on childhood and adolescence, the next four on Rose's life away from Hanratty, and the final two on her return to her place of origin (Martin, 98). But these two most apparent and conventional structural features can be seen to play both off one another and against readers' expectations: the chronological development is repeatedly disrupted not only by each discrete story but also by those large narrative blocks grouping stories of childhood, adulthood, and middle age;[5] and neither element (chronology or Aristotelian divisions) really accomplishes the illusion of continuity and coherence it usually does in novels. The stories of Rose are experienced by the reader more in stroboscopic flashes and flashbacks than in a steadily growing light, in piled reminiscences of memories in hindsight, with time sometimes looping back on itself like a claustrophobic Möbius strip, and with dead and freshly buried characters popping up in the opening of subsequent stories (as Flo does at the end of 'Spelling' and the beginning of 'Who Do You Think You Are?'). Thus is a life constructed and narrative time manipulated in the contemporary story cycle of character, in a way that ideally marries form and function for the postmodern sensibility.

Further regarding structure, Rose's conservatively circular journey is doubly framed by the question posed in both the book's title and the title of the final story, which is also asked in the first story by her stepmother, Flo (13), and in the return story by her English teacher, Miss Hattie Milton (196). And apart from the chronological development and those large groupings described by Martin, there are many other linkages among stories. For example, the middle section of four stories can be seen to form two groupings of companion pieces. The blatantly consumerist affair of 'Mischief' (see Mathews, 189; and Redekop, 131) follows consequentially from the failure of marriage recounted in 'The Beggar Maid'; that is, in 'Mischief' Rose is commodified in a manner that could be read as poetic justice for the way she uses Patrick in 'The Beggar Maid.' The titles of the final two stories of the middle section, 'Providence' and 'Simon's Luck,' obviously relate them as complementary, or juxtaposed (Heble, 114), stories on such important matters as the limits of self-determination and the role of happenstance in its mystical ('Providence') and mundane ('Simon's Luck') forms.

There may also be a principle of alternation at work in this story cycle (which I suggested is the primary organizational feature of Scott's *Viger*). The theme of the second story, 'Privilege,' the first flowing of Eros, recurs and is developed in the fourth, 'Wild Swans,' with its depiction of an act of complicit molestation, which theme recurs and is developed in the sixth story, 'Mischief,' with its tawdry failed affair and group sex, and is seen again in the eighth story, 'Simon's Luck' – and seen to doom that potentially redemptive relationship. Such Procrustean construing may seem less violent when it is considered that all the other stories of the first eight – 'Royal Beatings,' 'Half a Grapefruit,' 'The Beggar Maid,' and 'Providence' – are not about romantic-sexual relations. 'The Beggar Maid,' about Rose's meeting her husband, may seem to contradict this pattern, but it doesn't: it, like the other three stories in this alternate group – 1, 3, and 7 – is about acting as a means to Rose's empowerment in her search for and shaping of self-identity. All of which is to say, the first eight stories may alternate in exploring two possible avenues to answering the question of the book's title: acting and love. There are yet other possibilities, complementary and enriching, for viewing the organization of stories in *Who Do You Think You Are?* But suffice it to say that it is no wonder Munro was kept up all one weekend and busy for a week, at considerable eventual monetary expense, revising towards the final version of the book (C.S. Ross, 82). Although her first major revision of the 'Rose and Janet' manuscript, which neatly comprised six stories for each, had been to do away with the structural symmetry (Martin, 106) which, with various kinds of rigid ordering, is a *bête noire* of so much of Munro's fiction, it would appear that an organic, architectonic impulse is inherent in this artist, perhaps in all art, and beyond even the masterful Alice Munro's conscious control.

Over all, the stories of *Who* proceed in a way definitive of the story cycle's reliance on what Ingram first called 'the dynamic patterns of recurrence and development' (20). To give but one example of the book's many dynamic patterns: the imagery of concealment used to describe the molestation of fourteen-year-old Rose in 'Wild Swans' (60–2) is inverted in 'The Beggar Maid' when Rose assaults Patrick (79), is used again in 'Mischief' (113) and in 'Simon's Luck' (161), and ultimately in the title story (199). The recurrence of the imagery of concealment in these instances is not obvious, and its development from contexts of molestation to power games to complementary love to non-sexual bonding is even less so. In the first instance Rose is supposedly powerless; with Patrick she is bullying; with Clifford in 'Mischief' she is shown to be somewhat naive and victimized, though ultimately she again turns disadvantage to selfish advantage; in 'Simon's Luck' she is under the covers with a potential nurturing life mate, 'the man for my life!' as Rose says (164); and in 'Who Do You Think You Are?' Rose and Ralph Gillespie are secretly forming a bond that will ultimately tie Rose to Hanratty in affirming fashion. But *Who Do You Think You Are?* is woven tightly with imagery in such patterns of recurrence and development. A close reading of all the stories for the purpose of highlighting their many patterns would provide what is hardly called for any longer: evidence of Munro's artistry in layering meanings (see the subtitle of Carscallen's book, *The Other Country: Patterns in the Writing of Alice Munro*). What is worth remarking here, however, is the way in which short story sequencing generally, and the dynamics of the short story cycle especially, facilitate this strength of her literary art.

Another intriguing, and previously unremarked, formal feature of *Who* is the way that each individual story mimics the shape and movement of the whole cycle. The example of one story can adequately illustrate this final formal observation. 'Royal Beatings,' the first story, tells its tale of two beatings – the one, of Rose, melodramatic, female-orchestrated and cathartic; the other, of Becky Tyde's father, real, male, and murderous – and concludes with an epilogue of sorts (see Mathews, 185–6), a kind of literary coda.[6] The reminiscent narrative in the subjective third person, followed by a later reminiscent reflection (the coda), is typical of the structure of most of the stories in *Who*.[7] One purpose of these literary codas, and most didactically so in 'Royal Beatings' and 'Half a Grapefruit,' is to show how he who controls the representation of the past – in these two it's male members of the sensationalist/sentimentalist media – controls its presentation in the present, thereby enabling revision of the past and creation of self-serving histories within a dominant patriarchy. In a magnification of this movement, the whole cycle begins in Hanratty and childhood and moves steadily outward, to adolescence and high school across the bridge, to university in London (Ontario), to Canada's west coast, and swoops back to Hanratty in the final two stories. The concluding story, 'Who Do You Think You Are?,' functions similarly within the structure of the cycle to those reflective codas to most of the individual stories; and in it Rose – former TV hostess, popular actor – finally assumes a kind of creative control of the representation of her own history, establishing grounds for optimism for her present and her future. So, despite Magdalene Redekop's assertion that 'these stories cannot be construed as making up concentric circles like Dante's celestial rose' (129), *Who Do You Think You Are?* can nonetheless be conceived as cycling/spiralling away from the original site of self-formation constituted by Flo and Hanratty, reaching an apex of self-willed explorations, then dropping back to the place of origin (to Flo in 'Spelling,' the penultimate story, and to Hanratty in the last), which is seen now through Rose as affirmingly definitive and forgivingly redemptive. Excursus and recursus, the romantic quest pattern, whether in the *Odyssey* or *The Wizard of Oz*: as destabilizingly postmodern as *Who* can be in its interrogation of subjectivity, it is also finally quite conservative and conventional in its structure, and, in its conclusions about the basis of self-identity, quite reassuring. And such an appreciative reading may also account for Munro's simultaneous popularity with readers and paramount status among literary critics.

Who Do You Think You Are? is, then, not only a story cycle in terms of the genre label and in accordance with the theorizing of that genre, but also cyclical in its overall movement because, quite simply, it is a sequence of stories that begins in Hanratty and returns there. But much more than that: dizzyingly, it comprises cycles within cycles and utilizes the short story cycle's dynamic pattern of recurrent development to marked advantage in the exploration of its most obvious theme, which is posed neatly in its riddling title.

In fictionally formulating answers to its titular question, *Who Do You Think You Are?* emphasizes nurture over nature, especially (and perhaps inevitably in a version of the bildungsroman) the importance of the formative years, and focuses on place of origin as equally definitive of why you are who you are. Why else does the first story, 'Royal Beatings,' begin with Flo as a kind of primary speaker (see Heble, 97, 101, 109), with the remembered death of the biological mother, and with so much talk of eggs (1–2), if not implicitly to downplay the *ab ovum* argument in favour of the environmental? Of greater potential importance throughout the stories, however, is the role of love, all forms of love, but especially of romantic-sexual love, whose formation and exercise are determined both circumstantially and inherently. Why else is the character named Rose if not to underscore the potential importance of romantic-sexual love in the formation of her character and sense of self?[8] As Ildikó de Papp Carrington has observed, *Who Do You Think You Are?* 'constitutes an organic whole, and the humiliations of love are one of the major themes integrating and unifying it' (124).

The generative figure of romantic-sexual love in *Who Do You Think You Are?* is honey, which is soon figured as candy, and subsequently as all forms of sweets, and is used euphemistically in the epithet 'honey-dumper' to figure the fusion of the romantic-sexual and the scatological. (Undoubtedly Munro is playing seriously with those two stereotypical gifts of the romantic lover: flowers – Rose – and candy.) Following the introduction of the disarranged home environment in 'Royal Beatings,' the second story, 'Privilege,' details the formation and first expression of love in Rose. Here, the primary image of Eros as honey is given after the young Rose has her infatuation with an older girl, Cora, encouraged by Cora's teasing invitation to '*Come on up, honey*'(32):

> The opening, the increase, the flow, of love. Sexual love, not sure yet exactly what it needed to concentrate on. It must be there from the start, like the hard white honey in the pail, waiting to melt and flow. There was some sharpness lacking, some urgency missing; there was the incidental difference in the sex of the person chosen; otherwise it was the same thing, the same thing that has overtaken Rose since. The high tide; the indelible folly; the flash flood.   (33)

It would be difficult to overstate the importance of this passage or the story in which it occurs. The narrator is speculating on an essentialist view of Eros and stating regretfully ('the same thing, the same thing') that the pattern of love which 'Privilege' narrates becomes deterministically recurrent in Rose's life. Its sensually symbolic description of 'the hard white honey in the pail' that liquefies encourages the anticipation that Munro will be dealing exclusively with female desire, despite 'the incidental difference in the sex of the person chosen.' And although this narrator, here more third-person omniscient than subjectively Rose, will eventually return to a portrayal of romantic-sexual desire in suggestively Freudian-Lacanian terms – as a striving to satisfy either a biological or psycho-linguistic lack – Eros here is the inexplicable given of human nature. (As I will argue below in discussing the title story, Hanratty as place of origin is ultimately accorded similar generative/metaphysical significance.)

At the beginning of 'Privilege,' the very first unconscious rousing of Rose's proto-sexual interest is presented suggestively against a backdrop of tacit Freudian theorizing on the child's confusion of the excremental and procreative functions. In spying on Mr. Burns in his outdoor privy,

Rose 'thought she had seen testicles but on reflection she believed it was only a bum' (25); and the copulating brother-and-sister act, Shorty and Franny, 'perform' in an outdoor toilet (25–6). This scatological association of procreation and defecation, attended by postures of defenceless exposure, persists figuratively in Rose's romantic obsession with Cora. As the realist Flo sneers, Cora's grandfather is none other than the 'honey-dumper' (36), the cleaner of outdoor johns, with 'honey' now being a euphemism for excrement: 'Her grandfather was the honey-dumper. That meant he went around cleaning out toilets' (30). (Perhaps it is only fortuitous that the central passage above uses the word 'flow' twice to signal the beginnings of romantic-sexual love; but such use, if intentional, would be nicely ironic, because sharp-boned Flo is anathema to the kind of prostrate puddling being described; in fact, she provides the 'sharpness lacking,' if too cuttingly.)

I am guided here by Norman O. Brown's intriguing analysis-cum-defence of Swift's 'excremental vision' in *Life against Death*. Brown argues that the 'real theme' of Swift's scatological writings 'is the conflict between our animal body, appropriately epitomized in the anal function, and our pretentious sublimations, more specifically, the pretensions of sublimated or romantic-Platonic love' (186). Brown's citations from Freud's writings provide a compelling gloss on Munro's story of the birth of Eros (187–8), but suffice it here to say that in 'Privilege' Munro is no less intrigued by humankind's repressive repugnance at the knowledge that *inter urinas et faeces nascimur* than was the original speaker of the phrase, St Augustine, or Freud himself, or Brown.[9] In the 'conflict between our animal body' and 'our pretentious sublimations,' the body ultimately equals disruptive death in the 'life against death' war waged by neurotic consciousness. It is fitting, therefore, that the passage giving *Who*'s informing vision of Eros as honey is followed immediately by a description of 'the game of funerals,' which is played only by girls (33). In many of the stories of *Who Do You Think You Are?* the female body especially is associated paradoxically with death, with the scatological (for instance, the patriarchal principal in 'Half a Grapefruit' publicly refers to a Kotex napkin as a 'disgusting object' [40]), and with imagery of entropic tendencies towards disorder, against which struggle predominantly male notions of order and respectability.

Moreover, sexual desire becomes for Rose, as a consequence of her first love, decidedly narcissistic, in a way that will also persist deterministically through her various affairs. Rose's love for Cora is announced in an oddly phrased one-sentence paragraph: 'It was Cora Rose loved' (30). The

inverted construction of this sentence (not quite passively voiced) empha-
sizes.the subjective experience of loving at the expense of the object of
love, a condition that the central passage on Eros-as-honey makes clear
with its dismissal of the importance of such features as the sex of the
beloved, that 'incidental difference.'[10] Rose's loving Cora leads to a wor-
ship which expresses itself in a desire to *be* Cora, which can be seen as a
(suggestively Lacanian) wish to represent the object of desire to herself
(to Rose) as herself – there is never any real desire on Rose's part for a real
relationship. What Rose craves is to possess, to internalize and embody,
Cora's presence and power, and the high road to that empowerment is
imitation: 'Rose was obsessed. She spent her time trying to walk and look
like Cora, repeating every word she had ever heard her say. Trying to *be*
her' (32). Thus in her reaction to her first love – the initial 'high tide' and
'flash flood' – Rose finds what will become her life's vocation: acting. But
acting, the convincing assumption of other identities, though it may provide an expedient *modus operandi*, cannot furnish an answer to the crucial
question of identity. In ironic point of fact, such a career path leads
('indelible folly') in the very opposite direction, as much later in 'Simon's
Luck' Rose will flee her potentially ideal mate for an acting job.

The passage on Eros as honey is echoed immediately, amplifying its
importance, in the description of Rose longing for Cora: 'When she
thought of Cora she had the sense of a glowing dark spot, a melting center,
a smell and taste of burnt chocolate, that she could never get at' (34).
Apparently it is the possession, not of the real object of desire, but of the
sweet impossible ideal of that desire that is unattainable (and both Freud's
concept of the narcissist's unrealizable 'ego ideal' and Jacques Lacan's popular concept of the 'mirror stage' – the first objectifying of an elusive self –
come to mind). In the confused attempt to secure what is really the reflecting fabrication of Eros (or of libido) – its displacement in/cathexis of Cora
– Rose steals some candy from Flo's store and takes the bag to school, 'car-
rying it under her skirt, the top of it tucked into the elastic top of her
underpants' (34). Not to belabour the obvious, but the secreted location of
the bag of sweets makes obvious indeed that the sweets are to be read as a
love offering from Rose's brimming honey-pot (the image and fictional
logic *are* Munro's: 'hard white honey in a pail'). Everything goes wrong.
Rose's thievery and normal girlish foolishness is brutally exposed. And it is
Flo's role to dam the first flowing of romantic-sexual love in Rose, in effect
doing the seemingly impossible and making the flow of honey retreat. Flo
is seen to do so in a passage that, again, picks up on the central image of
Eros as an inherent lump of honey that melts. Following the exposure of

her crush, Rose's 'feelings were at the moment shocked and exposed, and already, though she didn't know it, starting to wither and curl up at the edges. Flo was a drying blast' (35). 'The candy was in no condition for eating, anyway. It was all squeezed and melted together, so that Flo had to throw it out' (35). But what is it that Flo finds so bemusedly repellent in Rose's romantic infatuation? The un-subjective third-person narrator gives the answer unequivocally: 'It was love she sickened at. It was the enslavement, the self-abasement, the self-deception' (35). The coda to 'Privilege' then compares Hanratty before and after the war, and concludes with the one-sentence paragraph, 'Cora's grandfather had to retire, and there never was another honey-dumper' (37). Readers can confidently conclude that there is no need for another honey-dumper because, in terms of this story's excrement-equals-honey-equals-a-generative-and-potentially-definitive-Eros trope, Rose has had all the honey dumped out of her. And the candy-disposing honey-dumper is Flo, her not so wicked stepmother, if one yet full of witchery.

The lesson that Rose learns in 'Privilege' comes hard, then, at the feet of Flo. It is not a lesson to encourage hope for the character's achieving stable selfhood via love, because it involves love intimately with humiliating exposure (prepared for at her real school in the confusion of the excremental and the procreative functions surrounding the unaware Mr 'Burns-your-balls'). To avoid the shame of exposure, Rose opts to pursue the path of actress, of disguise, mistakenly thinking she thereby acquires the power responsible for her humiliation, and unconsciously she now takes Flo for her model, the true perpetrator of the humiliation. Imitation/acting for Rose is a sincere form of flattery indeed, but what it flatters is power, and Rose's desire to act is a strategy of avoidance, deception, and empowerment. At the close of 'Wild Swans,' the story that gives the swan song of Rose's childhood, she is shown expressing envy of a woman who imitates the actress Frances Farmer. In the story's concluding sentences, imitation/acting is presented not in imagery of the fairy-tale ugly-duckling metamorphic, but in skin-shedding, reptilian imagery: '[Rose] thought it would be an especially fine thing, to manage a transformation like that. To dare it; to get away with it, to enter on preposterous adventures in your own, but newly named skin' (64). Prepared so at the end of childhood, like some shirking, serpent-supplanting Eve, Rose enters on the preposterous affairs of her adult life. Though Rose is never as scheming as Eloise Ruelle of *Viger*'s 'No. 68 Rue Alfred de Musset,' Scott's sardonic send-off line for Eloise would not be misapplied here to Rose: 'This was the beginning of her career' (49).

Because of the events of 'Privilege,' love continues for Rose as very much a narcissistic passion and pastime, with unfortunate repercussions in her various love affairs throughout the story cycle. The two best examples are with Clifford in 'Mischief' and with Simon in 'Simon's Luck.' With Clifford, Rose's attraction in her first and most unsuccessful adultery is clearly narcissistic. The description of Clifford's background by his wife, Jocelyn, shows it to be the mirror image of Rose's: 'the arthritic father, the small grocery store in a town in upstate New York, the poor tough neighborhood. [Jocelyn] had talked about his problems as a child; the inappropriate talent, the grudging parents, the jeering schoolmates' (110). Too obviously perhaps, this description could, with but an insignificant change of detail, accurately describe Rose's life. Reflecting on Jocelyn's information, Rose thinks, 'What Jocelyn called bitterness seemed to Rose something more complex and more ordinary; just the weariness, suppleness, deviousness, meanness, common to a class. Common to Clifford's class, and Rose's' (111). Rose's desire for romantic-sexual love from Clifford is mostly a greedy and selfish need, however justified by her situation in a bad marriage to the patriarchally named and honey-filled Patrick Blatchford (which marriage Rose nonetheless arranged). But the whole of 'Mischief,' easily the ugliest story of the cycle, portrays relationships in cannibalistic/consumerist terms, from the woman at the party who has written a play 'about a woman who ate her own children' (106) (and note Clifford's first words to Rose at that party: 'Oh Rose. Rose baby' [109]) to the concluding sexual threesome, which comes across more as a sort of witch's smorgasbord than as sexual pleasure or even voyeuristic titillation: 'Though Clifford paid preliminary homage to them both, [Rose] was the one he finally made love to, rather quickly on the nubbly hooked rug. Jocelyn seemed to hover above them making comforting noises of assent' (132). The deceptive, forest-dwelling Jocelyn of the 'foul fire' (131), who is also a maternal echo of stepmother Flo, can even be seen to have orchestrated this humiliating consumption of Rose by Jocelyn herself and the fiddling Clifford.

Having fallen into a *ménage à trois*, Rose, 'at some level she was too sluggish to reach for, [feels] appalled and sad' (132). Rose may be too weary to exercise her moral muscle, but as Redekop observes, 'surely the reader is urged not to be so sluggish a consumer' (131). The 'level' here gestured towards is the level at which Rose lives, or lived rather, in Hanratty, with Flo, both of whose prudish morality and proscriptions against public display, 'parading around' (191, 203), would have kept Rose from exposing herself on the nubbly rug. Furthermore, the spatial imagery of levels points to the concluding story of the cycle, whose title repeats the book's definitive question and substitutes place of origin for romantic-sexual love as foundational answer, employing in its closing lines the more comforting image of 'slots' over (277) in place of the vertical and disturbing levels down of 'Mischief.' But it is an ugly lesson in using other people that Rose adopts from her experience in 'Mischief,' as the ending makes clear in a rhetoric suggestive of trite self-affirmation movements: 'Sometime later she decided to go on being friends with Clifford and Jocelyn, because she needed such friends occasionally, at that stage of her life' (132). I would suggest that for Rose 'that stage' not only connotes the mistaken thespian trope but also something of an extending mirror stage. What 'Privilege' made clear, 'Mischief' confirms: Rose is not going to answer the titular question through romantic-sexual love, though love remains a powerful inducement – as had Clifford himself, the male tease – to that end. In 'Simon's Luck,' Rose is allowed one final, stumbling kick at the honeyed can.

With Simon, Rose is attracted at first because she thinks again that he is, as she says, '"Like me"' (159). But Simon soon emerges as more complement than reflection, and Rose declares that she has met the 'man for [her] life!' Indeed, there is no call to contradict her: Simon is practical, nurturing, and like Paul Farlotte a knowledgeable gardener (for this Rose): '"Learn not to be so thin-skinned," said Simon, as if he were taking her over, in a sensible way, along with the house and garden' (163).[11] And unlike the other men in *Who Do You Think You Are?* (such as Rose's unnamed father and Patrick Blatchford), with the notable exception of Ralph Gillespie in the concluding story, Simon is a good actor (161), one whose name connotes foundation in a new law of love. It may be, therefore, that the potentially ideal mate for Rose, Simon, is something of a reflection and a complement. But Rose ultimately rejects Simon, for involved reasons of selfish uninvolvement. All the parodic ratiocination accompanying her flight from Simon suggests that she is choosing to be finished finally with playing the woman-victim in romantic-sexual relationships – and that there is no other role for a woman in love other than the victim position, primarily because the aging of men's bodies is more acceptable, sexually speaking, than is that of women's. Or Rose's self-involved reasoning can be summed up more sympathetically as follows: emotionally she does not want to leave herself open to the humiliation that she first experienced at Flo's hands via the intermediation of Cora and at Jocelyn's via Clifford; and even if love with Simon would have proven to be the real thing, she finally prefers in her escape to recover 'the private balance spring' of which love, whether good or bad in the end, robs her; she desires now only to renew her somewhat neurotic affiliation with a 'little dry kernel of probity.' The deeply subjective third-person narrator turns abruptly, disruptively ironic, capping Rose's implicitly feminist line of reasoning thus: 'So she thought' (170), 'thus implying the possibility that Rose's wholesale rejection of love might, after all, be a mistake' (Carrington, 142). That 'little dry kernel of probity,' like the untouched 'level' of common (Hanratty/Flo) sense in 'Mischief,' is also a repetition in other form of the lump of 'hard white honey' symbolizing immature or dammed romantic-sexual love. To touch base with Hanratty/Flo can be redemptive, as it could have been before participating in the threesome at the end of 'Mischief,' and it can be tragic, as in Rose's flight from Simon.[12]

In a very real sense, then, Flo, by dumping the 'honey' out of Rose early in her life and damming what was left, has made Rose incapable of accepting the real thing when it comes along in the person of Simon. Although it may well sound like the cliché of a TV talk show on romance, Rose cannot permit herself to be vulnerable to potential humiliation for the sake of love, and Munro seems to be suggesting that such an open posture – authenticity, exposure – is prerequisite. A feminist reading might well argue that Rose must reject Simon if she is to achieve an autonomous identity as a woman, and such an argument may have something ideological to recommend it. For instance, Coral Ann Howells sees Rose's reconnoitring with 'the little dry kernel of probity' as 'the nearest that Munro ever comes to defining a subjective centre of being for her protagonists' (62). However, because of the weighty irony of the true fictional situation – Simon's dying – I cannot but agree instead with Carrington, who writes that Rose's running 'lament thus becomes a subtle parody of the feminist protest against the exacting standards of sexual attractiveness men apply to women but never to themselves.' Carrington goes so far as to call 'Simon's Luck' an 'anti-feminist story,' and observes too that 'Rose's protracted psychological struggle to free herself from Simon, to regain that "little dry kernel of probity," though undeniably crucial to her conception of herself, turns out to be a flight to free herself from a dead man' (143). It is as difficult to accept that Munro, perhaps the English-speaking world's reigning monarch on matters of the fictionalized female heart, would dismiss the benefits of, if not the ontological necessity for, romantic-sexual love. She did say in 1975 that 'doing without men is an impossibility ... obviously sex is the big thing, and the whole thing of emotions that radiate out from good sex, which seems to be so central in adult life, and so irreplaceable' (in C.S. Ross, 79; ellipsis in original).

Perhaps the most compelling argument in favour of my reading of Rose's life in love is the fact that Simon dies of pancreatic cancer (172). The repercussions of this piece of news are ironic and immense, more so even than Rose imagines. They involve, as the ending of 'Simon's Luck' makes clear and as Rose knows, the baselessness of much of her reasoning in making the momentous decision to abandon Simon because *she* feels abandoned, aging, and thus vulnerable to exposure and humiliation. Here it is the male, not the female, body that equals disruptive death ('*memento mori, memento mori*,' Simon intones to Rose in his role as The Old Philosopher [161]), as Rose is shown to learn at the end: 'It was preposterous, it was unfair ... that Rose even at this late date could have thought herself the only one who seriously lacked power' (173; see Carrington, 143). The piece of delayed information also comments, as this story turns at its conclusion to metafictional considerations, on the way stories work as literary art as opposed to how TV shows work, and how various forms of story-telling represent the unpredictability of reality. For my purposes, though, the piece of news about the cause of Simon's death again picks up that central image of Eros as honey which was first given in 'Privilege' and subsequently displaced in various ways. Which is to say, Simon's death from cancer of the pancreas involves the very organ that regulates sugar in the blood. Simon would have functioned as a kind of pancreas in Rose's life, for however long. It doesn't really matter to Rose that Simon dies; it matters everything that she kills her love for him.

(Because readers may suspect my ascription of such importance to the honey/sweets motif, before proceeding I would like to open this lengthy parenthesis rather than drop its information into a note. There are numerous repetitions and developments of the honey/sweets image that, when taken together, support the argument that it forms the telling pattern in the story cycle. Although it doesn't begin in earnest until the central passage in 'Privilege,' the image of compensatory sweets is introduced in the first story, 'Royal Beatings,' in relation to Rose's second model [after Flo], Becky Tyde. The performing Becky, another actress of a kind, 'would put a whole cookie in her mouth if she felt like it' [6], and does so only to stop herself from telling explicitly the mysterious tale that determines her mocking role in Hanratty [which itself anticipates sweets-snatching and carnivalesque Milton Homer in the title and return story]. The secondary displacement of Eros into sweets is shown later in this story when Flo placates the royally beaten Rose with rich treats [19], and Carrington

[126] suggests that Rose's solitary self-teasing behaviour with the syrupy treats is masturbatory. The sluttish Ruby Carruthers salvages what self-esteem she can by refusing the bribe of cupcakes [42]. Candy figures a number of times in 'Wild Swans,' but most significantly as part of the perverse undertaker's bribe for sex in Flo's incident-predicting story [57]. When in 'The Beggar Maid' Rose capitulates under various pressures to accept Patrick's proposal of marriage, she wakes up in the middle of the night craving sweets [80]; similarly after first having sex with Patrick, 'She thought of celebration. What occurred to her was something delicious to eat, a sundae at Boomers, apple pie with hot cinnamon sauce' [81]. The craving in this latter situation is typical of the way the image is used throughout the remainder of the stories: those who lack love, or those whose love has remained a little white lump of honey, crave the substitute, in a way that parallels [according to the Freudian theory of anal fixation] the misers' and millionaires' grasping after all filthy lucre. In 'Providence,' Rose feels guilty for giving her daughter Anna sweet breakfast cereals instead of the conventional mothering she believes Anna needs [140-1]; and later Anna, confused and recovering from illness, and perhaps feeling her mother's resentment, makes up a story about three colour-coded princesses, the brown one of whom 'had roast beef and gravy and chocolate cake with chocolate icing, also chocolate ice cream with chocolate fudge sauce' and grows '"rude things"' in her garden [144], thereby replicating Rose's girlhood confusion of the sweet and the scatological. In something of an ironic inversion, Rose's mistaken break from Simon is signalled to her in a restaurant's yonically shaped dessert containers: 'the thick glass dishes they put ice-cream or jello in. It was those dishes that told her of her changed state. She could not have said she found them shapely, or eloquent, without misstating the case. All she could have said was that she saw them in a way that wouldn't be possible to a person in any stage of love' [170]. She finds the significantly empty concave containers for [substitutive] sweets reassuring because she is heading away from – emptying herself of – the real thing, love with another, and moving towards a mistakenly desired, loveless independence. And of course she is also running towards that other wrong-headed alternative in her life, an acting job in a TV series that sounds very much like the old CBC program 'The Beachcombers' [171]).

By 'Spelling,' when the cycle begins the return movement to place of origin in Hanratty, returning Rose to Flo, Flo herself has developed a consuming, a revolting and, again, suggestively obscene craving for any sweets. She 'might tip the jug of maple syrup up against her mouth and drink it like wine. She loved sweet things now, craved them. Brown sugar by the spoonful, maple syrup, tinned puddings, jelly, globs of sweetness to slide down her throat' (175; see also 181–2). Well before this point in the cycle, such a craving can only signal a commensurate lack of love, the hungry absence which is attendant here on the abandonment that overtakes those who grow old in these stories.[13] Flo's craving is monstrous indeed. By the logic of this fiction, she grows the greatest obsessive-compulsive need for the sweet substitute for love because she is the character most without love (her only rival in this regard is Milton Homer, about whom more below). In Rose's dream of the old folks' home where Flo is to be committed, she sees the caged old people being offered 'choice' food: 'chocolate mousse, trifle, Black Forest Cake.' In the final cage, Rose discovers Flo, 'handsomely seated on a throne-like chair, ... and looking pleased with herself, for showing powers she had kept secret till now' (184). The queenly secret is, I believe, Flo's determining role in Rose's life, the subconscious 'spelling' that she worked, which is echoed in the queenly Cora with her two 'attendants' (31) and in Jocelyn's witchcraft in 'Mischief.' Flo's is a determining influence that the opening sentences of 'Royal Beatings' can, in hindsight, be seen to have established: '*Royal Beating*. That was Flo's promise. You are going to get one Royal Beating.' This can now be read both as prediction for Rose's life in love and as tribute to Flo's primary powers of suggestion.

As I have argued, the most damaging aspect of Flo's determining role is that she dried up the metaphorically and potentially definitive honey/love in Rose, acting as too severe a realistic check on Rose's romantic tendencies (which are evident immediately in the cycle when Rose plays with the phrase 'royal beating'). At the end of 'Spelling,' Flo is entering terminal senility, and in an increasingly delirious condition thinks she is in hospital for a gall-bladder operation.

> '... Do you know how many gallstones they took out of me? Fifteen! One as big as a pullet's egg. I got them somewhere. I'm going to take them home.' She pulled at the sheets, searching. 'They were in a bottle.'
> 'I've got them already,' said Rose. 'I took them home.'
> 'Did you? Did you show your father?'
> 'Yes.'
> 'Oh, well, that's where they are then,' said Flo, and she lay down and closed her eyes. (188)

This concluding scene, moving as it is, nonetheless argues fictionally that

Flo substituted a stone of gall for the lump of honey in Rose, a displacement which subsequently made love something of a non-starter in her life, and made her, at the crux of her relationship with Simon, opt for the return of the symbolically echoing 'little dry kernel of probity' (cf. Carscallen, 517). Observe too that at the end of Flo's life there is a return to the mothers and eggs of the opening pages of 'Royal Beatings.' The difference here is that where Rose's biological mother died with the feeling that she had ingested an egg (2), Flo has the gallish egg removed from her and passed on to Rose. What are the expressions of this stony gall? It suggests generally an embittered narcissistic retreat rather than a loving flow, with associations of withholding, distrust, fear of exposure, prudishness and prurience, impudence, bitterness, audacity, irritability, and (inevitably) biliousness – everything, in fact, that is Flo (though in the first story of the cycle 'hard pride and skepticism' are already given as part of 'Rose's nature' [5]). Contrarily, Rose's father gives the accounting of Flo's virtues: 'Flo was his idea of what a woman ought to be ... A woman ought to be energetic, practical, clever at making and saving; she ought to be shrewd, good at bargaining and bossing and seeing through people's pretensions. At the same time she should be naive intellectually, childlike, contemptuous of maps and long words and anything in books, full of charming jumbled notions, superstitions, traditional beliefs' (45). Interestingly, it is to this unnamed and long-dead patriarch, Rose's father, that Flo wants Rose to have shown the transferred gallstones. Perhaps Flo had also precluded warmer relations between Rose and her father; perhaps Rose, under Flo's tutelage, inadvertently became too much the kind of woman her father admired, for there is no mention of love in his catalogue. As Rose says of Flo's imaginary gallstones, using the key word of return stories, '"I took them home."'

Primarily, then, because of Flo's influence on who she is, love could never be definitive for Rose. That is why Flo is the first to put the essential question to her: 'Who do you think you are?' (13). In her quest to solve that riddle of identity, it is necessary for Rose at the end of 'Spelling' to recognize Flo's role in her life and to accept emotionally that romantic-sexual love is not going to provide an answer for her. This latter truth she had recognized intellectually in 'Simon's Luck,' and the impossibility of a definitive love in her life would appear to be Rose's luck, her bad luck: you do not get to choose your parents, biological or adoptive. But this is not to say that Munro is dismissing the potentially definitive role that romantic-sexual love can play in the construction and affirmation of self-identity, for men and women. Having recognized in this first of the two 'return stories' that conclude *Who Do You Think You Are?* the primary importance of Flo in making her who she is – in fact, Rose affirms this recognition with her simple 'Yes' response to Flo – Rose is prepared for her return home. If she is ever to have a sense of self confirmed, she must rely instead on her connection to place or origin, to Hanratty (see Howells, 64). That is why in the final story the third-person narrator at her most subjective is careful to dismiss any romantic-sexual element from Rose's feelings for Ralph Gillespie, who becomes Rose's key to the door home: 'She was enough a child of her time to wonder if what she felt about him was simply sexual warmth, sexual curiosity; she did not think it was' (205). That is about as declarative as Munro's fiction ever gets. As far as Rose's self-identity is concerned, we are no longer considering the reifying power of romantic love.

In 'Half a Grapefruit,' the mistake which had led to Rose's dreaded public shame had been her 'wanting badly to align herself with towners, against her place of origin' (38). Where 'Spelling' returned Rose to various sources – to Hanratty secondarily, but primarily to the font of her own spleen in Flo's gall (to overwrite it) – 'Who Do You Think You Are?' returns her most fully to her place of origin, returns the cycle to its titular riddle, and returns readers to that same question of identity. But the true subjects of a return story are the passage of time, the effects of, as Roberts puts it in 'The Tantramar Revisited,' 'the hands of chance and change' (51), and identity, the identity of an individual in relation to a region, a community, and/or a country – always to home. Viewed in these terms, 'Who Do You Think You Are?' is, like Leacock's 'L'Envoi: The Train to Mariposa' and Elliott's 'The way back,' exemplary of this distinguishing element of the Canadian short story cycle. What must appear remarkable, though, is that a contemporary short story cycle of character concludes by suggesting an answer to the riddle of self-identity that priorizes the definitive power of place-as-home in a turn that recalls not only Leacock's musings on the wider importance of 'Mariposa' but also, before him, Duncan Campbell Scott's on the value of 'Viger' and, more recently, Elliott's return story about '[t]he way back' to connection with the unnamed community of *The Kissing Man*.

Within 'Who Do You Think You Are?' the riddling question is asked in final framing fashion by one Miss Hattie Milton (196). She is very much a figure of origins, of what made Hanratty what it was and no longer is: 'Miss Hattie Milton taught at the high school. She had been teaching there longer than all the other teachers combined and was more important than the Principal. She taught English ... and the thing she was famous for was keeping order' (195). Thus, it could be said that the question of identity is finally asked of Rose *by* Hanratty itself through the person of Miss Hattie Milton. Because for Rose the answer to the riddle posed here figuratively by place *is* place, she must find a means of reconnecting herself affirmatively to Hanratty. And her only way to do so – to reconnect with her place of origin, and so to answer the question – lies through the grotesque figure of Miss Hattie's nephew, Milton Homer. So I must disagree here with Redekop, who writes, 'Hattie Milton's question "Who do you think you are?" – if directed at Milton Homer – would have no answer' (143). That is only literally true; figuratively, Milton Homer could answer that he is more mascot and scapegoat than village idiot; that he is also a figure of literal as well as Bakhtinian carnival, loudly and viciously mocking the pretensions of official Hanratty as it does that thing which it normally censures in its sober citizens: parades about (191–3). He is also one of Munro's richest creations: a ratty representative of Hanratty, an escaped emanation, symbolically evocative, yet nicely particularized. And as Heble observes, he 'is of particular interest to Rose because he represents something of a mythology of the past' (119). Appropriately by this point in the story cycle, Milton Homer, like Becky Tyde in the first story, is presented as one who is silent only with a mouth full of sweets (189); he also seriously snatches candy tossed for children at the parades (192), and gluttonously gobbles down sweets at the Milton sisters' annual graduating-class party (197). As the latest generation of the foundational Miltons, with his insatiable hunger for sweets which is matched only by Flo in 'Spelling,' Milton Homer (and was there ever a more foundational name than one that takes those of the two epic poets of the classical and the Christian traditions?) argues that Hanratty was and is a town without much love, or with but a grudging sort of love. And this is the only place that Rose has left, to return to.

The only way to Milton Homer for Rose – the way to touch base with her place of origin, and thereby to approach an answer to the story's and the book's and Flo's and Hattie Milton's and Hanratty's question of identity – lies through Ralph Gillespie, an old high school friend whom she meets again on returning to Hanratty. In keeping with the narcissistic bent of her attractions, Ralph is like Rose; a kind of inherent familiarity is what first drew them to one another in high school (199). Ralph is also one of those who showed Rose the power of imitation/acting by doing a distinguishing Milton Homer imitation for his classmates: deeply impressed, Rose 'wanted to do the same. Not Milton Homer; she did not want to do Milton Homer. She wanted to fill up in that magical, releasing way, transform herself; she wanted the courage and the power' (200). Unsurprisingly, Rose sees acting as an empowering activity, which it becomes for her (most damagingly so in her marriage to Patrick; and, recall, when she learns of Simon's death while she is acting, she wonders 'how she could have thought herself the only person who could seriously lack power' [173]). But where Rose also learns to construct an identity in the extra-Hanratty world by playing other roles, Ralph fails in the outside world, is radically injured in a navy accident and has to be rebuilt 'from scratch,' as Flo says (201). Finally, Ralph 'Milton Homer'd himself right out of a job' (202) at the Legion Hall, doing imitations none of the newer residents recognized, and mistakenly plunged to his death in its basement. Ralph Gillespie is for Rose, then, both a generative presence and a figure of entrapment within Hanratty, one who dies, as his obituary records, because 'he mistook the basement door for the exit door and lost his balance' (206). Rose found the exit, as in leaving Simon she recovered a too tight 'private balance spring' (170). So it is Ralph, not Simon, who can be read, if anyone can, as the measure to this point of Rose's liberated, non-gendered, limited success.

For present purposes, the more important aspect of this distant, deconstructed and reconstructed Ralph Gillespie is that he provides Rose's point of contact with and re-entry to what emerges as her redemptive place of origin in Hanratty. Rose's imitation of Milton Homer is, as was suggested earlier, an imitation of Ralph's imitation of Milton Homer.[14] And, to repeat, Milton Homer is himself 'a mimic of ferocious gifts and terrible energy' (192), whose subject is official Hanratty and its citizens at their most ostentatiously parading. Ralph is even associated with that other foundational character in Rose's life, Flo, who, resurrected now in the manner of return stories, claims that Ralph in his refusal to show pain is 'Like me. I don't let on' (201). With Ralph established as a distant figure of origins in Hanratty – and, via the much-imitated Milton Homer, as the only way back to remote Hanratty – the final few puzzling pages of *Who Do You Think You Are?* can be read as a conversation between Rose and Hanratty; or read as a narrative commentary on Rose and her relation to place of origin in Hanratty.

The narrator writes through Rose that Ralph/Hanratty does 'want something' from her, but that he/it is unable to find expression:

But when Rose remembered this unsatisfactory conversation she seemed to recall a wave of kindness, of sympathy and forgiveness, though certainly no words of that kind had been spoken. That peculiar shame which she carried

around with her seemed to have been eased. The thing she was ashamed of,
in acting, was that she might have been paying attention to the wrong things,
reporting antics, when there was always something further, a tone, a depth, a
light, that she couldn't get and wouldn't get. And it wasn't just about acting
she suspected this. Everything she had done could sometimes be seen as a
mistake. She had never felt this more strongly than when she was talking to
Ralph Gillespie, but when she thought about him afterwards her mistakes
appeared unimportant.   (205)

Rose's shame is that in her career as actress and retailer of Hanratty lore
she, like Ralph, had been Milton Homering, imitating only surface pecu-
liarities, and thereby missing in others as well as in herself the interior
lives and relations that also make us who we are. And not just in acting:
'Everything she had done could sometimes be seen as a mistake.' What a
monumental self-confession this is, linking her whole life to the falsifica-
tions of bad acting, entertaining the idea that her life has been poor enter-
tainment, confronting her with the possibility that she has never had an
authentic life. And note: such a possibility depends on the assumption –
the belief – that authenticity is possible. Whatever else can be said about
this character, it must be conceded that Rose's behaviour in the final pages
of the story cycle demonstrates enormous courage as she trains an
unflinching gaze on the mirror of who she is: Ralph Gillespie, Milton
Homer, Hanratty. What a tough act to follow. But graciously Ralph *as*
distant Hanratty does not confront her only with this possibility of
doomed inauthenticity; he also proffers a kind of redemption. For Rose's
revisioning memory finds, through Ralph to Milton Homer to the Misses
Milton to Hanratty, some vague sense of forgiveness for her sins of imita-
tive omission, a discovery which seems to entail a kind of confirmation of
the self-identity she has fled and sought throughout the cycle.

   Confirmation is the right word, because one of Milton Homer's 'public
function[s]' (191) is as a priestly figure whose mock-christening incanta-
tion stresses, in typical Hanratty fashion, the possibility of the death of
the newborn (see Redekop, 142). As such, the broadly named Milton
Homer can also be seen to fuse the functions of such figures from earlier
story cycles of small towns as *Viger*'s pedler and *The Kissing Man*'s Doctor Fletcher and grinder man. What gets confirmed at the end of *Who Do
You Think You Are?* is a middle-aged woman's acceptance of self-identity
as connected intimately to an unattractive place of origin. Although I
think that in the following comment Redekop is overly cautious, I nonetheless agree with the sense of her conclusion: 'The fact that no powerful

autonomous subject can be constructed does not negate the importance of knowing who you think you are, of knowing the limits of yourself, the place where the boundaries of self dissolve and flow into the self of some other. Munro pictures the pain of isolation and offers as comfort a sense of community – however small' (147). In line with such a modest reading, the enigmatic closing sentence of this story cycle is appropriately inter-rogative: 'What could she say about herself and Ralph Gillespie, except that she felt his life, close, closer than the lives of men she'd loved, one slot over from her own?' (206). 'Closer than the lives of men she'd loved' because, as I have argued, romantic-sexual love was, after the events of 'Privilege,' never potentially definitive for Rose. 'One slot over from her own' in terms of a spatial and temporal image that places Rose beside Ralph, who is one slot over from Milton Homer, who is one slot over from his aunts, who are one slot over from Hanratty – the place of origin which is posited here by Munro (one slot over from Rose?) very much as a metaphysical signifier with the power to bestow a reassuring degree of identity, meaning, and presence of self to self – a reifying self-consciousness (see Howells, 65).[15]

True, this signifier, 'Hanratty,' is itself quite unstable, always changing, and perhaps it will eventually threaten such a subject as Rose with 'Ralph Gillespie-ing' herself out of a snugly confirmed sense of selfhood – thus again the aptness of the closing question mark. But regardless of the hint of perpetual deferment suggested by the *mise en abîme* of imitations of imitations and the indeterminacy of that closing question, this short story cycle in its return to place of origin nonetheless strengthens Rose's self-possession, reinforces her constructed subjectivity, if you will. Unless some radically positive development occurs in the human brain, an evolu-tion which biologists tell us is most unlikely, there will never be a compel-lingly logical way to establish the ground of selfhood, whether in fiction or philosophy (the enigmatic closing pages of *Who* at least make that quite clear). But after Rose has recognized Flo's predominant role in her life and accepted that romantic-sexual love cannot be definitive for her, her obvious contentment at the end of the cycle, her sense of forgiveness and well-being, *can* be traced back to her relation to Hanratty as a sugges-tively reifying place of origin. Perhaps the sophisticated third-person sub-jective point of view is manipulated here to signal that what Rose cannot say, we as readers of educated imagination can nonetheless intimate. Con-sidered so, *Who Do You Think You Are?* emerges not as a philosophical writing of subjectivity as an eternally deferred sequence of signification, but as one masterful fiction writer's act of faith.

L'Envoi:
Continuity/Inclusion/Conclusion

I have long been impressed by Stephen Leacock's title for the index of *My Remarkable Uncle*, 'Index: There Is No Index,' and had toyed with the notion of borrowing it for this conclusion – Conclusion: There Is No Conclusion. But I wouldn't pretend to the requisite bravado of the man James Doyle's biography dubs 'the Sage of Orillia.' The fashionable slash marks the limit of my nerve in a title, and of course it's long past passé. Besides which, this is the kind of surveying study that requires a more considered conclusion. Or perhaps it's bravado enough to end this study of Canadian short story cycles with a brief return to *Sunshine Sketches of a Little Town*, the story cycle that first fired my interest in the subject and provides in the introduction a textbook illustration of cyclical structure and return story techniques.

The temptation to return to Leacock in connection with Munro's *Who Do You Think You Are?* proved irresistible because that last story cycle of character analysed here actually rounds off as a cycle that presents a difficult protagonist's self-integrity as grounded in place, as finally Munro reinscribes the pre-eminence of the small-town home in writing the riddle of identity for the thoroughly contemporary Rose. Although the continuum of the Canadian short story cycle begins properly with Duncan Campbell Scott's late nineteenth-century anatomy of communal place, *In the Village of Viger*, it was Leacock's *Sunshine Sketches of a Little Town*, and especially its concluding 'L'Envoi: The Train to Mariposa,' that most insistently portrayed the connection between the home place as small-town Ontario and identity – individual, communal, and national identity. Munro may have dodged J.R. (Tim) Struthers's repeated attempts to get her to admit a Leacockian influence in her work ('Material,' 17, 33–4), but Struthers was nonetheless on to something in detecting unmistakable ech-

oes of *Sunshine Sketches* in *Who Do You Think You Are?* (Given the curt-
ness of Munro's responses to Struthers, I would go so far as to impute
stirrings of a Bloomian anxiety of influence to Munro; Hugh Hood, on
the other hand, readily acknowledged the pre-eminence of Leacock's
influence in his own story cycle of place, *Around the Mountain* [1967],
claiming that as a child he 'just about memorized' *Sunshine Sketches*
[Struthers, 'Intersecting,' 11]). Such an influence, acknowledged or not,
may be unavoidable for any writer using the genre of the short story cycle
and a Canadian small-town setting after 1912. Still, some Mariposan turns
in *Who Do You Think You Are?* are particularly noteworthy.

In his humbly proud recounting of the reception given wealthy Patrick
Blatchford, the comically hickish Billy Pope, Flo's cousin, closely resembles the down-home Mariposans in their familiarity with the Prince of
Wales during a whistle stop: '"We just set him down and give him some
sausages,"' says Billy, '"don't make no difference to us what he comes
from!"' (86; compare *Sketches*, 120–1). And there would seem to be more
than a little of romantic Peter Pupkin in Patrick Blatchford when he and
Rose get engaged: 'Patrick gave her a diamond ring and announced that
he was giving up being a historian for her sake' (88). Compare the more
romantic, thus riches-despising, Zena Pepperleigh, who says of Pupkin's
diamonds that 'she would wear them for his sake' (116). Even Flo's
answer when Rose asks after the grotesque Milton Homer – '"He's out
there at the County Home and you can see him on a sunny day down by
the highway keeping an eye on the traffic and licking up an ice cream
cone"' (201) – remembers the close of the sketches portraying the
redemptive Pepperleigh-Pupkin romance, where Leacock's narrator
informs the reader, 'you can find them to this day. You may see Pupkin
there at any time cutting enchanted grass on a little lawn in as gaudy a
blazer as ever' (117). And of course 'you' can find such characters, by
opening 'such books as the present ones,' *Sunshine Sketches* and *Who Do
You Think You Are?* Such synchronicities can only be attributed to
shared subject and cultural context, to Frye's imaginative continuum.
Further, this very sharing led Leacock and Munro (and many another) to
choose the short story cycle – or to be chosen by it with its Bakhtinian
genre memory – as the most fitting form for bodying forth their imaginative conceptions of small-town Canadian life, of communal (and national)
and individual identity, and of the relationships among them.

Nowhere, though, is similarity-cum-continuity between the two books
more striking than in *Who's* concluding 'Who Do You Think You Are?'
In the first place, it too is the return story of a short story cycle, a return

story whose purposes are, as has been shown, fairly identical with those of 'L'Envoi: The Train to Mariposa.' But particularly as well, for such details as the various Hanratty parades, which provide the ideal stage for the carnivalesque Milton Homer, could have been taken from the opening of 'The Marine Excursion of the Knights of Pythias.' Leacock was first to describe the small town's ambivalent predilection for parading around (36–7), listing various nationalist occasions and commending the inclusiveness of small town life: 'That's the great thing about the town and that's what makes it so different from the city. Everybody is in everything' (36). How far from this in imaginative space and time is Munro?

> There used to be plenty of parades in Hanratty. The Orange Walk, on the Twelfth of July; the High School Cadet Parade, in May; the schoolchildren's Empire Day Parade, the Legion's Church Parade, the Santa Claus Parade, the Lions Club Old-Timers' Parade. One of the most derogatory things that could be said about anyone in Hanratty was that he or she was fond of parading around, but almost every soul in town – in the town proper, not West Hanratty, that goes without saying – would get a chance to march in public in some organized and approved affair.   (191)

Somewhat surprisingly, Hanratty's parade is not as inclusive as Mariposa's, and the parenthetical exclusion of the poor is relevant to what makes Rose who she is. Also, Leacock's is primarily a humorous, where Munro's is a realistic, fiction. But readers would be mistaken in thinking that Munro is only waxing nostalgic with the *ubi sunt* trope, 'There used to be ...' Besides, as 'L'Envoi' makes clear, Leacock was also already looking back to a pre-modern time of stronger communal values, and implying that 'such a book as the present one' (141), *Sunshine Sketches* – the product of imagination informed by accurate memory – could serve as a vehicle for recovering the worthwhile from the past. And it was Leacock's complex narrator in 'L'Envoi' who first prescribed periodic returns to 'home' for what ails the identity-challenged: 'Your face has changed in these long years of money-getting in the city. Perhaps if you had come back now and again, just at odd times, it wouldn't have been so' (145). That of course is what Rose does at the end of *Who*, goes back to Hanratty at an odd time in her life, returns home. Home made her who she is, and reaffiliating with home will enable her to become more than what she was. But not only Rose, and not only small-town Ontario, impressive as these similarities nonetheless are between two white Anglo-Protestant Ontario writers of short story cycles, the one a man at the beginning of the twentieth century and the other a woman more than half a volatile century later. For Will, the mixed-race hero of Thomas King's story cycle set in Alberta towards the end of the century, *Medicine River* (1989), is another character who has taken Leacock's advice to heart and returned home.

Medicine River is marketed as a novel. It is not a novel. King himself has said that he prefers 'to think of *Medicine River* as a cycle of stories' (Rooke, 63). More like Hood than Munro in this regard, he agreed with an interviewer's suggestion that his story cycle has a place in the continuum of Canadian short story cycles (Rooke, 63–4). King also insisted, though, that such features as the episodic structure and repetitions of *Medicine River* are characteristics of Native oral traditions. Fair enough. But these are also prime features of the short story cycle. In authentic oral traditions, repetitions are just that – repetition for memorial purposes – whereas in *Medicine River* repetition is actually recurrent development, which is of course one of the key features of the story cycle as originally defined by Ingram. Doubtless many aspects of literary story cycle form derive from older traditions (the Irish may provide the most apt instance), whether the oral traditions of folk tale, a nation's legends and history, liturgical calendars, or various cyclical forms such as medieval miracle plays and sonnet sequences. And doubtless *Medicine River* could be said distantly to mimic some features of Native oral story-telling. But the language and form of Thomas King's writing, and of *Medicine River* especially – its literary tradition – is the English-Canadian short story cycle. *Medicine River* is no more written in a Native oral tradition (and note the oxymoron in saying so)[1] than is Duncan Campbell Scott's *In the Village of Viger* (it could as well be said facetiously, given the long-serving deputy superintendent general of Indian Affairs' exposure to Native cultures in their purer forms, that Scott's *Viger* has the more convincing claim to the influence of Native oral traditions).

Medicine River is composed of eighteen chapters that readily stand alone as short stories but whose meanings are most fully understood in the context of the whole. These eighteen episodes are unified primarily, as are the stories of Munro's *Who*, by the continuing presence of the protagonist Will and the dominant setting of the titular small city of Medicine River. More important to Will, who is perhaps too obviously in quest of a self he can live with, is the Indian reserve that apparently shares the name of the city. For the half-breed Will, his identity quest is as much to grapple for understanding with the white half of himself, which was contributed by an absent father, as it is to recognize his place and find a home in the Native community of Medicine River. In *Medicine River*, place and identity, home and self, are connected in an evolving cause-and-effect process.

A key sign of the success of Will's journey is the framing symbol of a child's top (and of course framing with the first and final stories is a structural technique of the short story cycle). A top was supposedly sent to Will and his brother as a Christmas present from his father, but it never arrived. In the penultimate paragraph of this story cycle, Will has purchased a similar top for his surrogate daughter South Wing, thereby assuming the role of father which his own father had shirked. Notably, the biological non-Native father was a rodeo rider who chose a life of irresponsible vagabondia that is more in keeping with the American myth of rugged individualism than the conservative and domestic Canadian (recalling the Grove persona in the first half of *Over Prairie Trails*). Alone at Christmas, the homebody Will sets the toy top spinning and it makes 'a sweet, humming sound, the pitch changing as it spun in its perfect circle' (260–1). Literally come home, and home alone, in this story cycle Will has more truly willed himself into the perfect circle of a surrogate family and Native community. What Will does here in reconstituting and redefining family and its roles at the end of the erratic twentieth century is different only in time from the choice made by Paul Farlotte in *Viger* towards the end of the disruptive nineteenth century.[2]

And if Munro's *Who Do You Think You Are?* shares some striking similarities with Leacock's *Sunshine Sketches*, King's *Medicine River* can be seen to share an indebtedness to that earlier Canadian short story cycle that is at least as striking, and may well be yet more remarkable. As with the coincidental scenes between *Who* and the *Sketches*, I present the following similarities as a kind of conclusive, tangible intertextual evidence that a Frygean imaginative continuum does exist in Canadian literary culture and that the Canadian short story cycle does indeed possess Bakhtinian genre memory; and if 'evidence' sounds too material a term for such exegetical proof, I would ask readers to think of the way that verbal tics, word associations, and the interpretation of dreams are accepted as evidence of the existence of the intangible subconscious itself.

To begin broadly, I can think of no literary writer since Leacock other than King whose ironic tone and authorial attitude are so 'kind' – Leacock's term for the humour that bespeaks communal identification, *kinship* – and whose narratorial opinions can persist so enigmatically. Decoding the deceptively simple narration of such writers as Leacock and King, figuring out their attitude to their subjects, often necessitates extra-textual trips. So it is worth noting that King has stated that he feels protective towards the Native communities about whom he writes (Rooke, 72–3), just as in his preface to *Sunshine Sketches* Leacock insists on his affection for the Canadian originals that make up the composite Mariposa and its characters (xviii). Obviously, these are two writers unafraid to state that they cherish the places they anatomize with humorous satire.

Less evidently similar is the way in which comedy is always threatening to turn into tragedy in both books, or the way in which seriously dangerous matters are laughed into farce – the way in which Leacock and King are always rescuing their characters and readers from catastrophe.[3] For instance, 'The Mariposa Bank Mystery,' wherein a rumoured murder is slowly degraded (or upgraded) to the level of the ludicrous (110–12), is echoed clearly in *Medicine River*'s handling of an episode involving AIM (American Indian Movement), where a rumoured murder dissolves into the story of an Indian having fallen on a bottle he carried in his pocket (254). And to take but one more striking example from among the many revealing parallels and echoes, *Medicine River* has its own Mariposa Belle scene, where Will and his mother and brother find themselves sinking in a boat and fearing death by drowning in what turns out to be a few feet of water (246–7; the scene is simultaneously paralleled in Will and Harlen's misadventure in a canoe, which, I suspect, is a Native in-joke).

Most strikingly parallel of all, though, are the ways in which *Sunshine Sketches* and *Medicine River* privilege the connections between place as small town, home, and identity. The introduction to the present study has discussed the workings of *Sunshine Sketches*' return story, 'L'Envoi: The Train to Mariposa,' in this regard. In *Medicine River* it is Harlen Bigbear, the *spiritus loci* of Medicine River, who insists on a very real physical connection between place and identity, even with suggestions that place enables the performance of a best self (if in humorous reference to Native basketball competitions): '"That's why you miss them jump shots. That's why you get drunk on Friday night and can hardly get your shoes tied on Saturday. That's why we lose those games when we should be winning ... cause you don't know where you are"' (15). Where you should be to know where you are is 'home.' *Home* is a word that King plays on and repeats with almost as many ironies and typographical qualifications of quotation marks and inverted commas and italics as does trickster Leacock himself in the first few paragraphs of 'L'Envoi' (141). The following scene is presented some eighty pages after the passage just quoted, though it occurred earlier in fictional time, when Harlen was presumptuously trying to convince Will to return to Medicine River:

Harlen turned the radio down a bit. 'Can't see Ninastiko from Toronto,' he said. 'So, when you think you'll be moving back home?'

'Here?'

'Sure. Most of us figured that, with your mother and all [just buried], you'd be coming home soon.'

There was no logic to it, but my stomach tightened when Harlen said *home*.

...

'... You see over there,' Harlen said, gesturing with his chin. 'Ninastiko ... Chief Mountain. That's how we know where we are. When we can see the mountain, we know we're home.'   (93)

In *Medicine River*, and in Medicine River, to know where you are and where you belong is to be in sight of the reifying landmark Ninastiko, Chief Mountain. Good medicine indeed (which really does sound better than talk of a metaphysical signifier). And it's the same medicine that's been prescribed by our Carlylean literary physicians of the age from premodern Scott and Leacock to postmodern Munro and King.

This continuity of form and subject from Scott and Leacock to Munro and King should argue at least that the form of the short story cycle has proven itself adaptable to the literary needs of both genders and various racial groups. I am not arguing that King can serve for all ethnic Canadians, even if he is conveniently of mixed race ('a native writer of Cherokee, Greek and German descent,' as his book bio describes him). King's *Medicine River* provides a final compelling example of the short story cycle's adaptability, but King is certainly not the only available contemporary writer of Native or recent ethnic heritage to employ it in ways strikingly reminiscent of its uses throughout the history of Canadian literature. For as much as the short story cycle has served the needs of such writers as Sime, Grove, and Carr earlier in the twentieth century, it continues to serve writers from the diverse groups that continue to make Canadian communities and Canada. In an article on M.G. Vassanji's *Uhuru Street* (1991) as a short story cycle, Rocio G. Davis discusses the ways in which the story cycle is 'a literary genre exceptionally suited to the task of articulating and elaborating distinctiveness ... The dynamics of the short story cycle make it appropriate for the new definition of cultural pluralism that incorporates immigrant legacies while adapting to the practices of the culture in which these works are created' (7). In discussing the ways in which the Canadian 'ethnic short story cycle enacts the enigma of ethnicity by formally materializing the trope of doubleness, presenting the between-world condition via a form that itself vacillates between two genres' (8–9), Davis makes reference to such story sequences as Rachna Mara's *Of Customs and Excise* (1991), Shyam Selvadurai's *Funny Boy* (1994), Dianne Maguire's *Dry Land Tourist* (1991), Rohinton Mistry's *Tales from Firozsha Baag* (1987), and Wayson Choy's *The Jade Peony* (1997), which list she describes as 'a small sample of recent ethnic short story cycles' (10). Not all these works accord with the precise definition of the short story cycle given by the present study (perhaps only Vassanji's and Mistry's). But short story cycles are well suited to cross-sectioning places (small towns and variously defined communities) and conveying a character's fragmentary experiences: so the immigrant's experience as s/he adapts would be especially amenable to treatment in such a form because of the divisions (of loyalty and consciousness), losses, novelty, and episodic nature of that experience.

After the formally necessary elements of an independent-interdependent arrangement of short stories and the dynamic of recurrent development – features shared by the generic family from *Dubliners* to Louise Erdich's *Love Medicine* – the return movement can be seen to distinguish the Canadian short story cycle. For example, Thomas King's *Medicine River* could justifiably be described as a short story cycle composed entirely of return stories, recalling in this respect Grove's *Over Prairie Trails*. And it is easy to imagine why and how the return story would be especially apt and attractive to immigrants to multicultural Canada, this country of immigrants where self-identification by nationality often involves a hyphenated label. W.H. New writes in *Land Sliding* that 'Canadian writing recurrently takes characters on journeys home; far from the standard American model of eternal progress – "you can't go home again" – Canadian writing advises that you must return, in order to place the past apart, to read its other-centred rules in a fresh way, and to make the present and future home, whatever its relationship with a distant childhood, your own' (159–60). George Willard of the American Anderson's *Winesburg, Ohio* lights out like Huck Finn before him; such characters as Paul Farlotte, the Envoi's auditor, Grove's persona, and Rose either eventually stay put or yearn to return home. The aptly named Will of *Medicine River* abandons his money-getting in the city (Toronto, named here if unnamed in *Sunshine Sketches*) and returns to close proximity with his Albertan reserve community – his home – and there finds accommodation with self and other, with his past, and with the non-Native other within himself.

Of course, this fictional urge to return is also a deeply human desire in response to the psychic sense of diaspora, one that is as old as the *Odyssey*, *Paradise Regained*, and the numerous myths of reintegration in a wombing oneness. It might also be said that all writers, including literary critics, are dispositionally conservative and humanist, whatever their politics and critical-theoretical practices. It is a humanist-conservative impulse that urges writers to go after the good word, the new word, even the translated word (*Who*, 205–6) – *excursus* – and to bring the news home – *recursus*. When such spirit finds expression in Canadian short story cycles, its works argue fictionally that smaller communities of like-minded citizens support individual identity in ways too meaningful to be forgotten; that patriarchal definitions of society and gender roles must not be allowed to continue a crass capitalism's suppression of women and other workers; that the self may be a constructed entity that can blossom in an interdependent relationship with the natural world; that communal and individual rituals, symbols, and memories are necessary to cultural continuity; that self-identity and the process of self-realization may be connected forever to place of origin as home. Such lessons are reasonably humanist, broadly conservative, and distinctly, identifiably Canadian.

As I suggested in the introduction, the story cycle's definitive tension between the one and the many may form a large part of its attraction for the writers in English of a country, Canada, that was formed out of the tensions between the conservatism of both its founding parents, England and Royalist France, and the liberalism of its enterprising neighbour to the south (and later post-Revolutionary France) – a Canada whose defining myth became the middle-way. The distinguished English-Canadian short story in its extension to the story cycle – that middle-way genre of prose fiction – can also be figured now as mirroring most fittingly the distinctive yet closely linked regions of Canada, constituting a kind of geopolitical fictional linkage of abiding bonds and creative gaps *A Mari usque ad mare* as opposed to the continuous totalizing story written *E Pluribus Unum*. The mistakenly much-anticipated, ever-elusive Great Canadian Novel may actually have been written, or is yet to be written, as a great Canadian short story cycle. (Readers will forgive me if I humbly suggest *Sunshine Sketches of a Little Town* as our seminal site, much as humble Hemingway declared that modern American fiction flows from *The Adventures of Huckleberry Finn*.) Such half-facetiousness and serious speculation help to explain the continuing presence in Canadian literature of what Priscilla M. Kramer has called the 'cyclical habit of mind' (in Ingram, 24), a habit that we see expressed in explorers' journals and sketch books and long poems from the eighteenth century onwards, and in the shaping of interdependent stories into cyclical patterns of recurrent development and return by many of our best fiction writers: Duncan Campbell Scott, Stephen Leacock, J.G. Sime, Frederick Philip Grove, Emily Carr, George Elliott, Alice Munro, and Thomas King.

Notes

Introduction: The Canadian Short Story and Story Cycle

1 I prefer the term short story 'cycle' to 'sequence,' 'series,' or 'composite' because 'cycle' best captures the form's dynamic of recurrent development, because it best describes the return function of the Canadian cycle's concluding story, and because it carries enriching historical associations with other cyclical and seasonal models (oral traditions, calendars, liturgies, miracle plays, sonnet cycles, etc.), and even with larger drama and novel cycles. For others' preferences, see Luscher (149), Kennedy (vii–x), and Lunden. Lunden's book appeared too late for full incorporation into the present study; however, we do seem to share a view of the short story cycle as more interesting for its tension between the one and the many than solely for its strategies of coherence.

2 Kennedy (viii) argues that what he calls the 'story sequence,' which is defined so inclusively as to have room for mixed-genre literary collages, is an American genre: 'Although recent collections by such writers as Alice Munro, Angela Carter, Gabriel Garcia-Marquez, and Italo Calvino remind us that the proliferation of short story sequences is truly a global phenomenon, still the pragmatic affinity for short stories that shaped the literature of the United States decisively in the nineteenth century seems to persist in our national avidity for organized story collections. Perhaps the very determination to build a unified republic out of diverse states, regions, and population groups – to achieve the unity expressed by the motto *e pluribus unum* – helps to account for this continuing passion.' For now, I would indicate only that American culture, as distinguished from Canadian, has always stressed the *unum* over the *pluribus*, and thus its postcolonial obsession with identifying the great American novel. Here, Lunden's view is closer to Kennedy's than to mine.

3 For instance, Norman Friedman (29), after impressively surveying the subject of short story theories over some thirteen pages, concludes, 'For my own part, I do not really believe there is any such thing as the short story more specific than "a short fiction narrative in prose."' See also Ferguson.

4 See Bakhtin (*Dialogic*, 8): 'Faced with the problem of the novel, genre theory must submit to a radical re-structuring.'

5 I am grateful to Gwendolyn Guth for drawing my attention to this aspect of Bakhtin's writings.

6 It is no accident that Poe, with 'Murders in the Rue Morgue,' also invented the detective short story. Not only does his detective's method of deduction work backwards from an effect – the crime – in a manner that recalls Poe's instructions for composition, but the detective story is the ideal type to be conceived from end to beginning.

7 But this is not only a woman writer's explanation. In 'Fires' (23–5), the American minimalist short story writer Raymond Carver also cites domestic responsibilities as the cause of his writing short stories instead of novels. Carver recounts a poignant scene of genre choice, having been left in charge of his two children and a load of laundry.

8 Perhaps the most pertinent distinction is that between the sketch and the short story. See Carole Gerson and Kathy Mezei, who provide a working definition of the sketch as 'an apparently personal anecdote or memoir which focuses on one particular place, person, or experience, and is usually intended for magazine publication' (2). Thus the sketch, mainly an eighteenth- and nineteenth-century form (though practised still in the magazine profile, travel writing, and newspaper column), can be considered more personal than the short story, and more anecdotal, more tightly focused on one subject (a character, a natural event), perhaps also more obviously didactic, and supposedly less fictional. It is also the most important of the mini-forms that contributed towards the emergence of the short story as a distinct genre. See New (Introduction, 11–12) for a catalogue of seventeen forms of short fiction, and his summary observation: 'As Canadian writers began during the 19th century to experiment with short fiction, they tried out all of these forms, often bringing together several different ones into a single book-length miscellany ... It would be wrong, therefore, to claim a single source of Canadian short fiction, whether in anecdote and tale, or history and moral exempla, or fable and folk tale, or journal and sketch. It would also be wrong to ignore any of them.'

9 To digress (relevantly, I trust), it might be observed that the idea of a Canadian short story, and of course a Canadian literature, depends by definition on a healthy cultural nationalism. Sometimes expressed as virulent anti-Americanism, such is not really definitive of Canadian nationalism, or is but an incidental

feature of it; most often the cause of Canadian anti-Americanism is merely that the proximity of such a powerfully assured national entity makes for ready self-definition 'as against.' Historically in English-Canadian culture, Britain had served as the distant pole exerting an influence sufficient to keep Canada distinct from its near North American neighbour (as in matters of spelling). Often in the history of Canadian ideas and politics, this practice of self-definition has focused on the issue of trade reciprocity with the Americans. Previously whenever the call for freer trade went out, as in the federal elections of 1878 and 1911, Canadians were encouraged (and not always for idealistic reasons) to assert their tie to England, their Imperial loyalty, later their Commonwealth consciousness, and later still their distinct Canadian identity. In the 1860s the upsurge of Canadian cultural nationalism was the expression of movement towards, and then the attainment of, Dominion status. In the 1920s it was the result of pride in Canada's having acquitted itself honourably in the First World War. By the 1960s, the notions of a Canadian Britishness, Imperialism, and the Commonwealth had long since become untenable. In place of this un-American absence, the ongoing process of defining a Canadian identity became something of a cultural industry, and it thrived as a consequence of such nationalist factors as the Massey Report on Canadian culture of the early 1950s, the establishment of the Canada Council in the late 1950s, and the rebirth of anti-Americanism in the widespread feeling against imperialist America's involvement in the Vietnam War in the 1960s. However, and for reasons that remain incomprehensible to me, the notion of continually exploring a Canadian identity fell out of favour well before the 1980s. With nothing meaningful left with which to oppose closer ties with the Americans, and after over a century of failed attempts to strengthen economic union between the two primary trading partners, the North American Free Trade Agreement (NAFTA) was passed by Parliament in 1987, and since then ever-expanding trading agreements have proceeded apace. Of course, today we talk of plural Canadian identities, as should always have been the case; more and more we are becoming former prime minister Joe Clark's 'community of communities.' As the present study will suggest at a few points, the various pluralistic conceptions of a unified Canada are another reason why the short story cycle is such an apt form for us. Still, it is worth noting that genuine interest in Canadian literature also grew, and the Canadian short story flourished, during and after those three most active periods of Canadian cultural nationalism: the 1860s, the 1920s, and the 1960s.

10 See New (Introduction, 5–7) for a succinct survey of the contemporary period of the Canadian short story.

11 Cf. Ingram (24), Barth (218–38, 84–90, 258–81), Schroeder ('Fear,' 162), and New (*Dreams*, 10–12).

196 Notes to pages 16–19

12 In American literature, Sara Orne Jewett's *The Country of the Pointed Firs*, like *Viger* published in 1896, holds the distinction of being the first short story cycle, a fact which again points up the simultaneity of the new form's development.

13 See Meindl (19), who views the story cycle as pre-eminently a Modern form, one ideally suited to twentieth-century alienation: 'Modern alienation becomes palpable through the confinement of individuals to self-contained stories which in their aggregate suggest the societal, communal or family context which fails to function.'

14 See Luscher (153): 'The form's development has been spurred not only by Joyce and Anderson but also by the possibilities of unity demonstrated in American regional collections and by more recent experimentation with the novel'; and Meindl (17): 'Considering that the modern novel is above all characterized by a dissolution of consecutive temporal structure, by the breaking up of plot and story line, the short story cycle, which radicalizes this trend, becomes a key modernist genre'; and Godard (27): 'discontinuous narrative modes are privileged in contemporary English-Canadian literature where anecdotes are strung together in extended patterns that stretch the traditional story. They occur in two modes which have generally been considered to form distinctive genres, the short story cycle and the long poem.'

15 See Grace (448): the short story series 'retains the fragmentation of experiential reality while allowing the artist to shape and control material unobtrusively.'

16 Although Luscher (162) ultimately disagrees with Ingram's method of categorizing story cycles, he concedes that Ingram's terminology is the one 'critics most commonly use' (149). See also Kennedy's critique (ix).

17 F.R. Scott's 'W.L.M.K.' (60–1) offers in a satiric portrait of Canada's longest-serving prime minister, William Lyon Mackenzie King, a leftist critique of many of these traditionally Canadian characteristics, especially the willingness to compromise and the predilection for the middle way. I have always thought Scott's poem extremely ungenerous, mainly because Scott so eagerly sacrifices King's (and, by his own equation, Canada's) complexity to a simple ideology. For a fascinating and highly appreciative sketch of King, see J.G. Sime's little-known 'Three Meetings with Mr. Mackenzie King' (*Brave*, 155–65). I must quote an extensive passage from it, because even given subsequent revelations of King's eccentricities, this incident deserves a wider circulation.

Sometime about the mid-1930s, Sime is invited to dinner in Ottawa with the prime minister. It is a party of six, and towards its end Sime and two other women make an excuse to go upstairs 'in order to inspect some very lovely embroidered underwear that our hostess had brought back with her from her oriental travels.'

We were engrossed in our inspection when the voice of Mr. King, crying 'Are you coming?' fell upon our ears and the moment after, he himself appeared at the door. It was evident that he was still in his merry mood and was not in the least annoyed at our tardiness or anxious for us to hurry. Indeed when he saw that our hostess had just lifted a dressing-gown out of the drawer, he went up to her, took it from her with a smile, shook it out of its folds and then, slipping his arms through the kimono arm-holes and drawing the amplitude of the garment round his sizable waist with the sash, he surveyed us, the smile – and it really was a smile – still on his face. And we laughed.

It is impossible to say how funny he looked, the dressing-gown was so entirely feminine and he so utterly masculine. We laughed and laughed and he, spurred on by our ready participation in his doings, staged a little playlet – the impersonations of a lady arranging herself for going out, making herself up before the mirror and twisting from side to side so as to catch a glimpse all round the globe, as one might say. I don't suppose the performance lasted more than half a minute ... Mr. King had the faculty of presentation in a greater degree than anyone who has come my way; he put a thing before you so definitely that you felt you had it for your own. An invaluable talent for a Prime Minister to possess.

18 See Struthers ('Intersecting,' 16–30) for a critique of the limitations of Ingram's system with reference to Canadian short story cycles by Hood, Munro, Blaise, and Hodgins.

19 Luscher, in criticizing and attempting to improve Ingram's system of categorizing story cycles, arrives at a 'definition' of the form that is not nearly as useful because of its openness. For an even less useful inclusive approach to the necessary business of a working definition, see Kennedy (vii–xi).

20 See Luscher (149–50): 'These works should be viewed, not as failed novels, but as unique hybrids that combine two distinct reading pleasures: the patterned closure of individual stories and the discovery of larger unifying strategies that transcend the apparent gaps between stories.'

21 See Godard (30), who observes that the story cycle 'defamiliarizes the temporal conventions of the novel.' And again Luscher (150) is worth quoting: 'By operating without the major narrative unities of the novel, the writer of the short story sequence courts disunity in order to achieve "victory" over it by setting up a new set of narrative ground rules that rely heavily on active pattern-making faculties.' Godard (31) writes, too, that the 'manipulation of space and time [is] characteristic of the subgenre.'

22 See R. Davies ('Stephen Leacock,' 136) and Cameron (*Faces*, 138); this view of

Leacock is best represented by the title of Cameron's *Dalhousie Review* essay: 'Stephen Leacock: The Novelist Who Never Was.'

23 Functionally, return stories may derive from the tradition of the French *ballade*, where an *envoi* caps the poem with a refrain-like stanza that reiterates the poem's main theme, often incorporating preceding images and symbols, and can be in the voice of a direct address to the reader. Thus the title of the return story of Leacock's *Sunshine Sketches*, 'L'Envoi: The Train to Mariposa' (141). Hugh MacLennan's end-piece to his innovative use of serial-cyclical form in *Seven Rivers of Canada* is also titled 'L'Envoi' (169), which must seem more and more the best way to end a book.

24 In this regard the story cycle does accord with Bakhtin's description (quoted at greater length above) of other genres under the influence of novelization: 'the novel inserts into these other genres an indeterminacy, a certain semantic openendedness, a living contact with unfinished, still-evolving contemporary reality (the openended present)' (*Dialogic*, 7). Of course, Bakhtin is not thinking of short stories, let alone story cycles, but rather the classical genres.

1: 'In the Meantime': Duncan Campbell Scott's *In the Village of Viger*

1 *In the Village of Viger* was first published in Boston by Copeland and Day, and not published in Canada until the Ryerson Press edition of 1945. It has been published twice as a McClelland and Stewart NCL paperback, in 1973 and 1996 (page references in the present chapter are to the latest edition). For a bibliography of Scott, see Groening. All of the stories but two, 'No. 68 Rue Alfred de Musset' and 'Paul Farlotte,' were published in magazines before being arranged (Ingram's terminology) for *Viger* (Groening, 501–2). Interestingly, on 5 June 1944 Scott wrote E.K. Brown that he had given thought to writing another story cycle 'with Welly Legrave as a centre' (McDougall, 108). Welly Legrave is the hero of Scott's 'northern' short story, 'A Legend of Welly Legrave' (*Witching*, 178–97).

2 In the afterword to the most recent NCL edition of *Viger*, Tracy Ware (124–5) gives an amusing account of Morley Callaghan's unfavourable reaction, in a letter to Knister, to this tribute: 'What is the matter with you?' As Ware observes, 'Callaghan lived to receive a similarly cruel treatment from younger writers and critics who also would clear the ground of the past to allow the present to flourish.'

3 John Metcalf (*What*, 45–87) has argued at length, in a naïve and anxious attack, against the importance of *Viger* (see above, 5–7, and Dragland's response to Metcalf, *Floating*, 131–2).

4 Ware (Afterword, 120), in giving the themes of the story cycle, never mentions

the occurrence in every story of fractured and disrupted families: 'The main themes of *In the Village of Viger* are the appeal and the limitations of pastoral beauty, the dangers of oppressive traditions that threaten to stifle the present, and the continuities and discontinuities between European culture and the life of a small village.' Later (122), Ware does recognize that 'the Desjardins and other families in the book' are victimized by their own histories.

5 See New (*Land Sliding*, 157–8) for a discussion of the complex relation of city to small town in Canadian fiction.

6 Scott, born and raised in Ottawa, enjoyed a highly successful career in the Department of Indian Affairs, eventually rising to the position of deputy superintendent general; early in his career he was one of the department's chief treaty negotiators, and later the author of the government's policy statement, *The Administration of Indian Affairs in Canada* (1931).

7 Scott's suggestively Arnoldian understanding of the relation between literature and progress is best read in his 'Poetry and Progress: Presidential Address Delivered before the Royal Society of Canada, May 17, 1922' (*Circle*, 123–47).

8 An 'At the Mermaid Inn' column of 4 February 1893 (B. Davies, 254). Here Scott is citing Pater in reference to Gustave Flaubert's struggle to marry form and content, speculating that 'perhaps Flaubert was born with a musician's idea of form and was constantly searching for the absolute fusion of form and context which is found in no other art.' For a fuller account of Scott's ideas regarding music, see 'Poetry and Progress' (*Circle*, 139–40).

9 A look at the contents pages of *The Poems of Duncan Campbell Scott* finds the following titles: 'Night Hymns on Lake Nipigon,' 'The Piper of Arll,' 'Powassan's Drum,' 'Dirge for a Violet,' 'On the Death of Claude Debussy,' 'Improvisation on an Old Song,' 'Adagio,' 'Words after Music,' 'At the Piano,' and many another with the word 'song' in the title.

10 Musical metaphors and analogies do appear to translate well in discussions of the formal properties of story cycles. See Luscher (149): 'As in a musical sequence, the story sequence repeats and progressively develops themes and motifs over the course of the work; its unity derives from a perception of both the successive ordering and recurrent patterns, which together provide the continuity of the reading experience.' Godard (30) observes of the discontinuous narrative of story cycle form that 'the musical metaphor is an apt reminder that beauty lies in the intervening silences as well as in the notes sounded, as the composer John Cage has suggested.' And Patricia Morley's essay on Grove's *Over Prairie Trails*, the book which provides one of the two primary texts of chapter 3 below, is dominated by musical metaphors.

11 Purdy describes his experience of the north as 'like being born again into a world so different from the fat South' (*No Other*, 146).

12 See Clark Blaise, 'To Begin, To Begin' (22–6), who shows the ways in which a short story's opening paragraph can project the entire story. Blaise's own *A North American Education* (1973) is an excellent example of the contemporary Canadian short story cycle of character.

13 See *The Oxford Dictionary of Saints*. St Joseph is also the patron saint of all who desire a holy death (thus the high number of St Joseph's hospitals). Is Scott implying that a holy death is the most Viger can hope for? And if that suggestion is entertained, it can be joined by another that also sees in the name 'Viger' a root shared with 'vigil.' I am indebted here to David Bentley for directing me towards the importance of St Joseph.

14 I have in mind Erwin Panofsky's definition of humanism as 'an attitude which can be defined as the conviction of the dignity of man, based on both the insistence of human values (rationality and freedom) and the acceptance of human limitations (fallibility and frailty); from these two postulates results – responsibility and tolerance' (2).

15 See New (*Dreams*, 183): 'Arbique's Franco-Prussian quarrel with Hans over the Motherland masks a deeper quarrel – over the "possession" of Latulipe – that is sexual in origin, if political in expression, something which he sublimates past the point of recognizing.' Such a reading also supports the imputation of jealousy to Madame Arbique.

16 Again I want to direct readers to David Bentley's excellent articles on the turn-of-the-century 'mind-cure' movement as it relates to Carman's poetry ('Carman') and the short stories of Gilbert Parker, Roberts, and of Scott's *Viger* ('Thing'). In the second article, Bentley traces the influence of *symbolisme* and Maurice Maeterlinck on these writers (and I would note here, though some congruencies may be coincidental, the Christian name of Eloise's brother, Maurice). Also, it may be the likes of the Desjardins and Eloise Ruelle whom Michelle Gadpaille has in mind, somewhat mistakenly in her emphasis on Scott's realism and modernism, when she observes: 'In presenting character as dynamic rather than static, as something shaped by social, temporal, and geographical realities, Scott moved towards what has been called the "great modern subject", the disintegration of the human personality and consciousness' (15; See also Gerson, 'Piper's,' 138).

17 In showing the influence of Maurice Maeterlinck and *symbolisme* on Scott, Bentley ('Thing,' 41–2) argues that the intent in such a story as 'The Bobolink' is to be esoterically suggestive; he shows, moreover, that progressive supernaturalism is a sequential development in *Viger*, thereby discovering yet another organizing principle at work in the story cycle.

18 See the reactionary Michael Fischer (4–5), who outlines the history of this critique. Scott's close friend Archibald Lampman, who convinced Scott to write,

was a Fabian Socialist; his 'The Land of Pallas' (201–10) expresses the utopian hope of his Fabianism. Morris and Fabian Socialism are discussed at greater length in the following chapter on J.G. Sime's short story cycle, *Sister Woman* (1919). For an account of Morris's influence on Canada's Confederation Poets, see Bentley ('William Morris').

19 In its concern with the destructive consequences of the obsession with 'scientific' perfection at the expense of the 'human' element, 'Paul Farlotte' resembles any number of stories by Nathaniel Hawthorne, but see especially 'The Birthmark' (147–65). The scene where Farlotte comes upon Guy obsessing over his machine with the apparition of his father attending protectively (88) is especially reminiscent of Hawthorne.

20 Lyle Weis (50–1) has also noticed the relevance of St Joseph to Paul's reluctant assumption of the role of father. Weis has further observed a pun in the 'growing pear-tree' at the end of the story, against whose 'slender stem' Paul leans 'for support' (89), with the homonymic pun underscoring the *pairing* of Paul and the St Denis family. Weis has made me think that the pun may be even richer, and appropriately bilingual, as in *père*.

21 In a speech at Massey Hall, Toronto, in 1904, and subsequently published in the *Globe*, 15 October 1904. I am grateful to Lauren Walker for supplying this information.

2: Fabian Feminism: J.G. Sime's *Sister Woman*

1 But see Watt's whole dissertation ('Passing'), a biographical study, and Esther Lisabeth Bobak's dissertation (286–308), which includes Sime's *Our Little Life* as part of a study of the urbanization of the Canadian novel.

2 For a succinct biographical-bibliographical account of Sime, see New's entry in the *Dictionary of Literary Biography: Canadian Writers 1890–1920*. Another good source is the 'Publisher's Note' that concludes Sime's own short monograph *Thomas Hardy of the Wessex Novels* (55–8). Sime was born in Scotland in 1868 into a professional literary family. She moved with her family to London, England, in 1869, and through the ensuing years she regularly met many of the literary luminaries of the day. In 1907 she immigrated alone to Montreal, where she began writing and lived for most of the rest of her life. She returned to England towards the end of her life, where she died in 1958.

3 In an email to the author (17 April 2000), Watt suspects that Frank Nicholson, Sime's lifelong collaborator, contributed the title *Sister Woman*. In the unpaginated preface of her dissertation, Watt describes Nicholson as 'Georgina Sime's life-long friend, editor, amanuensis, and supporter.'

4 As to the number of stories, though, I would even go so far as to speculate that

Sime must have had either a higher or a lower number of sister-woman stories on hand and either subtracted from or added to that number to arrive at twenty-eight. Such purported numerological design may explain why a few of the stories of the cycle, and they are later ones, should have been omitted. 'The Wrestler,' 'Livin' Up to It,' and 'A Page from Life' are trite, condescending, and sentimental respectively.

5 In the form of its stories, *Sister Woman* also carries traces of Sime's first book, *Rainbow Lights: Being Extracts from the Missives of Iris* (1913), which is generically a sketch book, a miscellaneous collection of pieces (Watt Introduction, viii). But of course, as the introduction suggests, the eighteenth- and nineteenth-century sketch book was one source of the modern story cycle, as the sketch was one of the forms from which the short story itself developed.

6 As I mention in the introduction, Hugh MacLennan's *Seven Rivers of Canada* (1961) presents not only another innovative use of story cycle form (complete with 'L'Envoi') in a non-fictional genre but, in the context of Sime's prophecy, a fellow Montrealer's more formal approximation of the kind of literary art she forecast.

7 Frederick Kirchoff offers a compelling picture of Morris as proselytizer for the Fabian cause, giving a better idea than does Sime herself of what would have won her to his teaching: 'Morris discusses "work" in such an unabashedly personal fashion that it is difficult to argue with his premises. Here, as elsewhere, the voice that emerges from these lectures and essays is very much that of "a man speaking to men." Few literary spokesmen for revolution have argued in such down-to-earth terms. For Morris, socialism was not a matter of political theorizing, but one of the plain facts of human experience. He makes his case most cogently when he makes his audience most conscious of the complex, responsive personality behind his words. He is analytic without being obtruse, plainspoken without being condescending. And the result is the deep sincerity that characterizes the writings of his final twenty years' (117)

8 In *Bernard Shaw's Sister and Her Friends: A New Angle on G.B.S.*, Henry George Farmer quotes liberally from Sime's recollection of Shaw's sister.

9 Sime's relations with her own mother appear to have been cool and distant, though she does say of her, 'I don't know that my mother was a feminist, but she nearly always did take the woman's part' (*Brave*, 90). The appraisal sounds oddly like that of the more radical feminist and socialist: one is either for or against; the particulars of the issue are irrelevant.

10 At first this male interlocutor appears a promising representative of Shaw's enlightened man, described in his preface to the 1913 edition of *The Quintessence of Ibsenism*: 'Men are waking up to the perception that in killing women's souls they have killed their own' (101).

11 See Campbell (Introduction, x): 'The *persona* of the narrator in *Sister Woman* and many of its thematic concerns are rooted in Sime's own life. An Anglo-Scot who arrived in Quebec City in 1907 on the eve of her fortieth birthday, Sime, in her four decades of residence in Montreal, came to see herself a "near-Canadian", as she called herself in an interview [xxx n6]. She once described an immigrant as "a person who has definitely fallen between two stools, and, whether he likes it or not, has to stay there" [*Canada*, 177]. As an immigrant, as a woman alone, and as a writer, she was always conscious that she had a unique and marginalised perspective on the country that so fascinated her.'

12 In displaying the good-natured bettering of the man in this witty parrying, the prologue parallels the opening scene of Isabella Valancy Crawford's *Malcolm's Katie: A Love Story* (1884), where 'little Katie' at sixteen tactfully shows herself to be superior in intellect to her otherwise dominant fiancé, Max. And comparison of these two works is not valid only in the tolerant feminism displayed in their opening scenes; the Platonic-Christian idealization of love that constitutes the definitive myth of *Malcolm's Katie* is congruent with the idealization of love that climaxes 'Divorced,' the return story of *Sister Woman*, which will be discussed in detail below. Both loves are in the keeping of women. Both works offer subversive critiques of patriarchal capitalism (in *Malcolm's Katie* it is also subtextual). Both authors share subject positions as outsiders to the male, Anglo, Protestant establishment (Crawford being Catholic and Irish as well as female and unmarried).

13 See Dean (7), who, following the theorizing of Judith Butler (125), writes of the performative aspect of gender: 'Gender can't be done once and be done with; femininity is a practice which must *be* practised, be repeated over and over again because it can never be done "right," can never materialize as a natural attribute of a material body.' This is not a view with which either *Sister Woman* or Sime, I think (see Watt, Introduction, vii), would concur, though it provides a useful gloss on the repetitive aspect of the stories of *Sister Woman* and of the male interlocutor's failure/refusal to 'get it' in the epilogue.

14 See Kroetsch (*Lovely*) on the empowering strategies of being unnamed in Canadian fiction.

15 Campbell (Introduction, xxv) is worth quoting a length on this issue: 'The affirmation in these stories of a female love that transcends suffering derives from Sime's type of feminism, one typical of her time. Her handbook *The Mistress of All Work* (1916) expresses her conviction that "the central desire of the normal woman is to please some one of whom she is fond, and the more normal she is, the more will that desire occupy the inmost place in her heart" [137]. Twenty years later, in a memoir of the Laurentians, she was equally emphatic: "... whatever we [women] say and however feminist we become, it is

woman's nature to serve, and I think we are never happier than doing so"
[*Canadian Shack*, 206]. Such a viewpoint was shared by many of Sime's Canadian contemporaries. Women's historian Deborah Gorham has pointed out
[43–4] that early twentieth-century feminism in Canada was infused by a
"spirit of reconciliation," a maternal feminism in which "self-sacrifice was
central to women's role and the key to her psyche."'

16 It may be that in this instance Sime is influenced generally by Pre-Raphaelite
art and poetry, and perhaps more particularly by William Morris's poem *The
Defence of Guenevere* (1858). For a similar treatment of the legacy for Canadian female characters of medieval romance in its Victorian adaptations, and of
romance in its more pedestrian guise, see Lucy Maud Montgomery's humorous treatment in *Anne of Green Gables* (1908) and Margaret Atwood's more
satiric *Lady Oracle* (1978). 'The Beggar Maid' story of Alice Munro's *Who Do
You Think You Are?*, the cycle that provides the subject of chapter 5 of the
present study, is titled after Edward Burne-Jones's Pre-Raphaelite picture *King
Cophetua and the Beggar Maid*. See Bentley ('William Morris') for a discussion of Morris's influence on Canada's Confederation Poets.

17 See Bobak (305), who observes a similar recurrent metafictional interest in
Sime's novel *Our Little Life*: 'Sime may have found it amusing to write about
herself [the writer-persona in the novel] writing about Miss McGee [the hero-
ine]. In a larger sense, the entire novel is a comment on itself.' And later (308):
'Sime has done something in *Our Little Life*, however, which very few novels
about artists do – she has not only shown us the artist creating, but the creation itself (as in *The Diviners*).'

18 The title of the twenty-first story, 'The Social Problem,' does not refer to poverty or venereal disease, but to the coquetry of its subject, Donna, who, the
narrator observes, 'embodied all the things that I most dislike' (207). Donna is
probably *Sister Woman*'s prime figure of the female consumer consumed.
'"Say," she said, and turned her dark eyes on me again, "say, what's the good of
ut all? I keep goin'. And I'm goin' to keep goin'. And if this man don't suit I'm
goin' to have the next one – and that's goin' some, believe me! But it's" – she
sighed, and this time the sigh seemed to come from her very soul – "it's tirin',"
she said' (215). Donna's way of life is presented finally as metonymic of a
death wish in the broader culture.

19 Of course Marx's declaration, which is specifically in criticism of 'the narrow
horizon of bourgeois right' (*Gotha*, 10), has its source in the New Testament –
'and distribution was made unto every man according as he had need' (Acts
4:35) – and this confluence of sources itself may be seen to recall Sime's initial
recognition of a similarity between William Morris's socialist teaching and 'the
early Christians (*Brave*, 12). There are other places in *Sister Woman* that

apparently echo as well as critique Marx, such as 'Rose of Sharon,' which seems to be playing off the other popular Marxist belief that 'Religion ... is the opium of the people' (*Hegel's*, 131), while showing, this time at the expense of a somewhat materialistic narrator, that Rosie's nuisance evangelicalism is also sustaining of her simple soul.

20 I trust that readers will believe me when I say that the title of this chapter came to me before I'd found Weintraub's book, *Fabian Feminist: Bernard Shaw and Woman*. I mention this coincidence mainly because it supports my belief that Sime's socialism and her feminism were at this time directly influenced by Morris, Fabianism, and Shaw. And because that is the case, the coincidence is not remarkable.

21 See Weintraub (5, quoting from Shaw's letters): 'With her [Mrs Warren's] gains she has had her daughter highly educated and respectably brought up in complete ignorance of the source of her mother's income ... Nobody's conscience is smitten except, I hope, the conscience of the audience. My intention is that they shall go home thoroughly uncomfortable.' There are of course other works of the time, and earlier, that deal sympathetically with prostitutes on economic grounds (Defoe's *Moll Flanders*, say), and the 'whore with the golden heart' had already become a staple of melodrama. Nonetheless, the influence of *Mrs. Warren's Profession* on 'A Woman of Business' seems clear and direct, and it doubtless emerges from Sime's contact with Shaw, his work, and his sister Lucy. There are many other instances of possible influence, but only one other is too tempting not to remark. The obstreperously direct Lina Szczepanowska of Shaw's *Misalliance* (first performed 1910; first published in English 1914) seems to have provided a type for a number of Sime's young and not so young, stridently independent working women, especially the Lina who in her major speech towards the end of the play clarifies her Shavian views on marriage: 'I am an honest woman: I earn my living. I am a free woman: I live in my own house. I am a woman of the world ... And this Englishman! this linendraper! he dares to ask me to come and live with him in this rrrrrabbit hutch, and take my bread from his hand, and ask him for pocket money, and wear soft clothes, and be his woman! his wife! Sooner than that, I would stoop to the lowest depths of my profession [a daredevil] ... All this I would do sooner than take my bread from the hand of a man and make him the master of my body and soul' (*Bodley Head*, 5:249–50). Sime's working women often speak paler versions of Lina's declaration, or have them spoken for them by the narrator at her most third-person subjective: Bertha Martin and her 'sisters' in 'Munitions'; Phyllis Redmayne of 'An Irregular Union'; the unnamed dying woman of 'The Wrestler,' who is, like Lina, a circus performer; Tryphena of 'The Bachelor Girl,' who is named similarly to Hypatia

of *Misalliance* but talks like Lina; even Ella Hume of 'Divorced,' the return story of *Sister Woman*.

3: Fabulous Selves: Two Modern Stort Story Cycles

1 Grove, who adapted the conventions of naturalism to a Canadian fictional context, is generally recognized as Canada's first Modern novelist, as something of a Canadian hybrid of Émile Zola, Thomas Hardy, and Theodore Dreiser.

2 Margaret Stobie observes a similar movement in *Trails* from the early to the later stories, and sees this movement paralleled by a loss of directness in Grove's writing style (72). K.P. Stich describes the overall movement as one from 'certainty to uncertainty' ('Narcissism,' 32). Some forty-five years after *Trails*, fellow Manitoban writer Margaret Laurence, in *A Bird in the House*, will portray her autobiographical character, Vanessa MacLeod, developing through the same changes from romantic to realistic writer (see Stovel).

3 Despite the reference to 'definite notes' in the following, Grove concedes as much: 'I have often doubted my memory here, and yet I have my very definite notes, and besides there is the picture in my mind. In spite of my own uncertainty I can assure you, that this is only one quarter a poem woven of impressions; the other three quarters are reality. But, while I am trying to set down facts, I am also trying to render moods and images begot by them' (*Trails*, 53). See Stobie, who remarks 'the free altering of facts to create fiction in *Over Prairie Trails*,' and suggests that 'perhaps Grove considered himself a fiction' (74); Keith ('Grove's,' 76), who compares Grove to George Borrow and George Moore as a writer intent 'upon remoulding his own character on paper'; Eli Mandel, who supposes that 'Grove's life was created by his own fiction, his novels that – it seems now – literally wrote him into existence' (58); and New, who, in analysing the 'narrative vocabulary' of 'Snow,' describes Grove's project in *Trails* as a 'transformation tale' ('Geography,' 60–1).

4 Grove also wrote a cycle of poems, *Poems: In Memoriam Phyllis May Grove*, in memory of his daughter, who died in 1927 at the age of twelve. This work, a finished manuscript, remained unpublished until Gaby Divay made it part of her Master's thesis at the University of Manitoba (Divay, xxviii). After *Klee Wyck*, Carr published two other books of memoirs and vignettes, *The Book of Small* (1942) and *The House of All Sorts* (1944); though fascinating in their own right and with their pieces obviously arranged to purpose, neither of these is a short story cycle. Carr's other works, her journals, were published posthumously.

5 Later (Afterword, 357), Wiebe modestly concedes that his term is 'clumsy' and

that he might prefer yet another term, 'bio-fiction' (358). Wiebe's afterword to *Fruits of the Earth* is not only one of the best in the NCL series but the most astute, if all too brief, commentary on form in Grove and in Canadian fiction generally. He connects Grove's writing with Anderson's *Winesburg, Ohio*, Scott's *Viger*, Leacock's *Sunshine Sketches*, Birdsell's two cycles of Agassiz stories, Alford's *A Sleep Full of Dreams*, Laurence's *A Bird in the House*, and Munro's *Who Do You Think You Are?* Wiebe observes how these works refuse to level experience into the novel's 'chronological continuum ... by taking dramatic connected moments and letting them imply massive wholes.' It is interesting to watch Wiebe search for an appropriate generic term for these works – 'what can they be called? – story spirals, whole-book sequences? Inter-connected stories? discontinuous narratives?' – and not hit upon the term story cycles (356–8). Of course, Wiebe is not only one of Canada's prime chroniclers but also the author of a story cycle, *The Blue Mountains of China* (1970).

6 Stich, too ('Narcissism,' 37), is interesting in this regard, remarking of the end of *Trails* that 'as a creative writer, Grove has come to a recognition of how thoroughly his veiled rationalizations about his past life as a failed German writer motivate his creation of *Over Prairie Trails*, and how his emergence as a Canadian writer depends on creative transformations of his self-consciousness.'

7 Oddly, the Clarke Irwin edition of *Klee Wyck* (1951; pb. 1962) has only twenty stories, whereas the original Oxford UP edition of 1941 and *The Complete Writings* (1997), which I take to be definitive, include 'Martha's Joey' in the seventeenth position. I can find no reason for the deletion, doubtless an error, in the Clarke Irwin, unfortunately the most widely known edition.

8 Robert Kroetsch's poem 'F.P. Grove: The Finding' provides similar commentary on Grove's true project in *Trails* and on 'Snow' specifically, deflatingly giving the last word to Mrs Grove: '"You had a hard trip?"' I was directed to Kroetsch's poem by New ('Geography,' 53).

9 Although he never uses the term 'story cycle,' Stich ('Narcissism,' 36) nonetheless recognizes that cyclical structure underlies the psychological movement of *Trails* when he supposes that 'it is as if Grove, the artist-analyst, were caught in a cycle of transference and countertransference while re-cultivating his past in an archetypal New World context.'

10 Grove's only book of poetry published during his life was the German *Wanderungen* (1902), whose title translates into English as 'Wanderings' or 'Travels'; the German *wandern* is the verb 'to travel' (or even the English 'to wander'). Wandering, or ostensibly aimless travelling on the open road, was the therapeutic charm of Vagabondage. I am grateful to Gwendolyn Guth and Klaus Peter Stich for their help with the German. On Carman's popularity and

the popularity of his and Hovey's Vagabondia volumes, see McGillivray (8 especially). And see Spettigue (199) on Grove's poetry: 'The early "wanderings" that show the poet a lonely, aloof Werther-figure ...'

11 Divay (lxxxiii) describes Grove's/Greve's German poetry in this way: 'Neoromantic and symbolist motifs in the guise of medieval, exotic, or sacral allusions are favoured, and myths, dreams, and supernatural elements occur frequently as well ... Greve's poems adhere to all of these themes.'

12 See Stich ('Narcissism,' 31–2), who, quoting Robert D. Stolorow, remarks that the Grove of *Trails* 'reminds one of a child whose "earliest object relationships *of necessity* serve a basically narcissistic function ... to consolidate [his] rudimentary self-representation."'

13 See New (*Land Sliding*, 103) on this same passage: 'Clearly, in his prose, [Grove] does "garden" – not just by representing landscape as a painting but also by accepting the aesthetic priorities of a particular painting school: one that champions the necessity of foreground, the picturesque validity of the curved line, and the convention of perspective.' In discussing both *Trails* and *A Search for America* (1927), New similarly remarks the contradictions in Grove's attitudes respecting such subjects as wealth and land ownership.

14 Knönagel (88–91) views the movement of *Trails* as expressing Grove's coming to terms with the limitations of his Nietzschean conception of himself. It is an intriguing argument and one that, like the present one, recognizes that there is a controlled development in the Grove persona through *Trails*.

15 Consider, for instance, the maudlin figure displayed when he realizes that he has not harmed an owl: 'Oh, how I felt reassured! I believe, tears welled in my eyes. When I come to the home of frog and toad, of gartersnake and owl and whip-poor-will, a great tenderness takes possession of me, and I should like to shield and help them all and tell them not to be afraid of me; but I rather think they know it anyway' (26). Divay describes a parallel development in Grove's poetry from a *l'art pour l'art* Decadent style to 'a realistic ideal of art' (lxxxix).

16 According to Stobie (47), by 1 March 1918 Grove 'was teaching at Ferguson school, four and a half miles from Mrs. Grove ... and was living with his family in the Falmouth teacherage'; so the last trip of *Trails* would probably have been made in February.

17 New sees yet another structuring principle at work: 'The initial (relatively uneventful) journey, that is, immediately precedes one that hints at danger (fog making the distance seem longer, space troped by time). Then follows a sketch suggesting that danger is readily dealt with, three sketches that refute this interim conclusion by intensifying danger (representing it by means of blizzard, squall, and illness), and a final sketch in which "drift" (the slide in and out of alertness, on and off the trail) interrupts the ostensible security that

experience, preparedness, knowledge, and familiarity might have been expected to lay claim to. "Snow" itself appears in the central narrative position; it is this position, as well as the narrative stance it adopts and the acquired resonance of its title image, that makes the artifice of this episode so instructive' ('Geography,' 54).

18 Most interestingly, Keith ('Grove's,' 80) sees Grove here mimicking the reader as observer of his objectified self: 'At the same time, the sensation of looking upon his own adventure from the outside anticipates the reader's stance and openly reveals Grove's habitual method of observing himself from different angles.'

19 See New ('Geography,' 62–4) for analysis of Grove's gendering of persona and wilderness landscape: 'the journey ... functions as a test or proof of the narrator's manliness in addition to being the medium through which he becomes transformed' (62).

20 There is a contradiction here as well, as Grove digresses to outline a somewhat nihilistic-cum-fatalistic philosophy of life, and does so at the expense of his wife and child. In some of the least attractive self-characterization of the cycle, he reflects on how the 'most serious-minded men' become 'profoundly impressed with the futility of' life (131), and on how life, self-deluding and meaningless, 'slips by, unlived.' He then breaks out with, 'if my child was taken from me, it meant that my future was made meaningless,' exhibiting a self-centredness that is rendered understandable by his fear that his child is in mortal danger. Still, it must be wondered: how is his child to make meaningless life meaningful? He then characterizes his wife – half his future readership, recall – in the most patronizing, even insulting, of terms: 'True, my wife was something like a child to me. I was old enough to be her father, older even in mind than in actual years. But she, too, by marrying an aging man, had limited her own development, as it were, by mine. Nor was she I, after all. My child was. The outlook without her [his child] was night. Such a life was not to be lived.' Here Grove is indeed the fatalist he claims he is, and something of a pedestrian nihilist (*pace* Knönagel) – yet he would outwit fate and meaninglessness by acting as his daughter's mentor and model? Such an ambitious delusion may support my argument that in *Trails* Grove is shaping and playing with a duplicitous image of his self. Divay's thorough account of the influences of German turn-of-the-century culture on Grove's/Greve's thinking also supports this view: 'The underlying philosophical premises in Grove's poetry are indebted to Nietzschean and neo-Kantian positions current at the time of Greve's upbringing. They are marked by a blend of "Lebensphilosophie" [life philosophies](as already announced in Goethe), nihilism (prepared by Kierkegaard), a strong sense of relativity (most influentially popularized by

the physicist Ernst Mach), and the concurrent loss of a well-centred sense of self which had formerly been provided through religion.' Earlier, Divay suggests that this ethos encouraged in Grove a lasting chameleon-like approach to authorship: 'Grove did later not entirely relinquish old-standing habits – in theory, at least – such as adopting a variety of identities, masks, and roles ... he toyed with the idea of using an Andrew Rutherford pseudonym around 1922 for his first book publication *Over Prairie Trails*' (lxxiii). Apart from these speculations, it is always disheartening when reading 'A Call for Speed' to remember that Grove's daughter, Phyllis May, died in 1927 at the age of twelve.

21 As Stobie (149–52) tells it, while working in Ottawa for Graphic Publishers in 1930, Grove claimed to have 'manoeuvered' (Grove's word) Knister's winning first prize and $2500 in a novel contest for his fictionalization of Keats's life, *My Star Predominant*. Graphic went bankrupt before Knister could collect all his prize money.

22 See Keith ('Grove's,' 79): 'If [the reader] is expecting either the consistent portrait offered by a traditional novelist or the reliable persona of the familiar essayits [*sic*], he will be disappointed; if, on the other hand, he will be less troubled by the devious methods of a cumulative self-portrayal.' There is more than just a typo wrong with this expression, but the observation is nonetheless clear and correct.

23 For an informed discussion of the virtues and limitations of such thematic approaches in Canadian criticism, see John Moss's account, 'Bushed in the Sacred Wood,' which, among much else properly contextualized, has this to say about Frye's contribution: 'Frye responded to the same socio-cultural conditions as the others [thematic critics]; he did not create them. Frye on Blake, Milton, and Shakespeare is a very different phenomenon from Frye on Canadian literature, about which he generalizes with as much careless aplomb as the least of his apparent followers' (16). I trust that my analysis, perhaps particularizing to a fault, avoids the temptation to generalize.

24 See H. Thomas (19): '*Klee Wyck* undoubtedly raises questions about the appropriation of the experience of a marginalized people. What sets it apart from works that presume to speak for or about aboriginal people is that Carr is speaking as much for herself as for them, and she does not pretend to objectivity or detachment. She responds as an artist.'

25 In her summing up of 'The Indian Presence' in Carr's painting (*Emily Carr*, 137–8), Shadbolt reaches conclusions similar to those I observe of that presence and the 'dark' view of nature in *Klee Wyck*. She is certainly worth quoting at length: 'She felt the overall expressive character of native art: its tightness, its restraint, its inner tension, its mysterious, sober and dark spirit that was some-

times daemonic, sometimes quiescent. And so she took on the Indian's dark-ness in her canvases, closing them in with weighty and darkened skies, or with claustrophobic forests even when fidelity to her subject did not require her to do so. In seeking out the poles in their abandoned and overgrown locations and in creating painted environments that empathized with their character, she was drawn deeply into nature's dark side. And in probing one aspect of nature so deeply there opened up for her a vision of nature that embraced all moods, a possibility not previously envisioned.'

26 As Rimstead (50) notes, Carr's third encounter with D'Sonoqua is actually with the mistaken figure of a chief, and a male.

27 Along with the passages already quoted, see the following: 'the overlap of sub-ject and author is direct; the books are about herself' (*Complete Writings*, 6); 'accurate chronological recording has no part in her intentions'; 'the self-mir-roring quality that characterizes much of the writing. It is as though when [Carr is] ostensibly narrating an incident or describing a place, there is frequently present the underlying purpose of creating herself through and by means of the incident. So the books are about herself in a special kind of way' (7). As can be seen, those remarks come from a two-page range. And the following comes from Shadbolt's earlier *Emily Carr*: 'The conscious storyteller in her, altering situation and exaggerating characters for literary effect' (21); 'the books ... sub-stantiate the self-image she needed to authorize her life and art' (23).

28 In this respect, *Klee Wyck* is similar to a number of earlier and later works in the continuum of Canadian literature dealing with Native subjects: Duncan Campbell Scott's pastoral elegy for his artist friend, 'Lines in Memory of Edmund Morris' (*Selected*, 58–65); Al Purdy's 'Lament for the Dorsets' (*Being*, 50); and the end especially of Guy Vanderhaeghe's novel *The English-man's Boy*. See Robert Fulford (37), remarking on an address that Carr deliv-ered in Victoria in 1935: 'By the end of her talk it was clear that she was speaking a lament for a dead culture, one which she had been fortunate enough to glimpse and portray in its dying moments before the last great poles col-lapsed of their own weight and were reclaimed by the rain forests.' And Tho-mas (5): 'Like most of her contemporaries, Carr undoubtedly believed that native culture was doomed to extinction, and that the aboriginal peoples must either adapt to modern ways or die out entirely.' For some reason, perhaps because a non-Native male implicated in the governing structure is viewed safely as fair game, only Scott seems regularly to catch it for such attitudes as describing his 'Onondaga Madonna' as part of 'a weird and waning race' (*Selected*, 14); of course 'weird' does not mean odd but fated (as it does for *Macbeth*'s fate-serving 'weird sisters' [1.3.32]).

29 One of the more subtle ways in which Carr insinuates identity between Klee

Wyck and the Indians is in the repeated use of the temporally lax expression 'By and by' (for Klee Wyck), or 'Bymby' (for the Indians).

30 In his frequently reprinted foreword to *Klee Wyck*, Ira Dilworth quotes a passage from Carr's diary entry for late October 1936, and it is worth repeating here for the light it sheds on Carr's view of art and life as process: 'There's words enough, paint and brushes enough and thoughts enough. The whole difficulty seems to be getting the thoughts clear enough, making them stand still long enough to be fitted with words and paint. They are so elusive – like wild birds singing above your head, twittering close beside you, chortling in front of you, but gone the moment you put out a hand. If ever you do catch hold of a piece of a thought it breaks always leaving the piece in your hand just to aggravate you. If one only could encompass the whole, corral it, enclose it safe – but then maybe it would die, dwindle away because it could not go on growing. I don't think thoughts *could* stand still – the fringes of them would always be tangling into something just a little further on and that would draw it out and out. I guess that is just *why* it is so difficult to catch a complete idea – it's because everything is always on the move, always expanding' (19).

4: 'To keep what was good and pass it on': George Elliott's *The Kissing Man*

1 The other article is a version of the present chapter published in *Studies in Canadian Literature* (1997). Clara Thomas has published an interesting essay comparing *Sunshine Sketches* and *The Kissing Man* (1986). And John Moss's entry on *The Kissing Man* in his *A Reader's Guide to the Canadian Novel* (98–100) is appreciative and insightful, as is David Jackel's article on Elliott in *The Dictionary of Literary Biography* (124–6), though both are understandably limited by the format.

2 Apart from a couple of poems in the literary magazine *New Quarterly* and two published short stories – 'Four Little Words' in *76: New Canadian Stories* (1976) and 'Side Trip' in the *Canadian Forum* (June–July 1986) – Elliott's only book-length publication to 1994 was the text for the coffee-table book *God's Big Acre: Life in 401 Country* (1986). This book, whose subject is the farming communities along the southern Ontario highway, covers territory familiar to readers of *The Kissing Man*, and Elliott's text provides an interesting gloss on his fiction. Not long before his death in 1996, he published two books of fiction with Tim Struthers's Red Kite Press of Guelph, Ontario: *The Bittersweet Man* (1994) and *Crazy Water Boys* (1995). As its title suggests, *The Bittersweet Man* is something of a companion story cycle to *The Kissing Man*.

3 See C. Thomas (102) for evidence that the town is based closely on Strathroy, Ontario.

4 See Magee, who provides a highly informed and succinct account of the development of local-colour fiction, one that views Jane Austen's novels as the British epitome of the vogue.

5 Hood himself has drawn attention to the influence of the nineteenth- and twentieth-century sketch-book form/genre on *Around the Mountain* (Struthers, 'Intersecting,' 13–14), as well as to the influence of *Sunshine Sketches* (Struthers, 11).

6 Surrealist-absurdist fictions, usually satires, were popular in North America in the 1950s and 1960s, as witness for example such works as the American Terry Southern's *The Magic Christian* (1960), or in Canada the aforementioned *Beautiful Losers* (1966), or Richler's *The Incomparable Atuk* (1963) and *Cocksure* (1968).

7 Shadbolt (*Emily Carr*, 217) similarly describes Carr's eclectic approach to art: 'Her intuitive sense of her own needs enabled her to interpret and adapt such modernist international movements to her own Canadian West Coast vision without becoming enmeshed in their historical theoretical aspects. She was fortunate in being able to take from them what was relevant to her purpose while remaining in the best sense an innocent.'

8 See Gerson ('Piper's,' 140), who observes a similar comparison: '[Scott's] matter-of-fact narration of Paul Farlotte's visions and Paul Arbique's well-timed death brings his tales of the unknown closer to the understated domestic mysteries of George Elliott's *The Kissing Man* than to the more elaborate gothicism of Poe and Hawthorne. Hence in his tales which draw on traditional legendary material ... Scott blurs any distinction between reality and unreality, with the effect of emphasizing the power of a communal belief in magic to transform myth into everyday reality.' Gerson seems as if she would like to say, *à la* Borges, that Elliott influenced Scott towards an anticipation of magic realist fictional techniques. I think she undervalues their common source in the tale, and even in the tales of Poe and Hawthorne. See page 201n19 above.

9 'Sedan,' recall, presents outspoken racism. Leacock was such a British Imperialist, and so ardent a promoter of Canada within a greater empire, that his racism is fairly global in its inclusiveness, mostly good humoured and, like Carr's, seldom ugly. In *Sunshine Sketches*, the barber Jefferson Thorpe, the only Mariposan (with Josh Smith being an interloper) obsessed with getting rich ('It was probably in him from the start' [24]), wears a skullcap (22). Despite Leacock's prejudice, Thorpe is presented positively, as resilient and communally beneficial.

10 Froody is the first to hear Doctor Fletcher at his secret rites. Her new baby brother was delivered by Fletcher eight days before the day on which she

overhears him (42). At story's end, Doctor Fletcher is returning to the hospital 'to fix up Mrs. Scorrel's baby boy' (47), an 'eight-day-old baby boy' (48). To this, add Froody's witnessing 'something tiny and pink' (42) falling from the cotton pad that the Doctor holds, and Fletcher's cryptic admonition: 'Nourish him the way you do all of us. Be patient with him because you'll get the rest of him soon' (44). The phrase 'the rest of him soon' implies that a part of him is now being commended to the earth's keeping. On the day that Froody observes the act, that part would be her baby brother's foreskin.

11 Perhaps Doctor Fletcher attempts too much. In T.S. Eliot's definition, culture, the 'incarnation of [a people's] religion' (*Notes*, 27), is tripartite. There is a culture of the individual, a culture of the group, and a culture of the society, in a rising dependency based on an organic (not to say a feudal) model. Which is to say, society cannot do culturally what the individual contributes to the whole, and vice versa. So perhaps Doctor Fletcher has overreached in trying to make a private ritual serve a much larger function. In 'A room, a light for love,' Alison Kennedy may succeed at a similar bridging of the personal and the communal, but her purposes remain more personal, less grandly ambitious than Doctor Fletcher's. Or it may simply be that one succeeds and the other fails.

12 See Flores (190, 191) on the manipulation of time in magical realism generally: 'the reader is thrown into a timeless flux and/or the inconceivable, freighted with dramatic suspense'; 'time exists in a kind of timeless fluidity and the unreal happens as part of reality.' One further note, which may as well go here. George Elliott worked for a long time in the advertising business in the United States, and in the States 'johnson' is a euphemism for penis. So I wonder if Elliott might not have been intending a mildly salacious pun with the name Johnson Mender for the mysterious character who desires to recover the value of babies.

5: No Honey, I'm Home: Alice Munro's *Who Do You Think You Are?*

1 As Hoy documents so fascinatingly (59–62), three of the stories from the 'Rose and Janet' manuscript – 'Connection,' 'The Stone in the Field,' and 'The Moons of Jupiter' – became part of *The Moons of Jupiter* (1982); other Janet stories, which had begun life as Rose stories, were translated back into Rose stories; 'Simon's Luck' was added; and 'Who Do You Think You Are?' was written to end the revised manuscript.

2 With the exception of her first collection of stories, *Dance of the Happy Shades* (1968), all Munro's collections exhibit varying degrees of coherence and design (what Ingram calls 'arrangement'), with such a collection as *Open Secrets* (1994) perhaps coming closest to being a story sequence, if not a cycle.

But *Lives of Girls and Women* (1971) is a novel. Munro has frequently said, too humbly, that it remains her one attempt at a novel. None of its chapters appear in her *Selected Stories*. Furthermore, *Lives* impresses me as clearly being an instance of the bildungsroman as novel, one whose chapters cannot stand alone as stories, and where at the end the heroine, Del Jordan, is prepared to light out on her life's adventures. Any thought of return she entertains is but a projection whose meaning is wholly literary (Jubilee transformed into a future subject of the developing writer) as opposed to Jubilee figuring as the self-confirming site of the relation between place and identity that the Canadian short story cycle inscribes.

3 Another interesting bit of publishing lore about *Who Do You Think You Are?* is that its American and British publishers changed its title to *The Beggar Maid: Stories of Rose and Flo* because they feared their readers would not understand the implied put-down in the Canadian phrase (Struthers, 'Material,' 29). As is probably too well known to warrant mention, Hanratty is based on the southwestern Ontario town of Wingham, Munro's home town, as is Jubilee in the novel *Lives of Girls and Women*.

4 See Blodgett (99), who views Rose's ill luck in arranging a rendezvous with her lover Tom as a providential parallel to the pay-phone money.

5 The opening sentences of stories seem almost to flout readers' expectations of coherence: 'Rose wrote the Entrance, she went across the bridge, she went to high school' ('Half a Grapefruit,' 38); 'Patrick Blatchford was in love with Rose' ('The Beggar Maid,' 65); 'Rose gets lonely in new places; she wishes she had invitations' ('Simon's Luck,' 152).

6 The sadomasochistic beating of Becky Tyde's father eerily recalls the drunken mob that, for racist reasons, goes to beat Hans Blumenthal in 'Sedan' of *Viger*. Not only do the two events show the exclusively prejudicial (even the psychosexual) underside of small town life, but the incident in *Viger* demonstrates that Hans, had he not been saved by Latulipe, might have met the same end as Mr Tyde.

7 Oddly, Gerald Noonan thinks the point of view first person, persistently speaking of 'Rose, the narrator in all ten stories' (168). See Heble (103–4) for an enlightening analysis of a textual site where the narrative does slip from third-person subjective to first-person plural.

8 See Redekop (126–30) for an extended discussion of Rose's name.

9 See Carrington (43–8) for a discussion of 'Royal Beatings' in terms of Freud's 'A Child Is Being Beaten.'

10 Freud's convenient, and controversial, distinction between 'object libido' and 'ego libido' (*Narcissism*, 6–11) comes to mind as a useful gloss. The narcissist is one whose libido turns from cathecting objects to cathecting the ego, which

word 'ego' is used in the *Narcissism* essay as we use the word 'self.' I am grateful to Dr David Fairweather for drawing my attention to the *Narcissism* essay.

11 See Carrington (138–42) for a discussion of imagery of warmth in this story.

12 It might be objected that Simon is the one who leaves Rose, since he doesn't
contact her and eventually dies. But the story is told only from Rose's point of
view, and from Rose's perspective her decision to leave constitutes a flight
from Simon and the demands of reciprocal love (not, as Coral Ann Howells
mistakenly reads it, as a 'chasing after him hundreds of miles by car' [62]).
Moreover, the reasons for her decision to flee have only to do with her own
unwillingness to submit to the exposure that enduring intimacy entails. Given
the immediate cause of her self-centred flight west – one weekend's silence
from Simon – her action is rash, perhaps even hysterical. See the long internal
'monologue' that begins tellingly with 'She could not remember what they had
said about Simon coming again' (164) and concludes with what I read as an un-
subjective third-person irony: 'So she thought' (170). Finally, had Rose fought
her fear and held out, she might have discovered that Simon, stricken with cancer, was attempting to spare her the pain of his ultimate departure.

13 The aged, whose senses fail generally of course, have a diminished sweet taste
especially. Workers in old folks' homes report that they have to watch their
charges closely at the dessert course lest the elderly cover their chocolate fudge
with sugar, claiming they can't taste it otherwise. I am grateful to Angela
Arnold for bringing this gerontological information to my attention. Readers
who are interested in old age and the Canadian short story cycle should read
Edna Alford's *A Sleep Full of Dreams*.

14 Remarking this sequence of imitators, Heble sees something similar, if getting
it backwards: 'this movement away from a sense of an origin is re-enacted
many years later when Rose meets up with Ralph at the Legion Hall in
Hanratty' (120).

15 Apologies for yet another lengthy note, but I want here to address the suggestively autobiographical aspect of *Who Do You Think You Are?* Questions of
representation crop up throughout this story cycle, becoming most apparent
at the end of 'Simon's Luck' and in 'Spelling,' whose title could be said to
return language itself to its basic arbitrarily signifying components as Rose is
returned to spell-casting Flo and Hanratty. Such self-reflexive sites recur at the
end of the title story, too, which worries the problem of 'translating' the inner
lives of people and their communities. Thinking of Ralph Gillespie, Rose
reflects on the difficulty of conveying 'feelings which could only be spoken of
in translation; perhaps they could only be acted on in translation' (205–6). In
an unpublished interview with Thomas Tausky, Munro similarly observes
that, for her, 'fiction was a way of being able to translate a kind of rapture that

I think everybody feels. The thing is to find a way of expressing it' (in C.S. Ross, 45). So connected, these suggestive writerly swerves in *Who* can justifiably be read as metafiction. Further, an actress is an artist of sorts, which further posits Rose as a possible autobiographical figure in this bildungsroman that can also be read as a künstlerroman. It is not too far a stretch, then, to read the final pages of the story cycle as Munro worrying like guilty Rose about the way she has exploited small town lives for her literary art; and only a little further to read the conclusion as wish-fulfilling fiction that creates, like Rose's revisioning memory of her conversation with Ralph, significant forgiveness and confirmation for, at worst, an essentially parasitic vocation (fiction writing). I would note further that Munro has described 'Privilege,' the story to which I have ascribed something of a determinant status in the cycle, as 'an autobiographical piece, not fiction at all' (Gerson, Review-Interview, 7; see also Struthers, 'Material,' 21). And in shakiest support of these biographical suppositions, I observe that the *Wingham Advance-Times* reported that a resident 'fell down a cellar stair' in the week Munro was born (in C.S. Ross, 23), a coincidence which helps indeed to situate Munro but one slot over from Rose, who is one slot over from similarly fallen Ralph. See Redekop (141), who gives a ten-item list sequencing 'figures that can be extrapolated from the last two stories,' beginning with '1 Homer (blind)' and ending with '10 Munro doing them all.'

What is difficult to consider for long, though, is that Alice Munro, expert in the painstaking nuancing of inner lives, could wonder for long about the legitimacy of her marvellous art. I think, rather, that the autobiographical element is intended instead to implicate the author more fully in the affirmation of the importance of place to self-identity – which is especially pertinent to one such as Rose who has had obviated that other potentially definitive element, romantic love. (Here, the Rose character is decidedly un-autobiographical, since Munro is long married and living in Clinton, Ontario, near her place of origin in Wingham, thereby combining the best of the two definitive elements, love and place [C.S. Ross, 92–3].) In answer to interviewer Harold Horwood's question about her attachment to her own place of origin in southwestern Ontario, Munro said, 'Love isn't the word really, because that sounds like I'm going out looking at sunsets and pretty views; it's not that. It's just that it's so basic like my own flesh or something that I can't be separated from. I always felt when I lived in Vancouver and Victoria that I had to go home to die, because life on the west coast wasn't real in the same way' (Horwood, 135). The flesh image fortuitously recalls its negative use as a reptilian image of transformation at the conclusion of 'Wild Swans,' where Rose craves empowering metamorphosis into a sly actress and freedom from Hanratty. Apparently Munro was not inclined to shed her Wingham skin permanently. But in her answer to Horwood, Munro uses the flesh image to underscore what *Who Do You Think You Are?* illustrates positively: the relation between place and the maintenance of an identity. And I think what Munro means (if I may be so presumptuous) is that she, like Rose, had to go home to live and reconfirm her art.

L'Envoi: Continuity/Inclusion/Conclusion

1 King ('Godzilla,' 13) uses the term 'interfusional' to describe 'that part of Native literature which is a blending of oral literature and written literature.' I think, though, an earlier statement in the same article demonstrates the Orwellian sin against plain speaking – from the plain-writing King – that occurs when he discusses the nomenclature for Native literature's indebtedness to Native oral traditions: 'If we are to use terms to describe the various stages or changes in Native literature as it has become written, while at the same time remaining oral, and as it has expanded from a specific language base to a multiple language base, we need to find descriptors which do not invoke the cant of progress and which are not joined at the hip with nationalism.' Cant aside, see Hertha D. Wong (172–4) for an illuminating discussion of the relation between short story cycle form and Native oral traditions. Wong proceeds to focus her discussion on the American Native writer Louise Erdich's 'short story sequence' *Love Medicine* (1984). *Love Medicine*, revised and expanded in 1993, is part of a much longer sequence of stories, a tetralogy of books; and it has a more legitimate claim to connection with Native oral traditions, if only for the fact that its stories, often the same stories, are told by a multiplicity of narrators.

2 Scott's many Indian poems just about always present a situation of mother and child, often a sick child, with no father in the picture. The implications for the future of Native peoples, in Scott's view, are obvious. But it should be remembered that the families of the village of Viger are in a similar state of disruption, transition, and 'assimilation'; and of course that King has made the absent father a dominant feature of *Medicine River*.

3 See King (Rooke, 65): 'There is a level of disaster in each of those episodes that I feel helpless to prevent.'

Works Cited

Alford, Edna. 'Fear of the Novel.' In Probert. 173–9.

– *A Sleep Full of Dreams*. Lantzville, BC: Oolichan, 1981.

Anderson, Sherwood. *Winesburg, Ohio*. 1919. Rpt. Ed. Malcolm Cowley. New York: Penguin, 1976.

Atwood, Margaret. *Lady Oracle*. Toronto: McClelland and Stewart, 1976.

– *Survival: A Thematic Guide to Canadian Literature*. Toronto: Anansi, 1972.

Bakhtin, M.M. *The Dialogic Imagination: Four Essays*. Trans. Caryl Emerson and Michael Holquist. Austin: U Texas P, 1981.

– *Problems of Dostoevsky's Poetics*. 1963. Rpt. Trans. and ed. Caryl Emerson. Minneapolis: U Minnesota P, 1984.

Barnes, Julian. *The History of the World in 10½ Chapters*. New York: Knopf, 1989.

Barth, John. *The Friday Book: Essays and Other Nonfiction*. New York: G.P. Putnam's Sons, 1984.

Bentley, D.M.R. 'Carman and Mind Cure: Theory and Technique.' In Lynch, *Bliss Carman*. 85–110.

– *Mimic Fires: Accounts of Early Long Poems on Canada*. Montreal and King-ston: McGill-Queen's UP, 1994.

– 'A New Dimension: Notes on the Ecology of Canadian Poetry.' *Canadian Poetry: Studies, Documents, Reviews* 7 (Fall/Winter 1980): 1–20.

– 'The Poetics of Roberts' Tantramar Space.' In *The Charles G.D. Roberts Sym-posium, Mount Allison University*. Ed. Carrie MacMillan. Halifax: Nimbus, 1984. 17–41.

– '"The Thing Is Found to Be Symbolic": *Symboliste* Elements in the Early Short Stories of Gilbert Parker, Charles G.D. Roberts, and Duncan Campbell Scott.' In Lynch and Arnold-Robbeson. 27–51.

– 'Watchful Dreams and Sweet Unrest: An Essay on the Vision of Archibald Lampman, Part II.' *Studies in Canadian Literature* 7:1 (1982): 6–15.

– 'William Morris and the Poets of the Confederation.' *Journal of Pre-Raphaelite Studies* 6/7 (Fall/Spring 1997/8): 31–44.

Bhabha, Homi K. *The Location of Culture*. London: Routledge, 1994.

Birdsell, Sandra. *Ladies of the House*. Winnipeg: Turnstone, 1984.

– *Night Travellers*. Winnipeg: Turnstone, 1982.

Birney, Earle. *Ghost in the Wheels: The Selected Poems of Earle Birney*. Toronto: McClelland and Stewart, 1977.

Blaise, Clark. *A North American Education*. Toronto: Doubleday, 1973.

– 'To Begin, to Begin.' In *The Narrative Voice: Short Stories and Reflections by Canadian Authors*. Ed. John Metcalf. Toronto: McGraw-Hill Ryerson, 1972. 22–6.

Blodgett, E.D. *Alice Munro*. Boston: Twayne, 1988.

Bloom, Harold. *The Anxiety of Influence: A Theory of Poetry*. New York: Oxford UP, 1973.

Bobak, Esther Lisabeth. 'The Artist and the City.' 'Attitudes towards the City in the Canadian Realistic Novel of the Twenties.' Diss. Dalhousie University, 1981. 286–373.

Borges, Jorge Luis. 'Nathaniel Hawthorne.' In *Other Inquisitions 1937–1952*. Trans. Ruth L.C. Simms. Austin: U Texas P, 1964. 47–65.

Brown, Norman O. *Life against Death: The Psychoanalytical Meaning of History*. Middletown, CT: Wesleyan UP, 1959.

Bryant, William Cullen. *Poems of William Cullen Bryant*. London: Oxford UP, 1914.

Butler, Judith. *Bodies That Matter: On the Discursive Limits of 'Sex.'* New York: Routledge, 1993.

Cameron, Silver Donald. *Faces of Leacock*. Toronto: Ryerson, 1967.

– 'Robertson Davies: The Bizarre and Passionate Life of the Canadian People.' In *Conversations with Canadian Novelists, Part One*. Toronto: Macmillan, 1973. 30–48.

– 'Stephen Leacock: The Novelist Who Never Was.' *Dalhousie Review* 46 (Spring 1966): 15–28.

Campbell, Sandra. 'Gently Scan: Theme and Technique in J.G. Sime's *Sister Woman* (1919).' *Canadian Literature* 133 (Summer 1992): 40–52.

– Introduction. *Sister Woman*. By J.G. Sime. Ottawa: Tecumseh, 1992. vii–xxxvii.

Campbell, Sandra, and Lorraine McMullen, eds. *'New Women': Short Stories by Canadian Women 1900–1920*. Ottawa: U Ottawa P, 1991.

Canby, H.A. *A Study of the Short Story*. New York: Holt, 1913.

Carman, Bliss. *The Poems of Bliss Carman*. Ed. John Sorfleet. Toronto: McClelland and Stewart, 1976.

Carpenter, David. 'Fear of the Novel: The Linked Sequence of Short Stories in Saskatchewan Fiction.' In Probert. 155–161.

Carr, Emily. *The Complete Writings of Emily Carr*. Vancouver/Seattle: Douglas and McIntyre/U Washington P, 1997.

– *Klee Wyck*. Toronto: Oxford UP, 1941. Rpt. Toronto: Clarke, Irwin, 1952.

– 'Modern and Indian Art of the West Coast.' *Supplement to the McGill News* (June 1929): 18–22.

Carrington, Ildikó de Papp. *Controlling the Uncontrollable: The Fiction of Alice Munro*. DeKalb: Northern Illinois UP, 1989.

Carscallen, James. *The Other Country: Patterns in the Writing of Alice Munro*. Toronto: ECW, 1993.

Carver, Raymond. 'Fires.' In *Fires: Essays, Poems, Stories*. Santa Barbara, CA: Capra, 1983. 19–30.

Chanady, Amaryll. 'The Origins and Development of Magic Realism in Latin American Fiction.' In Hinchcliffe and Jewinski. 49–60.

Charters, Ann. 'Poe's Legacy: The Short Story Writer as Editor and Critic.' In Lounsberry. 97–8.

Choy, Wayson. *The Jade Peony*. Vancouver: Douglas and McIntyre, 1997.

Clay, Charles. Rev. of *Klee Wyck*. *Canadian Historical Review* 23 (1942): 90–1.

Cole, Margaret. *The Story of Fabian Socialism*. Stanford: Stanford UP, 1961.

Coleridge, Samuel Taylor. *On the Constitution of the Church and State*. London: Hurst, Chance, 1830.

– *The Statesman's Manual*. In *Lay Sermons*. Ed. R.J. White. *Collected Works*. Ed. Kathleen Coburn. Princeton: Princeton UP, 1972.

'Concluding Panel.' In Hinchcliffe and Jewinski. 113–24.

Coover, Robert. See Iftekharuddin.

Cortázar, Julio. 'The Present State of Fiction in Latin America.' In *The Final Island: The Fiction of Julio Cortázar*. Ed. Jaime Alazaraki and Ivar Ivask. Oklahoma City: U Oklahoma P, 1978. 26–36.

Crawford, Isabella Valancy. *Collected Poems*. Literature of Canada: Poetry and Prose in Reprint. Toronto: U Toronto P, 1972.

Creighton, Donald Grant. *The Commercial Empire of the St. Lawrence, 1760–1850*. Toronto: Ryerson, 1937.

Currie, Robert. *Night Games*. Moose Jaw, SK: Coteau, 1983.

Currie, Sheldon. *The Glace Bay Miner's Museum*. Ste Anne de Bellevue, QC: Deluge, 1979.

Davey, Frank. 'Genre Subversion in the English-Canadian Short Story.' In *Reading Canadian Reading*. Winnipeg: Turnstone, 1994. 137–50.

Davies, Barrie, ed. *At the Mermaid Inn: Wilfred Campbell, Archibald Lampman,*

Duncan Campbell Scott in 'The Globe' 1892–93. Literature in Canada. Toronto: U Toronto P, 1979.

Davies, Robertson. *Fifth Business.* Toronto: Macmillan, 1970.

– 'Stephen Leacock.' In *Our Living Tradition.* First series. Ed. Claude T. Bissell. Toronto: U Toronto P, 1957.

Davis, Rocio G. 'Negotiating Place: Identity and Community in M.G. Vassanji's *Uhuru Street.*' *Ariel* 30:3 (1999): 7–25.

Dean, Misao. *Practising Femininity: Domestic Realism and the Performance of Gender in Early Canadian Fiction.* Toronto: U Toronto P, 1998.

Derrida, Jacques. *Writing and Difference.* Trans. Alan Bass. Chicago: U Chicago P, 1978.

Dilworth, Ira. Foreword. *The Complete Writings of Emily Carr.* 17–22.

Divay, Gaby. Introduction. *Poems.* By Frederick Philip Grove. xvii–lxxxix.

Doyle, James. '"Just above the Breadline": Social(ist) Realism in Canadian Short Stories of the 1930s.' In Lynch and Arnold-Robbeson. 65–73.

– *Stephen Leacock: The Sage of Orillia.* Toronto: ECW, 1992.

Dragland, S.L. *Floating Voice: Duncan Campbell Scott and the Literature of Treaty 9.* Concord, ON: Anansi, 1994.

– Introduction. *In the Village of Viger and Other Stories,* by Duncan Campbell Scott. Toronto: McClelland and Stewart, 1973.

Duffy, Dennis. 'George Elliott's *The Kissing Man.*' *Canadian Literature* 63 (Winter 1975): 52–63.

Dyer, Klay. 'Passing Time and Present Absence: Looking to the Future in *In the Village of Viger.*' *Canadian Literature* 141 (Summer 1994): 86–106.

Eliot, T.S. *The Complete Poems and Plays, 1909–1950.* New York: Harcourt, Brace and World, 1971.

– *Notes towards the Definition of Culture.* New York: Harcourt, Brace and Company, 1948.

– 'Tradition and the Individual Talent.' In *The Sacred Wood.* London: Methuen, 1920. 47–59.

Elliott, George. *The Bittersweet Man.* Guelph, ON: Red Kite, 1994.

– *Crazy Water Boys.* Guelph, ON: Red Kite, 1995.

– 'Four Little Words.' In *76: New Canadian Stories.* Ed. Joan Harcourt and John Metcalf. Ottawa: Oberon, 1976. 53–62.

– *God's Big Acre.* Toronto: Methuen, 1986.

– *The Kissing Man.* Toronto: Macmillan, 1962.

– 'Side Trip.' *Canadian Forum* June–July 1986: 36–9.

Erdich, Louise. *Love Medicine.* New York: Holt, Rinehart and Winston, 1984; rev. New York: HarperPerennial, 1993.

Farmer, David Hugh, ed. *The Oxford Dictionary of Saints*. 2nd edition. Oxford: Oxford UP, 1987.

Farmer, Henry George. *Bernard Shaw's Sister and Her Friends: A New Angle on G.B.S.* Leiden: E.J. Brill, 1959.

Ferguson, Suzanne C. 'Defining the Short Story: Impressionism and Form.' In May. 218–30.

Fischer, Michael. *Does Deconstruction Make Any Difference? Poststructuralism and the Defense of Poetry in Modern Criticism*. Bloomington: Indiana UP, 1985.

Flores, Angel. 'Magical Realism in Spanish American Fiction.' *Hispania* 38 (May 1955): 187–92.

Fowler, Alistair. *Kinds of Literature: An Introduction to the Theory of Genres and Modes*. Cambridge: Harvard UP, 1982.

Freud, Sigmund. *The Interpretation of Dreams*. 1900. Trans. A.A. Brill. Rpt. New York: Random House, 1950.

– *On Narcissism: An Introduction*. 1914. Trans. J. Strachey. Rpt. New Haven: Yale, 1991.

Friedman, Norman. 'Recent Short Story Theories: Problems in Definition.' In Lohafer and Clarey. 13–31.

Frye, Northrop. Conclusion. *Literary History of Canada*. 1965. Rpt. in *The Bush Garden: Essays on the Canadian Imagination*. Toronto: Anansi, 1971. 213–51.

– *Fables of Identity: Studies in Poetic Mythology*. New York: Harcourt, Brace and World, 1963.

Fulford, Robert. 'The Trouble with Emily: How Canada's Greatest Woman Painter Ended Up on the Wrong Side of the Political Correctness Debate.' *Canadian Art* 10 (Winter 1993): 32–9.

Gadpaille, Michelle. *The Canadian Short Story*. Toronto: Oxford UP, 1988.

Gallant, Mavis. Introduction. *Home Truths: Selected Canadian Stories*. Toronto: Macmillan, 1981. xi–xx.

Gardner, John. *The Art of Fiction: Notes on Craft for Young Writers*. 1984. Rpt. New York: Random House, 1991.

Garfield, Viola E. Rev. of *Klee Wyck*. *Pacific Northwest Quarterly* 34 (1943): 101–2.

Gerson, Carole. 'The Piper's Forgotten Tune: Notes on the Stories of D.C. Scott and a Bibliography.' *Journal of Canadian Fiction* 16 (1976): 138–43.

– *A Purer Taste: The Writing and Reading of Fiction in English in Nineteenth-Century Canada*. Toronto: U Toronto P, 1989.

– 'Who Do You Think You Are?: Review-Interview with Alice Munro.' *Room of One's Own* 4:4 (1979): 4–7.

Gerson, Carole, and Kathy Mezei. Introduction. *The Prose of Life: Sketches from Victorian Canada*. Ed. Gerson and Mezei. Toronto: ECW, 1981. 1–15.

Godard, Barbara. 'Stretching the Story: The Canadian Story Cycle.' *Open Letter* 7 (Fall 1989): 27–71.

Goldsmith, Oliver. *The Rising Village*. 1825; rev. 1834. Rpt. ed. Gerald Lynch. London: Canadian Poetry P, 1989.

Goldsmith, Oliver. *The Vicar of Wakefield*. 1766. Rpt. London: Oxford UP, 1974.

Gorham, Deborah. 'The Canadian Suffragists.' In *Women in the Canadian Mosaic*. Ed. Gwen Matheson. Toronto: Peter Martin, 1976. 23–55.

Grace, Sherrill. 'Duality and Series: Forms of the Canadian Imagination.' *Canadian Review of Comparative Literature* 7:4 (Fall 1980): 438–51.

Grady, Wayne, and Matt Cohen, eds. *The Quebec Anthology, 1830–1990*. Canadian Short Story Library 19. Ottawa: U Ottawa P, 1996.

Groening, Laura. 'Duncan Campbell Scott: An Annotated Bibliography.' In *The Annotated Bibliography of Canada's Major Authors*. Vol. 8. Ed. Robert Lecker and Jack David. Toronto: ECW, 1994. 469–576.

Grove, Frederick Philip. *Over Prairie Trails*. 1922. Rpt. Toronto: McClelland and Stewart, 1991.

– *Poems/Gedichte by/von Frederick Philip Grove/Felix Paul Greve und Fanny Essler, With 16 facsimiles*. Ed. Gaby Divay. Winnipeg: Wolf, 1993.

Guth, Gwendolyn. '"A World For Women": Fictions of the Canadian Female Artist, 1840–1870.' Diss. U Ottawa, 1999.

Haliburton, Thomas Chandler. *The Clockmaker, or the Sayings and Doings of Sam Slick of Slickville*. 1836. Rpt. Series 1, 2, and 3. Ed. George L. Parker. Ottawa: Carleton UP, 1995.

Hancock, Geoff. 'Magic or Realism: The Marvelous in Canadian Fiction.' In Hinchcliffe and Jewinski. 30–48.

Hawthorne, Nathaniel. *Hawthorne's Short Stories*. Ed. Newton Arvin. New York: Knopf, 1946.

Heble, Ajay, *The Tumble of Reason: Alice Munro's Discourse of Absence*. Toronto: U Toronto P, 1994.

Heble, Ajay, Donna Palmateer Pennee, and J.R. (Tim) Struthers, eds. *New Contexts of Canadian Criticism*. Peterborough, ON: Broadview, 1997.

Hemingway, Ernest. *The Green Hills of Africa*. New York: Charles Scribner's, 1935.

Hiebert, Paul. *Sarah Binks*. 1947. Rpt. Toronto: McClelland and Stewart, 1995.

Hinchcliffe, Peter, and Ed Jewinski, eds. *Magic Realism and Canadian Literature: Essays and Stories*. Waterloo: U Waterloo P, 1986.

Hodgins, Jack. *Spit Delaney's Island*. 1976. Rpt. Toronto: Macmillan, 1987.

Hood, Hugh. *Around the Mountain: Scenes from Montreal Life*. Toronto: Peter Martin, 1967.

Horwood, Harold. 'Interview with Alice Munro.' In Miller. 123–35.

Howells, Coral Ann. *Alice Munro*. Manchester: Manchester UP, 1998.

Hoy, Helen. '"Rose and Janet": Alice Munro's Metafiction.' *Canadian Literature* 121 (Summer 1989): 59–83.

Huggan, Isabel. *The Elizabeth Stories*. 1984. Rpt. Toronto: HarperCollins, 1990.

Hutcheon, Linda. *Splitting Images: Contemporary Canadian Ironies*. Toronto: Oxford UP, 1991.

Iftekharuddin, Farhat. 'Interview with Robert Coover.' *Short Story*. New series 1:2 (Fall 1993): 89–94.

Ingram, Forrest L. *Representative Short Story Cycles of the Twentieth Century: Studies in a Literary Genre*. Paris: Mouton, 1971.

Jackel, David. 'George Elliott.' *Dictionary of Literary Biography. Canadian Writers, 1920–1959*. Vol. 68. First series. Ed. W.H. New. Detroit: Gale, 1988. 124–6.

Jewett, Sarah Orne. *The Country of the Pointed Firs and Other Stories*. 1896. Rpt. Garden City: Doubleday, 1954.

Jones, D.G. *Butterfly on Rock: Images in Canadian Literature*. Toronto: U Toronto P, 1970.

Joyce, James. *Dubliners*. 1914. Rpt. Markham, ON: Penguin, 1977.

Keith W.J. *Canadian Literature in English*. London: Longmans, 1985.

– 'Grove's *Over Prairie Trails*: A Re-Examination.' *Literary Half-Yearly* 13 (July 1972): 76–85.

Kennedy, J. Gerald, ed. *Modern American Short Story Sequences: Composite Fictions and Fictive Communities*. New York: Cambridge UP, 1995.

King, Thomas. 'Godzilla vs. Post-Colonial.' *World Literature Written in English* 30:2 (1990): 10–16.

– *Green Grass, Running Water*. Toronto: HarperCollins, 1993.

– *Medicine River*. 1989. Rpt. Toronto: Penguin, 1995.

– *One Good Story, That One*. Toronto: HarperCollins, 1993.

King, Thomas, ed. *All My Relations: An Anthology of Contemporary Canadian Native Prose*. Toronto: McClelland and Stewart, 1990.

Kirchhoff, Frederick. *William Morris*. Boston: Twayne, 1979.

Klein, A.M. *Selected Poems*. Ed. Zailig Pollock, Seymour Mayne, and Usher Caplan. Toronto: U Toronto P, 1997.

Klinck, Carl F., et al., eds. *Literary History of Canada: Canadian Literature in English*. 2nd edition. 3 vols. Toronto: U Toronto P, 1976.

Knister, Raymond. 'A Canadian of Canadians.' In Pacey, *Frederick Philip Grove*. 11–17.

– Introduction. *Canadian Short Stories*. 1928. Rpt. Freeport, NY: Books for Libraries P, 1971. xi–xix.

Knönagel, Axel. *Nietzschean Philosophy in the Works of Frederick Philip Grove.* European University Studies. New York: Peter Lang, 1990.

Kramer, Priscilla M. *The Cyclical Method of Composition in Gottfried Keller's Sinngedicht.* New York: Lancaster, 1939.

Kroetsch, Robert. 'F.P. Grove: The Finding.' 1975. Rpt. in *An Anthology of Canadian Literature in English.* Revised and abridged. Ed. Russell Brown, Donna Bennett, and Nathalie Cooke. Toronto: Oxford UP, 1990. 451–2

– *The Lovely Treachery of Words: Essays Selected and New.* Toronto: Oxford UP, 1989. 41–52.

Lacan, Jacques. *The Four Fundamental Concepts of Psycho-Analysis.* Trans. Alan Sheridan. Ed. Jacques-Alain Miller. New York: W.W. Norton, 1978.

Lampman, Archibald. *The Poems of Archibald Lampman (including 'At the Long Sault').* Ed. Margaret Coulby Whitridge. Literature of Canada: Poetry and Prose in Reprint 12. Toronto: U Toronto P, 1974.

Lane, Patrick. Afterword. *Over Prairie Trails.* By Frederick Philip Grove. 1991. 159–64.

Laurence, Margaret. *A Bird in the House.* 1970. Rpt. Toronto: McClelland and Stewart, 1989.

Leacock, Stephen. *Arcadian Adventures with the Idle Rich.* London: John Lane, 1914.

– *Essays and Literary Studies.* London: John Lane, 1916.

– *My Remarkable Uncle.* 1942. Rpt. Toronto: McClelland and Stewart, 1965.

– *Sunshine Sketches of a Little Town.* 1912. Rpt. A critical edition. Ed. Gerald Lynch. Ottawa: Tecumseh, 1996.

Lears, T.J. Jackson. *No Place of Grace: Antimodernism and the Transformation of American Culture, 1880–1920.* New York: Pantheon, 1981.

Logan, J.D., and Donald G. French. *Highways of Canadian Literature: A Synoptic Introduction to the Literary History of Canada (English) from 1760 to 1924.* Toronto: McClelland and Stewart, 1924.

Lohafer, Susan, and Jo Ellyn Clarey, eds. *Short Story Theory at a Crossroads.* Baton Rouge: Louisiana State UP, 1989.

Lounsberry, Barbara, et al., eds. *The Tales We Tell: Perspectives on the Short Story.* Westport, CT: Greenwood, 1998.

Lunden, Rolf. *The United Stories of America: Studies in the Short Story Composite.* Amsterdam and Atlanta: Rodopi, 1999.

Luscher, Robert M. 'The Short Story Sequence: An Open Book.' In Lohafer and Clarey. 148–67.

Lynch, Gerald, ed. *Bliss Carman: A Reappraisal.* Ottawa: U Ottawa P, 1990.

Lynch, Gerald. 'An Endless Flow: D.C. Scott's Indian Poems.' *Studies in Canadian Literature* 7:1 (1982): 27–54.

– *Stephen Leacock: Humour and Humanity*. Montreal and Kingston: McGill-Queen's UP, 1988.

– '"To keep what was good and pass it on": George Elliott's Small Town Memorial, *The Kissing Man.*' *Studies in Canadian Literature* 22:1 (1997): 69–95.

Lynch, Gerald, and Angela Arnold-Robbeson, eds. *Dominant Impressions: Essays on the Canadian Short Story.* Ottawa: U Ottawa P, 1999.

MacKendrick, Louis K, ed. *Probable Fictions: Alice Munro's Narrative Acts.* Downsview, ON: ECW, 1983

MacLennan, Hugh. *Seven Rivers of Canada.* Toronto: Macmillan, 1961.

MacLulich, T.D. *Between Europe and America: The Canadian Tradition in Fiction.* Toronto: ECW, 1988.

Magee, William H. 'Stephen Leacock, Local Colourist.' *Canadian Literature* 39 (Winter 1969): 34–42.

Maguire, Dianne. *Dry Land Tourist.* Toronto: Sister Vision, 1991.

Mandel, Eli. *Another Time.* Erin, ON: Porcépic, 1977.

Mann, Susan Garland. *The Short Story Cycle: A Genre Companion and Reference Guide.* New York: Greenwood, 1989.

Mara, Rachna. *Of Customs and Excise.* Toronto: Second Story, 1991.

Martin, Walter. *Alice Munro: Paradox and Parallel.* Edmonton: U Alberta P, 1987.

Marx, Karl. *Critique of the Gotha Program.* 1891. Rpt. New York: International Publishers, 1938.

– *Critique of Hegel's 'Philosophy of Right.'* 1927. Rpt. Cambridge: Cambridge UP, 1970.

Mathews, Lawrence. '*Who Do You Think You Are?* Alice Munro's Art of Disarrangement.' In MacKendrick. 181–93.

May, Charles E., ed. *The New Short Story Theories.* Athens: Ohio UP, 1994.

McBriar, A.M. *Fabian Socialism and English Politics, 1884–1918.* London: Cambridge UP, 1962.

McCormack, Derek. *Dark Rides: A Novel in Stories.* Toronto: Gutter, 1996.

– *Wish Book: A Catalogue of Stories.* Toronto: Gutter, 1999.

McCormack, Eric. *Inspecting the Vaults.* Toronto: Viking, 1987.

McCulloch, Thomas. *The Letters of Mephibosheth Stepsure.* Halifax: H.W. Blackadar, 1869. CIHM microfiche no. 49067.

McDougall, Robert L., ed. *The Poet and the Critic: A Literary Correspondence between D.C. Scott and E.K. Brown.* Ottawa: Carleton UP, 1983.

McGillivray, Mary B. 'The Popular and Critical Reputation and Reception of Bliss Carman.' In Lynch, *Bliss Carman.* 7–19.

McLeod, Les. 'Canadian Post-Romanticism: The Context of Late Nineteenth-Century Canadian Poetry.' *Canadian Poetry: Studies, Documents, Reviews* 14 (Spring/Summer 1984): 1–37.

McMullin, Stanley E. '"Adam's Mad in Eden": Magic Realism as Hinterland Experience.' In Hinchcliffe and Jewinski. 13–22.

Meindl, Dieter. 'Modernism and the English-Canadian Short Story Cycle.' *RANAM* 20 (1987): 17–22.

Metcalf, John. *What is a Canadian Literature?* Guelph, ON: Red Kite, 1988.

Metcalf, John, and J.R. (Tim) Struthers, eds. *How Stories Mean*. Erin, ON: Porcupine's Quill, 1993.

Miller, Judith, ed. *The Art of Alice Munro: Saying the Unsayable*. Waterloo: U Waterloo P, 1984.

Milton, John. *John Milton: Complete Poems and Major Prose*. Ed. Merritt Y. Hughes. New York: Odyssey, 1957.

Mistry, Rohinton. *Tales from the Firozsha Baag*. Toronto: Penguin, 1987.

Montgomery, Lucy Maud. *Anne of Green Gables*. 1908. Rpt. Toronto: McGraw-Hill Ryerson, 1942.

Morley, Patricia. '*Over Prairie Trails*: "a poem woven of impressions."' *Humanities Association Review* 25:3 (1974): 225–31.

Morson, Gary Saul, and Caryl Emerson. *Mikhail Bakhtin: Creation of a Prosaics*. Stanford: Stanford UP, 1990.

Morton, W.L. 'The North in Canadian Historiography.' *Transactions of the Royal Society of Canada*. Series 4, vol. 8 (1970): 31–40.

Moss, John. 'Bushed in the Sacred Wood.' 1981. Rpt. in *The Paradox of Meaning: Cultural Poetics and Critical Fiction*. Winnipeg: Turnstone, 1999. 13–28.

– *A Reader's Guide to the Canadian Novel*. 2nd edition. Toronto: McClelland and Stewart, 1987.

Munro, Alice. *Dance of the Happy Shades*. Toronto: McGraw-Hill Ryerson, 1968.

– *Lives of Girls and Women*. Toronto: McGraw-Hill Ryerson, 1971.

– *The Moons of Jupiter*. Toronto: McClelland and Stewart, 1982.

– *Open Secrets*. Toronto: McClelland and Stewart, 1994.

– *Selected Stories*. Toronto: McClelland and Stewart, 1996.

– *Who Do You Think You Are?* Toronto: Macmillan, 1978.

Nesbitt, Bruce. Introduction. *Recollections of Nova Scotia: The Clockmaker; or The Sayings and Doings of Samuel Slick, of Slickville*, by Thomas Chandler Haliburton. Ottawa: Tecumseh P, 1984. 1–16.

New, W.H. 'Back to the Future: The Short Story in Canada and the Writing of Literary History.' In Heble et al. 249–64.

– *Dreams of Speech and Violence: The Art of the Short Story in Canada and New Zealand*. Toronto: U Toronto P, 1987.

– 'Fiction.' In Klinck. 3:233–83.

– 'A Geography of "Snow": Reading Notes.' *Studies in Canadian Literature* 23:1 (1998): 53–74.

– Introduction. *Canadian Short Fiction*. Ed. W.H. New. 2nd edition. Scarborough, ON: Prentice-Hall, 1997. 1–14.

– 'Jessie Georgina Sime.' *Dictionary of Literary Biography: Canadian Writers, 1890–1920*. Vol. 92. Ed. W.H. New. Detroit: Gale, 1990. 356–61.

– *Land Sliding: Imagining Space, Presence, and Power in Canadian Writing*. Toronto: U Toronto P, 1997.

Noonan, Gerald. 'The Structure of Style in Alice Munro's Fiction.' In MacKendrick. 163–80.

O'Brien, Flann. *The Third Policeman*. London: Macgibbon and Kee, 1967.

O'Connor, Frank. *The Lonely Voice: A Study in the Short Story*. 1962. Rpt. London: Macmillan, 1963.

O'Hagan, Howard. *Tay John*. 1939. Rpt. Toronto: McClelland and Stewart, 1974.

Oxford Dictionary of Saints. 2nd edition. Ed. David Hugh Farmer. Oxford: Oxford UP, 1987.

Pacey, Desmond. 'Fiction 1920–1940.' In Klinck. 1:168–204.

Pacey, Desmond, ed. *Frederick Philip Grove*. Critical Views on Canadian Writers. Toronto: Ryerson, 1970.

Panofsky, Erwin. *Meaning in the Visual Arts*. Chicago: U Chicago P, 1955.

Parker, George L. Editor's Introduction. *The Clockmaker*. 1995. xvii–ci.

Patterson, Nancy-Lou. 'The Spiritual Eye: Magic Realism in Art.' In Hinchcliffe and Jewinski. 23–9.

Peterman, Michael. *James McCarroll, alias Terry Finnegan: Newspapers, Controversy and Literature in Victorian Canada*. No. 17. Peterborough, ON: Peterborough Historical Society, 1996.

Poe, Edgar Allan. *Selected Writings of Edgar Allan Poe: Poems, Tales, Essays and Reviews*. Ed. David Galloway. Harmondsworth: Penguin, 1982.

Pratt, Annis. 'Affairs with Bears: Some Notes towards Feminist Archetypal Hypotheses for Canadian Literature.' In *Gynocritics: Feminist Approaches to Canadian and Quebec Women's Writing*. Ed. Barbara Godard. Toronto: ECW, 1987. 157–78.

Pratt, Mary Louise. 'The Short Story: The Long and the Short of It.' In May. 91–113.

Probert, Kenneth G, ed. *Writing Saskatchewan: 20 Critical Essays*. Regina: Canadian Plains Research Center, 1989.

Purdy, Al. *Being Alive: The Selected Poems of Al Purdy*. Toronto: McClelland and Stewart, 1978.

– *No Other Country*. Toronto: McClelland and Stewart, 1977.

Redekop, Magdalene. *Mothers and Other Clowns: The Stories of Alice Munro*. London and New York: Routledge, 1992.

Reid, Ian. *The Short Story*. Critical Idiom, no. 37. London: Methuen, 1977.

Richler, Mordecai. *The Street*. 1969. Rpt. Toronto: Penguin, 1985.

Rimstead, Roxanne. '"Klee Wyck": Redefining Region through Marginal Realities.' *Canadian Literature* 130 (Autumn 1991): 29–59.

Roberts, Charles G.D. *Selected Poetry and Critical Prose*. Ed. W.J. Keith. Toronto: U Toronto P, 1974.

Rooke, Constance. 'Interview with Thomas King.' *World Literature Written in English* 30:2 (1990): 62–76.

Ross, Catherine Sheldrick. 'At Least Part Legend: The Fiction of Alice Munro.' In MacKendrick. 112–26.

Ross, Malcolm. Introduction. *Over Prairie Trails*, by Frederick Philip Grove. Toronto: McClelland and Stewart, 1970. v–x.

Russell, Bertrand. *A History of Western Philosophy*. New York: Simon and Schuster, 1945.

Schroeder, Andreas. 'Fear of the Novel: The Linked Short Story in Saskatchewan Fiction.' In Probert. 162–9.

– *The Last Man*. Port Clements, BC: Sono Nis, 1972.

Scott, Duncan Campbell. *The Administration of Indian Affairs in Canada*. Toronto: Canadian Institute of International Affairs, 1931.

– *The Circle of Affection*. Toronto: McClelland and Stewart, 1947.

– *In the Village of Viger*. 1896. Rpt. Toronto: McClelland and Stewart, 1996.

– *The Poems of Duncan Campbell Scott*. Toronto: McClelland and Stewart, 1926.

– *Selected Poems of Duncan Campbell Scott*. Ed. Glenn Clever. Ottawa: Tecumseh, 1974.

– *The Witching of Elspie: A Book of Stories*. Freeport, NY: Books for Libraries, 1923.

Scott, F.R. *Selected Poems*. Toronto: Oxford UP, 1966.

Selvadurai, Shyam. *Funny Boy*. Toronto: McClelland and Stewart, 1994.

Shadbolt, Doris. *Emily Carr*. Vancouver: Douglas and McIntyre, 1990.

– Introduction. *The Complete Writings of Emily Carr*. 3–14.

Shaw, George Bernard. *The Bodley Head Bernard Shaw: Collected Plays with Their Prefaces*. 7 vols. London: Bodley Head, 1970–4.

– *Shaw and Ibsen: Bernard Shaw's 'The Quintessence of Ibsenism' and Related Writings*. Ed. J.L. Wiesenthal. Toronto: U Toronto P, 1979.

Sime, J.G. *Canada Chaps*. Toronto: S.B. Gundy, 1917.

– *In a Canadian Shack*. London, Toronto: Lovat Dickson, 1937.

– *The Mistress of All Work*. London: Methuen, 1916.

– *Orpheus in Quebec*. London: George Allen and Unwin, 1942.

– *Our Little Life*. 1921. Rpt. Ottawa: Tecumseh, 1994.

– *Sister Woman*. 1919. Rpt. Ottawa: Tecumseh, 1992.

- *Thomas Hardy of the Wessex Novels: An Essay and Biographical Note.* 1928. Rpt. Folcroft, PA: Folcroft Library Editions, 1975.
Sime, J.G., and Frank Nicholson. *Brave Spirits.* London: Privately printed, 1952.
Smith, A.J.M. 'Eclectic Detachment: Aspects of Identity in Canadian Poetry.' *Canadian Literature* 9 (Summer 1961): 6–14.
Spettigue, Douglas O. *FPG: The European Years.* Ottawa: Oberon, 1973.
Steiner, George. *Real Presences.* Chicago: Chicago UP, 1989.
Stich, K.P. 'Narcissism and the Uncanny in Grove's *Over Prairie Trails.*' *Mosaic* 19:2 (1986): 31–41.
- 'Painters' Words: Personal Narratives of Emily Carr and William Kurelek.' *Essays on Canadian Writing* 29 (1984): 152–74.
Stobie, Margaret R. *Frederick Philip Grove.* New York: Twayne,1973.
Stovel, Nora. '"Love and Death": Romance and Reality in Margaret Laurence's *A Bird in the House.*' In Lynch and Arnold-Robbeson. 99–114.
Struthers, J.R. (Tim). 'Intersecting Orbits: A Study of Selected Story Cycles by Hugh Hood, Jack Hodgins, Clark Blaise, and Alice Munro, in Their Literary Contexts.' Diss. University of Western Ontario, 1981.
- 'The Real Material: An Interview with Alice Munro.' In MacKendrick. 5–36.
Sutherland, Ronald. *Frederick Philip Grove.* Canadian Writers no. 4. Toronto: McClelland and Stewart, 1969.
Szanto, George. *The Underside of Stones: A Story Cycle.* Toronto: McClelland and Stewart, 1990.
Thomas, Clara. 'The Roads Back: *Sunshine Sketches of a Little Town* and George Elliott's *The Kissing Man.*' In *Stephen Leacock: A Reappraisal.* Ed. David Staines. Ottawa: U Ottawa P, 1986. 97–105.
Thomas, Dylan. *The Poems of Dylan Thomas.* Ed. Daniel Jones. New York: New Directions, 1971.
Thomas, Hilda. '*Klee Wyck*: The Eye of the Other.' *Canadian Literature* 136 (Spring 1993): 5–20.
Thompson, David. *David Thompson's Narrative, 1784–1812.* Ed. Richard Glover. Toronto: Champlain Society, 1962.
Tippett, Maria. *Emily Carr: A Biography.* Toronto: Oxford UP, 1979.
Todorov, Tzvetan. *The Fantastic: A Structural Approach to a Literary Genre.* Trans. Richard Howard. Cleveland: P of Case Western Reserve U, 1973.
Trehearne, Brian. *Aestheticism and the Canadian Modernists: Aspects of a Poetic Influence.* Montreal and Kingston: McGill-Queen's UP, 1989.
Vanderhaeghe, Guy. *Man Descending.* Toronto: Macmillan, 1982.
- 'Poetic Desire and Authentic Rendering: Linked Collections.' In Probert. 170–2.
Vassanji, M.G. *Uhuru Street.* Toronto: McClelland and Stewart, 1992.

von Helmoltz-Phelan, Anna A. *The Social Philosophy of William Morris.* Durham: Duke UP, 1927.

Walker, Stephanie Kirkwood. *This Woman in Particular: Contexts for the Biographical Image of Emily Carr.* Waterloo: Wilfrid Laurier UP, 1996.

Ware, Tracy. Afterword. *In the Village of Viger,* by Duncan Campbell Scott. 1996. 119–25.

– Rev. of *New Contexts of Canadian Criticism.* Ed. Heble et al. *English Studies in Canada* 25 (1999): 236–9.

Watson, Sheila. *The Double Hook.* 1959. Rpt. Toronto: McClelland and Stewart, 1969.

Watt, Ian. *The Rise of the Novel: Studies in Defoe, Richardson and Fielding.* London: Chatto and Windus, 1957.

Watt, K. Jane. Email to Author. 17 April 2000.

– Introduction. *Our Little Life.* By J.G. Sime. Ottawa: Tecumseh, 1994. vii–xl.

– 'Passing Out of Memory: Georgina Sime and the Politics of Literary Recuperation.' Diss. University of Alberta, 1997.

Weintraub, Rodelle, ed. *Fabian Feminist: Bernard Shaw and Woman.* University Park: Pennsylvania State UP, 1977.

Weis, Lyle P. 'Bipolar Paths of Desire: D.C. Scott's Poetic and Narrative Structures.' *Studies in Canadian Literature* 12:1 (1987): 35–52.

Weiss, Allan. 'Rediscovering the Popular Canadian Short Story.' In Lynch and Arnold-Robbeson. 87–97.

Wellek, René, and Austin Warren. *Theory of Literature.* 3rd ed. New York: Harcourt, Brace, Jovanovich, and World, 1962.

Wiebe, Rudy. Afterword. *Fruits of the Earth,* by Frederick Philip Grove. Toronto: McClelland and Stewart, 1989. 351–9.

– *The Blue Mountains of China.* Grand Rapids, MI: Eerdman, 1970.

Wilson, Robert R. 'The Metamorphoses of Space: Magic Realism.' In Hinchcliffe and Jewinski. 61–74.

Wong, Hertha D. 'Louise Erdich's *Love Medicine*: Narrative Communities and the Short Story Sequence.' In Kennedy. 170–93.

Wood-Martin, W.G. *Traces of Elder Faiths in Ireland: A Folklore Sketch; A Handbook of Irish Pre-Christian Traditions.* 2 vols. London: Longmans, Green and Co., 1902.

Wordsworth, William. *Selected Poems and Prefaces.* Ed. Jack Stillinger. Boston: Riverside–Houghton Mifflin, 1965.

Index